Seminole Voices

Indians of the Southeast

SERIES EDITORS

Michael D. Green
University of North Carolina

Theda Perdue
University of North Carolina

ADVISORY EDITORS

Leland Ferguson
University of South Carolina

Mary Young
University of Rochester

Seminole
Voices

Reflections on Their Changing Society, 1970–2000

Julian M. Pleasants and
Harry A. Kersey Jr.

University of Nebraska Press • Lincoln & London

Library of Congress Cataloging-in-Publication Data
Pleasants, Julian M.
Seminole voices : reflections on their changing society, 1970–2000 / Julian M. Pleasants and Harry A. Kersey, Jr.
   p. cm. — (Indians of the Southeast)
Includes bibliographical references and index.
ISBN 978-0-8032-2986-0 (cloth : alk. paper)
1. Seminole Indians—Social conditions. 2. Seminole Indians—Education. 3. Seminole Indians—Religion. 4. Seminole Indians—Medicine. 5. Seminole Indians—Housing. 6. Seminole Indians—Rites and ceremonies. 7. Seminole Indians—Ethnic identity. 8. Social change—Florida. 9. Florida—Social conditions—20th century. I. Kersey, Harry A., 1935– II. Title.
E99.S28.P54 2010
975.9004'973859—dc22
2009041201

Set in Dante by Kim Essman.

For Rod, Steve, and Jessica—JMP

For Shaina, my favorite
granddaughter—HAK

Contents

Illustrations

Series Preface

The Seminoles were among the pioneers of Indian gaming, and today they own one of the most successful gaming enterprises in the country. The Seminoles are also the most culturally conservative of the South's Native peoples. They continue to live in the Everglades, where their ancestors took refuge during the Seminole wars. Although Seminoles no longer live in open-sided chikees located on hammocks or depend on hunting and subsistence farming for their livelihood, the memory of such an existence is fresh. Many Seminoles speak their own language, and, for many, the traditional Green Corn Ceremony is central to their lives. At the same time, gaming revenues have sparked economic development, a renewed emphasis on education, an increase in family incomes, and an expansion of tribal services. How can Seminoles seize the opportunities at hand and still hold onto the beliefs and practices that defined them as Seminole? In *Seminole Voices*, distinguished historians Julian Pleasants and Harry Kersey give the Seminoles an opportunity to describe how the changes brought by gaming have affected their lives. The authors have constructed the narrative by focusing on specific topics—economic change, education, religion and medicine, family structure and living conditions, language, and culture—but they draw heavily on interviews, conducted under the auspices of the Samuel Proctor Oral History Program at the University of Florida, to allow Seminoles to explain how they are coping with change in each of these areas. We are pleased to have this work join the Indians of the Southeast series.

Theda Perdue
Michael D. Green
University of North Carolina

Preface

This book project had its origins many years ago when Dr. Samuel Proctor, then director of the University of Florida Oral History Program (subsequently renamed the Samuel Proctor Oral History Program in his honor), was awarded a grant of $170,935 from the Doris Duke Foundation to help compile an oral history of Indians in the southeastern United States. Beginning in 1971, Dr. Proctor supervised the collection of some 900 interviews with Cherokees, Choctaws, Catawbas, Creeks, and Lumbees. For our purposes, the most important part of this academic enterprise was the 200 interviews (roughly 3,800 transcribed pages) with members of the Seminole Tribe of Florida.

The original Seminole interviews were done in 1969, 1970, and 1971, although a few were completed in the mid-1970s, the 1980s, and the 1990s. We appreciate the efforts of those academics who conducted the majority of the initial interviews, especially Sam Proctor, John Mahon, Harry Kersey Jr., Billy Cypress, William Boehmer, and Jean Chadhuri. Tom King lived among the Seminoles in 1972 and 1973 and provided several insightful and significant interviews. Dr. King used much of this information in the compilation of his dissertation at the University of Florida, "The Florida Seminole Polity: 1858–1977."

In 1998 and 1999, the Proctor Oral History Program, with the assistance of two grants totaling $20,000 from the Division of Historical Resources, Florida Department of State, began a series of new interviews to document how the Seminoles had changed or preserved their culture over the last generation. We wanted to compare the views and comments of our most recent interviews with those of the earlier interviews. In both cases, we interviewed individuals who exhibited a wide range of ages, gender, religious beliefs, occupations, and socioeconomic background. The grant from the Division of Historical Resources enabled the program to add forty-seven "new" interviews to the project. The second group of interviewees included a few tribal members (James Billie, Joe Dan Osceola, Billy Osceola, Mary Frances Johns, and Betty Mae Jumper, among others) who had discussed their history and culture with us during 1969, 1970, and 1971.

The Proctor Oral History Program formally proposed a series of new interviews with Tribal Chairman James Billie in a letter of January 16, 1998. In mid-February 1999 the director of the Proctor Program, Dr. Julian Pleasants, accompanied by James Ellison and Rosalyn Howard, traveled to the Big Cypress Reservation and met with Billy Cypress, director of the Ah-Tah-Thi-Ki Museum, and with museum employees Carol Cypress, Ruby Hamilton, and David Blackard to discuss the project and get advice from the tribe regarding whom to interview and what questions to ask. We then sent Billy Cypress a preliminary list of interview questions and a list of possible interviewees grouped by categories. Based on feedback from Billy Cypress and other members of the tribe, we then revised and modified the questions. We agreed to transcribe all the interviews and send the unedited transcript back to the interviewee for additions and corrections. We would take the final edit of the transcript, put it into our collection, and provide both the interviewee and the museum a copy. We explained our Deed of Gift, which would be signed by each person participating in the interview. This document gave the Proctor Oral History Program the legal ownership of the interviews. In addition, we included an informed consent document, which explained about confidentiality and indicated that participation was voluntary.

We agreed to allow the Seminole Tribe to use the interviews in any way they chose—teaching, research, preservation, museum exhibits, and so forth—except for compiling a volume that would overlap the project that resulted in this book. We also agreed to pay all costs in compiling the interviews, such as transcription and editing (around $800 for a three-hour interview) and all travel, food, and housing expenses. The project did not cost the tribe any funds. We agreed to hire a consultant from the tribe, Daisi Jumper, for $1,000, to assist in arranging the interviews and in modifying the questions. We obtained approval of the project and the questions from the Institutional Review Board at the University of Florida in March 1999.

By the end of March 1999, Tribal Chairman Billie had approved the project after the discussion and changes made at the request of Billy Cypress and the other museum employees. At the suggestion of the chairman and others, we expanded and revised the list of possible interviewees. Chairman Billie brought the matter up before the Tribal Council, indicated he was satisfied with the changes, and encouraged tribal members to speak with the interviewers. Rosalyn Howard, who holds a doctorate in anthropology and has extensive experience in oral history, did a majority of the second group of interviews. Rosalyn, an African American and part Indian, brought expertise in the field, as she had written her dissertation on the black Seminoles. James Ellison, at the time a doctoral student in anthropology, did an excellent job in arranging the interviews, acting as a liaison with the tribal authorities, and conducting some of the interviews. Neither of these interviewers was Seminole, but the tribe largely determined the questions they asked and their choice of subjects.

Our initial purpose was to compare the earlier interviews with the 1999 interviews to determine how the tribe has changed from 1970 to 2000. More importantly, we wanted to learn how tribal members themselves perceived what had occurred. However, there were not enough individuals who provided tapes in both 1970 and 1999 for a true pre- and post comparison. Moreover, the earlier tapes did not always address the tribal issues that were deemed pertinent nearly thirty years later. Therefore, we decided to meld the old and new tapes to provide the broadest perspective possible on the period. Most of those interviewed were in their mid- to late forties and early fifties at the time of the interviews in 1999. The average age of those interviewed was 47.5 (we were unable to determine the ages of several of the interviewees), so most of those who participated in this study grew into adulthood during the period from 1970 to 2000. Many were teenagers or in their early twenties in 1970 but were adults with families by 1999, and several held leadership positions in the tribe. These Seminoles lived through the dramatic changes and were in the best position to describe how these changes affected them and the tribe. Sometimes in historical research serendipity trumps good planning to yield an even better result.

The director of the Proctor Oral History Program, with assistance from James Ellison, chose the forty-six interviews to be used in this book. There are more than two hundred interviews in the Proctor Collection, but some of the interviews did not have a Deed of Gift and others did not contain information relevant to our study. The areas emphasized included a personal history of the interviewee, tribal education, economic changes, government, medicine and religion, preservation of culture and language, and housing and family values. In essence, the book chapters are organized around these topics, which the Seminoles considered most relevant. We therefore chose the forty-six participants based on their knowledge of the above categories.

In the earlier interviews there are conversations with non-Indians such as Virgil Harrington, who was the superintendent of the Seminole Indian Agency; William Boehmer, who taught for sixteen years at the Brighton Reservation school; Ivy Stranahan, a confidante and supporter of the tribe; and Bob Mitchell, part Mohawk Indian and a close friend and observer of the Seminoles since 1916. All of these individuals had a close working or personal relationship with the Seminoles, and we thought it instructive to get the viewpoint of some whites, especially for the pre-1950 period. Otherwise, most interviews are with members of the Seminole Tribe. Eighteen of the interviewees are female. Seminole society is matrilineal, and all of these women had a unique perspective about how they dealt with the changes that affected them and their families. We wanted the women's view on how family values, housing, the status of women, and cultures changed, so we included Daisi Jumper, Louise Jumper, Sadie Cypress, Marie Phillips, Mary Frances Johns, and Nancy Shore. Alice Johns Sweat worked with the elderly members of the tribe and had a unique insight into their issues. Betty Mae Jumper was the first female chairman of the Tribal Council. In education, Louise Gopher, the first female university graduate, was a counselor at the Brighton Reservation. Two non-Indian leaders in education were also interviewed: Vivian Crooks had a college degree and directed the tribe's Learning Resource Center, and Dr. Sharon Byrd-Gaffney supervised school operations.

The remainder of the selected group were males and came from varied backgrounds, ages, and interests. James Billie and Mitchell Cypress were chosen because of their leadership positions as chairman of the Tribal Council and president of the Seminole Tribe, respectively. Jim Shore served as the tribe's general counsel for many years and commented on legal matters. Sonny and Josie Billie had a vast knowledge of medicine men and healing. Many males expressed a traditional view of the place of women in the tribe.

The authors chose some tribal members for the specific information they could supply about life on the reservation. Victor Billie worked at the Swamp Safari, while Lorene Gopher, Paul Bowers Sr., and Stanlo Johns were experts on the cattle business. Billy Cypress, Brian Billie, and Jeannette Cypress worked at the museum and as such had a vast understanding of the tribe's history and cultural heritage. Richard Bowers Jr. and Don Robertson had valuable information on natural resources, while Andy

Buster's work in the rehabilitation program and Helene Johns Buster's career as a nurse gave them an intimate familiarity with the tribe's current medical problems. We selected other subjects because we found their comments to be both interesting and instructive.

Once we had decided on the interviews to use, we began the long and complicated process of selecting the most usable and relevant material from each interview. We put any cogent or insightful comment in the appropriate category, that is, medicine or religion or education.

Finally, we cobbled the most enlightening comments together in the proper chapter, omitting similar material to avoid redundancy. For the most part, we have used quotation marks for comments by individuals, but we have frequently summarized their opinions.

The 1999 interviews, when examined alongside those of an earlier period, suggest that the changes over the last generation created unique dilemmas for tribal members by combining unprecedented opportunities (primarily through gambling revenue) to achieve a higher standard of living with the increased likelihood of the loss of language and culture. The various ways Seminoles have explained their attempts to assimilate these changes while trying to preserve their heritage have provided us with new insights and unique perspectives on cultural evolution among Indians of south Florida. We have tried, with the use of archival resources and secondary materials, to situate these interviews into a broad socioeconomic and historical context and to provide some conclusions about the meaning of the changes over the period from 1970 to 2000 for the Seminole Tribe.

We decided it would be prudent to bring the history of the tribe up to the present since there was a series of dramatic changes and events during the final completion of the manuscript. The wealth and economic influence of the tribe increased significantly during those years, and there were major reforms in tribal government and leadership. We do not have any oral history interviews with the Seminoles for the period after 1999, but we relied on the *Seminole Tribune* and others newspapers and articles for up-to-date information.

We are extremely grateful to all the interviewees who took the time to share their history and life experiences with us. James Billie and the late Billy Cypress graciously supported the project. Without their help and support, this project would not have come to fruition.

In compiling the final version of the book, we are grateful to a large number of individuals who provided good advice and helped with transcribing the interviews and editing the book. First among these is James Ellison, who conducted some of the interviews, collected research materials, helped organize all the interviews, and created an outline for the book. Rosalyn Howard visited the reservation several times and produced valuable interviews. Jennifer Langdale wrote the initial grant, went to Tallahassee for the presentation to the Division of Historical Resources, and helped with setting up interviews. Alan Bliss worked on the second grant. Ann Smith, one of our valued and valuable volunteers, transcribed several of the interviews, and Gerrit Blauvelt helped with research. Diane Fishler indexed and wrote summaries of all the Seminole interviews, and Dan Simone, coordinator of the Proctor Oral History Program, assisted with various duties. As always, office manager Roberta Peacock provided expert technical help and excellent advice and helped organize the manuscript.

Dr. Theda Perdue, editor of the Indians of the Southeast series along with Michael D. Green, read the manuscript twice, and her suggestions improved the manuscript considerably. We also appreciate the valuable comments made by three other readers. Finally, thanks to Matthew Bokovoy, Elisabeth Chretien, Sabrina Stellrecht, Alison Rold, and Jonathan Lawrence of the University of Nebraska Press for their help and support.

We have worked diligently to enable the Seminoles to tell their own story. Too often in the past the Seminoles have been seen through white eyes, and their culture and history have been interpreted by non-Indians. We not only present the perspectives of a few tribal members, but we have, in essence, added our interpretation by choosing and editing the interviews. We had initially considered taking ten or twelve members of the tribe and allowing each one to give a more comprehensive analysis of how the tribe had evolved in the last forty years. These interviews would have had to be edited for space, and we would have had a smaller sample to draw from. We decided to use the current format and organize by topics so that more members could contribute to the telling of their story. Although interviews were conducted by whites and the writing and editing were done by non-Indians, this book does give tribal members a long-overdue opportunity to express their unique points of view.

When quoting individuals, we have used ellipses to indicate where material was omitted from the original transcript. When summarizing comments by the interviewee, we have tried to reflect accurately the meaning and context of the statements. Some observations have, of necessity, been presented out of sequence to support a theme or to solidify comments on specific topics. Any factual material supplied by the authors is in brackets. On rare occasions we have changed the tense of a verb or added a word to clarify the meaning of the quoted material, but never at the cost of changing the meaning or the context of the interviews.

The Samuel Proctor Oral History Program, the coordinating and organizing unit for this project, was founded in 1967. The repository at the University of Florida in Gainesville, Florida, currently has more than 4,000 interviews and close to 100,000 pages of transcribed interviews, making it one of the major collections in the country. Some of the material has been digitized and is available online. These transcribed materials are available for use by students, research scholars, journalists, gene-alogists, and other interested groups. The purpose of the program has always been to preserve for future generations these "spoken memories," which provide a firsthand account of the social, economic, political, religious, and intellectual life of the state of Florida.

Both authors have been closely associated with the Samuel Proctor Oral History Program virtually since its inception. Julian Pleasants served as director from 1996 to 2007. Harry Kersey, one of the original field operatives gathering interviews in the late 1960s and the early 1970s, has used its archival materials in several award-winning books on the Florida Seminoles.

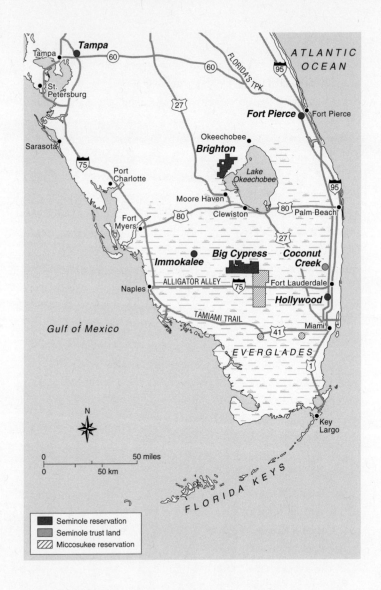

Seminole reservations in Florida. Created by Mapping Specialists Ltd., used by permission of Jessica Cattelino, and reprinted from *High Stakes: Florida Seminole Gaming and Sovereignty* (Durham NC: Duke University Press, 2008).

Introduction

During three tumultuous decades between 1970 and 2000, the Seminole Tribe of Florida underwent a dramatic transformation that affected virtually every aspect of the people's lives. Within a little more than one generation the tribe moved from relative obscurity to unimaginable notoriety, primarily as a result of the wealth derived from its highly successful gaming and other business ventures. This ended decades of endemic poverty for Florida Indians extending back well before the Great Depression. The Seminoles had been marked for "termination" in the early 1950s and only narrowly escaped that fate with strong support from Florida's congressional delegation. Although the Seminole Tribe of Florida received federal recognition in 1957 and operated with a constitution and business charter, neither the tribal government nor individual Indians were considered economically successful prior to gaming. The Tribal Council depended heavily on funding from the Bureau of Indian Affairs (BIA) to conduct its health, education, and social programs as well as for maintenance of infrastructure on the three Florida reservations. At that time most tribal members lived at the Brighton Reservation (northwest of Lake Okeechobee), the Big Cypress Reservation (near Alligator Alley), and the Hollywood Reservation (southwest of Fort Lauderdale), which was also the seat of tribal government.

In 1970 the tribe realized its major source of independent income for tribal government from a tourist village and handicrafts shop at the Hollywood Reservation, and that was highly seasonal. A few individual Seminoles were successful cattle owners who grazed their herds on tribal pastureland. Members of the Cattlemen's Association formed an economic and political

elite within the tribe in the late 1960s, and their interests dominated tribal government deliberations. Cattle owners were the
only group within the tribe approximating financial self-suffi-
ciency; most others either worked for the tribe or BIA in low-
skill jobs or engaged in agriculture-related labor.

Things changed rapidly following passage of the Indian Self-
Determination Act of 1975, which gave both form and substance
to President Richard Nixon's pronouncement five years earlier
shifting federal Indian policy from paternalism to one allowing maximum tribal independence. Taking their lead from the
Colville Tribe of Washington, the Seminoles soon exercised the
right to operate "smoke shops" on the reservations, selling tax-
free cigarettes. Officials of Broward County (Fort Lauderdale/
Hollywood) challenged the tribe's ability to sell cigarettes by the
carton without collecting Florida sales tax, but state courts ruled
that sales on the reservations were not taxable. Later, the Florida Legislature enacted a law specifically exempting the Seminoles from collecting the tax.

Buoyed by that initial success, the Seminoles opened the nation's first tribally operated high-stakes bingo hall at the Hollywood Reservation in 1979. This enterprise was immediately challenged by the sheriff of Broward County, and the case made its
way forward in federal court. In *Seminole Tribe of Florida v. Butterworth* (1981), the Fifth District Court of Appeals found that
Seminole bingo activities were not subject to state regulation
and that the tribe could operate a gaming enterprise. The federal courts thus freed the Seminole Tribe of Florida to compete
in the lucrative world of gaming. By 2006 the tribe operated six
casinos in Florida, and gaming revenues had reportedly reached
$1 billion. The following year the Seminoles became major play-
ers on the worldwide gaming/entertainment scene when they
purchased Hard Rock International for $965 million.

Numerous historians, anthropologists, journalists, and government officials examined the economic, political, and social

dynamics of this transformative era, and a substantial literature emerged. Those publications range from caustic newspaper exposés by the *St. Petersburg Times* and *South Florida Sun-Sentinel* of alleged individual and governmental corruption brought on by new wealth, to scholarly assessments of gambling's impact on the tribe such as Jessica Cattelino's *High Stakes: Florida Seminole Gaming, Sovereignty, and the Social Meanings of Casino Wealth* (2008). Unfortunately, many accounts lacked any real attempt to explore the personal dimension. While tribal leaders came under intense scrutiny, few writers bothered to ask ordinary Seminole people how they felt about the ways their lives were changing. Therefore, the goal of this book is to recount the story from a Seminole perspective by utilizing oral histories of individuals who lived through the period and experienced these events firsthand. The information culled from these interviews answers an essential question: What impact did these social and economic developments have on the everyday life of tribal members?

The most salient result was an explosive increase in both tribal and individual wealth. The Seminole tribal government effectively employed the new largesse to expand its casinos and other commercial ventures as well as to improve living conditions on the reservations. However, this immediate increase in disposable income had a variety of unanticipated outcomes for individuals, families, and the Seminole community as a whole. Many interviewees expressed concern that the new wealth would diminish the motivation of school-age youngsters to complete their education or to pursue gainful employment. By 2000 many of the older adults had not radically altered their lifestyle—most bought new trucks or other high-end vehicles and upgraded their homesteads—but they were still not accustomed to being wealthy. However, younger adults (primarily those in the under-thirty cohort) began to take windfall profits for granted and were engaged in conspicuous consumption; moreover, they were passing this attitude down to their children. This led Seminoles to ask: What is the motivation for an Indian child to attend school and work hard if he or she already has a trust fund?

Ironically, one positive tangible result of the tribe's new-found wealth was the upgrading of educational opportunities for Seminole youngsters. Shortly after World War II, children from the Brighton and Hollywood reservations began attending public schools, while the BIA operated an elementary school on the isolated Big Cypress Reservation. But for the most part, the result was low achievement, poor attendance, and only a handful of Indian high school graduates. Many of those interviewed provided striking accounts of being members of an Indian minority in white school systems. The Seminoles who seized political control of tribal government in the late 1970s made education a priority. The Tribal Council took control of the Indian school at Big Cypress Reservation in 1982, built a state-of-the-art facility, and instituted far ranging curricular and personnel changes. A tribal education department began close liaison with public schools and also made scholarships available for Seminole children attending private K–12 schools and for higher education. These advances in education and their impact on a generation of Indian children are documented in the interviews.

The appearance of substantial new homes on the reservations—some belonging to tribal leaders and bordering on gaudy excess—was the logical extension of a process that the government began in the 1960s to move Seminoles into modern housing with electricity and indoor plumbing. At that time most Seminole families on the outlying reservations still occupied thatched-roof structures known as chikees, which had been their primary shelter for well over a century. First, a number of concrete-block structures were constructed for cattle-owning families who could afford to assume mortgages for their improved accommodation. Then a turnkey housing project from the Department of Housing and Urban Development provided chikee-inspired wooden structures for less-affluent families. The transition in how people lived was not achieved without a social cost, however. Most adult Seminoles, especially those from the Big Cypress region, were accustomed to life in the traditional matrilineal clan camp, headed by the *posi* (clan matron) and surrounded by their close relatives. These extended-family camps were a culturally unifying factor in Seminole life, and when they disappeared, the task of raising children became more difficult, especially for single mothers. The reservation communities that emerged following the move to modern housing were decidedly more stratified by class and less egalitarian. Many of the interviewees decried the loss of a close-knit family structure and the individualism that replaced traditional camp life.

Religious divisions within the tribe were exacerbated during this time, with those who accepted Christianity—mostly members of the Baptist Church—strongly condemning individuals who attended the Green Corn Dance. From the time the first Creek/Seminole Indian Baptist missionaries arrived from Oklahoma in 1907, there was a struggle between the forces of Christianity and traditional Seminole beliefs represented by the Green Corn Dance and medicine men. Much of this acrimony existed because over the years the ceremony became identified with alcohol consumption and raucous behavior. Nevertheless, many Seminoles interviewed who professed to be Christians also attended the Green Corn Dance, which they viewed more as a cultural artifact rather than a religious observance. The retention of both language and ritual played a particularly important role in the formulation of Indian identity in an age of Red Power and self-determination.

The political leadership that took the Seminole Tribe on its unprecedented economic expansion in the 1970s was more secular in outlook than the men and women who led during the early years of organization. For the first twenty years of tribal government the elected leaders were predominantly Baptist ministers or devout church members. They, in turn, had supplanted the medicine men as political leaders acknowledged by the people. Then a younger, generally well educated generation of Seminoles, some of them Vietnam War veterans, came to the fore as both businesspeople and elected leaders. The Seminole Tribe became actively involved in local and state politics, formed a political action committee, and aggressively defended its rights in the courts and legislative halls. Assessments of various tribal political leaders figure prominently in the interviews.

It is fitting that Seminole voices will now be heard. Like most other Indian tribes, the Seminoles have a rich oral tradition for transmitting their history and culture in their native language. Until the late nineteenth century, the small remnant group of Seminoles, who survived three wars with the United States and eluded removal to Indian Territory, secluded themselves in the vast Everglades and avoided contact with the outside world. There the medicine men conducted the Green Corn Dance and associated ceremonies in the tribal languages. Even when Seminole men began to learn English to facilitate trade and legal negotiations with white settlers, women of the tribe remained cultural conservators charged with passing along the language and lore to the young.

Apparently, women did a good job of retaining and transmitting historical knowledge. A white boy whose family befriended the Indians in the early twentieth century recalled that his father took the son of a medicine man on a visit to Fort Marion in St. Augustine, where Osceola had been held prisoner, and discovered that *"Leek-a-lee* knew the story and more about the fort than we did."

The two languages spoken by Seminoles—most speak Mikasuki, but the people of the Brighton Reservation use Muskogee (Creek)—establish a strong link with the past and reaffirm their cultural origins in the Creek Confederacy. The Creek Confederacy was a polyglot collection of semi-autonomous towns that gradually coalesced into a nation beginning in the late eighteenth century. Each town was a ceremonial and political center with associated outlying villages. By the 1700s there were some sixty Creek towns in Georgia and Alabama. These were divided into Upper Towns and Lower Towns according to their location relative to the main trading route from Charleston. The language of the politically dominant Upper Towns, located along the Alabama River and its tributaries, was Muskogee (Creek), while some Lower Towns, sited near the Chattahoochee and Flint rivers in Georgia, were Mikasuki-speaking.

The inhabitants of those towns, which collectively became known as Seminole, either drifted into Spanish Florida to take advantage of economic opportunities or fled there in the aftermath of the Creek War of 1813–14. Like the Creek Confederacy, the Seminoles at the time of their southward migration were a people who spoke two distinct languages, so they established separate towns. Even ensconced in Spanish territory, the Seminoles were not safe, as General Andrew Jackson's forces attacked them there during the First Seminole War (1817–18). After Florida became a territory of the United States in 1821, the Seminoles were confined to a huge reservation in the interior of the peninsula, while the territorial legislature and federal officials placed great pressure on them to leave. Then Congress passed the Indian Removal Act of 1830, requiring all Indian tribes living east of the Mississippi River to move to Indian Territory in present-day Oklahoma and Kansas. The Seminoles refused to yield to that mandate, and the Second Seminole War (1835–42) ensued. Some four thousand Indians were killed or removed west during the conflict, but a few were never defeated. A third conflict (1855–58) further reduced the Indian population to several hundred individuals who secluded themselves in the wild interior wetlands of southern Florida.

Following the wars and removal, most of the survivors who remained in Florida were Mikasuki-speakers, with a small minority retaining the Muskogee language. Even though most Seminoles who use a native language today speak Mikasuki, it is notable that the Green Corn Dance ceremonial is still conducted primarily in Muskogee, as it was in the Creek Confederacy—another significant link to their cultural past. Moreover, both the Muskogee and Mikasuki languages are taught to youngsters formally in tribal schools and to some extent informally by families at home. A number of the adult Seminoles interviewed are fluent in one or both of the languages and encourage efforts to perpetuate them among the young people.

Throughout the remainder of the nineteenth century the Seminoles evolved a unique culture in the Florida wetlands. This transition from the prewar lifestyle they had known in north and central Florida required an adaptation to the semi-tropics. Rather than living in villages with wooden cabins and cultivating large communal fields, they established extended-family camps on fertile tree islands known as hammocks where they planted family gardens of corn, squash, beans, and bananas. If the corn crop failed they could gather the wild zamia plant to make *coontie*, a flour that was the key ingredient in their staple food *sofkee*. Gone were the large cattle herds of Spanish origin that roamed the prairies of north Florida; the largest animals found on the hammocks were generally pigs and dogs. These, along with household goods, could be transported from camp to camp in long canoes fashioned from cypress logs that Seminoles poled along watery trails through the tall saw grass. There were different types of canoes used in hunting, transporting goods and families, or rigged for sailing over open water. The chikee, an open-sided structure of saplings topped with a thatched roof made of palm fronds, provided the Seminoles' basic housing. There were different types of chikees in a camp. Some had raised platforms for storing goods and also served as sleeping quarters. Within a cooking chikee the traditional log spoke fire was set on a dirt floor and allowed women to work sheltered from rain and sun. There were even birthing chikees where women went to deliver their children.

The Seminoles also adapted their clothing to the climate and ecosystem. Instead of long trousers, flannel shirts, and buckskins that they wore in north Florida, Seminole men adopted a lightweight knee-length "big shirt" that allowed them to enter the shallow Everglades water to push their stuck canoes or dispatch alligators, otters, and other objects of the hunt. Indian women also created a new dress fashion that included a light cape and bare midriff to provide relief from the stifling south Florida heat. When the Indians began trading at frontier stores in Miami, Fort Lauderdale, and Fort Myers, they bought yard goods such as gingham and calico, and by the turn of the century, hand-cranked sewing machines appeared in most camps. Both Indian men and women learned to sew, and around 1917 the elaborate "Seminole Patchwork" items were being sold to tourists who came to Florida for the winter season. A number of the interviewees in this study stressed the importance of preserving and wearing Seminole clothing as a manifestation of their "Indianness."

In addition to providing the Indians' main source for processed foods and manufactured goods, the frontier trading posts proved to be their key point of cultural contact with the outside world. There Seminole men interacted with whites on a basis of economic equality, as the commodities they brought to sell, such as alligator hides, otter pelts, and bird plumes, were prized in the international fashion industry and thus highly profitable to the storekeepers. The Indians did not "trade" in the sense of bartering their commodities for manufactured goods; rather, they sold pelts and hides to merchants for cash, then purchased the items they wanted while saving the surplus to spend later. Lasting friendships were formed between some of the merchants, such as Frank Stranahan and William Brickell, and their Seminole clients, and a few even adopted their anglicized names.

There was also a degree of social parity in the frontier contact communities that grew around the trading posts. Indians frequented these small settlements selling huckleberries, bananas, venison, and handicrafts and were generally well accepted by the residents. They were often present at community gatherings as well as church meetings, and many visited in private homes. This cross-cultural acceptance began to wane with the rapid growth of white population after the Florida East Coast Railway arrived at Miami in 1896. Nevertheless, the residue of goodwill developed during this era carried over into the twentieth century to resurface when the Seminole Tribe was threatened with termination during the 1950s.

The Seminole hunting-trapping-trading economy collapsed in the early twentieth century for three reasons. First, the rapid growth of population in south Florida forced the Indians to abandon their hunting grounds and campsites near the Atlantic Coast. Therefore they had to range farther afield to find game. Second, in 1905 the state initiated a project to drain the Everglades and convert it into a vast agricultural area. This lowering of the water table was disastrous for the wildlife of the region and made it difficult for Indians to sustain their hunting. Third, the outbreak of World War I brought a temporary cessation for the international fashion industry centered in Europe. The Audubon Society and federal anti-pluming laws ended the traffic in bird feathers from Florida, and when the market for pelts and hides resumed in the 1920s, white hunters with better equipment worked the Everglades, and Indians were no longer a major factor in the trade.

By the time the nation entered the Great Depression, Seminoles were a destitute minority. Most traditional Mikasuki-speakers kept to their chikee camps in the Everglades near the Tamiami Trail, where they survived by hunting, fishing, and subsistence agriculture and followed the political and religious leadership of the old medicine men. They rebuffed all government efforts to have them included in programs for the reservations. A few Indian families became itinerant agricultural workers who lived on or near the farms where they were employed. However, nearly two-thirds of the nine hundred Seminoles had taken up residence on one of the three federal reservations. There they learned to work with a beef cattle herd provided by the federal government, or worked on Works Progress Administration and Civilian Conservation Corps programs. The families also received medical care from government contract doctors, and some permitted their children to attend the government day schools. A large number of the reservation residents also accepted Christianity and attended the Baptist churches. The Brighton Reservation became the home for Muskogee-speakers, while the Big Cypress Reservation was predominantly populated by Mikasuki-speakers who had moved there from the Tamiami Trail area when their medicine man converted to Christianity. The small Dania Reservation (renamed Hollywood in 1966) became the site of the Seminole Indian Agency in 1926, and its small population worked primarily for federal or tribal programs. In many respects there were three different Seminole communities with more agendas (linguistic, cultural, economic, and political) that divided them than united them as a tribe. Thus many of the issues that still faced the Seminole people in the 1970s were prefigured some forty years earlier.

Understandably, the Seminoles' interpretation of their history reflected in the interviews, particularly among the older people, is often strikingly different from that of Western historians. As the late Tewa scholar Alfonso Ortiz reminds us, the Indian view of time is predominantly cyclical and repetitive rather than irreversible and linear. For Indians, the time that has elapsed between an event and its recurrent manifestation is less important than the event itself. For example, a historian who worked on the reservation several years ago and returns today is likely to be greeted by his Indian friends as though he had never left.

From an Indian perspective, what is important is not the passage of time between visits but that a friend had returned. Likewise, Indians measure events in terms of their impact on preserving language and religion. Thus they viewed the contemporary religious conflict between Seminole traditionalists and Christians not as something new, but as the repetition of a problem from five decades past and beyond. A few of the Indians interviewed found it irrelevant that three decades had passed since the tribe first began to earn money from "smoke shops" and bingo, and the current distribution of huge dividends; unexpected windfall profits, regardless of the source or amount, led to the same social problems. Their criticisms of language loss and culture decline, as well as a lack of personal initiative first voiced in the 1970s, were only magnified in 2000. Therefore, Indians continually return to the historical origins of issues for a clearer understanding of contemporary options.

Unequivocally, the most important point arising from this body of interviews is the Seminoles' perception of themselves as a people who, although they have radically altered their social and economic condition, retain their core values. When Mary Jene Coppedge, having offered a candid assessment of issues within modern tribal life, concluded by saying, "And my values, to me, are still there," she articulated the sentiments of most Seminole adults of that day. The Seminole people are by nature survivors; historically they evinced an unparalleled ability to adapt to changing conditions and to turn adversity to their advantage, from adapting to life in the Everglades, developing a hunting-trading economy, and when that failed, moving to reservations and taking up cattle herding. The tribe's entry into high-stakes gaming should be viewed as just the latest stage in a long developmental process. Yet, despite the inevitable dislocations brought about by the rapid introduction of great wealth, the Seminoles have retained a communal spirit and have used their wealth for both individual advancement as well as the common good.

This unifying tendency is verified in anthropologist Jessica Cattelino's recent study on the fungibility of monies through a case study of Seminole gaming revenue distribution in the form of per capita dividends. Cattelino contends that in the fiscal politics of indigeneity, the Seminoles use money to structure their relations internally as well as with the larger society, but always in ways that reinforce indigenous political authority and autonomy. The availability of seemingly ever increasing gaming revenues allows the Tribal Council to allocate substantial sums, free of federal constraints, to run the tribal school and myriad social services and programs that virtually all tribal members utilize. Furthermore, there is a profound commitment to retaining tribal history and culture by funding the state-of-the art Ah-Tah-Thi-Ki Museum plus associated historical/archaeological research and preservation units. All of these activities promote the cohesiveness of the Seminole polity.

The distribution of per capita dividends "for the general welfare" further maximizes the tribal government's autonomy under provisions of the Indian Gaming Regulatory Act of 1988, while at the same time promoting individual and household autonomy through discretionary spending. Seminoles were accustomed to receiving per capita distributions from the cattle program or BIA, so gaming dividends are a natural extension of that process. Moreover, some Seminoles claim that the act of allocating dividends is itself consistent with their tradition of hunting and then distributing meat to clan camps at the time of the Green Corn Dance. There are other signs of indigenous value loading in the process. Rather than using available direct bank deposit, most Seminoles prefer to receive their distribution checks in person on "Dividend Day," which has taken on aspects of a festival or social gathering at the reservations. Therefore, the Seminoles use gambling wealth to reinforce their indigeneity

and cultural distinctiveness, thus challenging the widely held assumption among non-Indians that gambling is antithetical to retaining "Indianness." While some individuals remain concerned
that gambling is the source of their income stream, most are in-
different to gaming; it is just a way to make money and escape
poverty. Nevertheless, the Seminoles are keenly aware that it is
"our money," not federal largesse, additionally reinforcing the
concept of "The Tribe."

In retrospect, then, Coppedge's words from 1999 were haunt-
ingly prescient. Indeed, the Seminoles of Florida have once again
found a way to survive in the white man's world by adopting economic strategies that are congruent with their own value system. This book offers them an opportunity to relate how that
happened in their own way. It is a tale well worth recounting.

1. Economic Change

From 1971 to 1979, the initiation and successful development of such lucrative enterprises as tax-free cigarette stores (known as "smoke shops") and high-stakes bingo halls dramatically changed the modern economy of the Seminole Indians. The tribe continued to support the older standbys of cattle, tourism, and crafts, but it also encouraged economic diversification by providing both capital and a safety net for entrepreneurs desirous of branching out into new endeavors. The Seminole Tribe of Florida, Inc., channeled funds into a variety of business ventures, including citrus groves, cane sugar, ecotourism and safari tourist attractions, commercial real estate, a Sheraton Hotel in Tampa, and the Micco Aircraft Company, a commercial aircraft business.[1] Most significantly, since 1988 the Seminoles have expanded their casino operations. The Coconut Creek Casino opened in 2001, and in 2004 the Seminoles built two Hard Rock Hotels and Casinos—one in Tampa and one in Hollywood. In 2006 the tribe acquired the Hard Rock International chain for $965 million.

Tribal leaders have used the profits from these businesses to enhance tribal health, education, and social welfare programs, making up to some degree the cutbacks in federal funding during the Reagan administration. Under the leadership of James Billie the tribe instituted a revenue-sharing program. In the 1990s a monthly dividend was distributed to tribal members, thus boosting the standard of living for families. The Seminoles' new business ventures and a commitment to free enterprise created a foundation for widespread economic security among Seminoles that had not existed previously. The new revenues brought increased opportunities for education and training, which in turn enabled the younger generation to vie for new jobs in both the public and private sector.

By 2006, most tribal members had access to modern housing and health care. In addition, the tribe spent over $1 million per year on education alone, including grants-in-aid to promising Seminole college students and the operation of the Ahfachkee School. Other tribal funds had been allocated for such projects as the Seminole Police Force; gymnasiums at Brighton and Big Cypress; a senior citizens center; the Cultural Heritage Project; and building of the Ah-Tah-Thi-Ki Museum. More than three hundred tribal members were employed in dozens of governmental departments, including law enforcement and legal services. By employing Seminoles in the "smoke shops," bingo halls, and government positions, the tribe reduced the unemployment rate by 50 percent. The 1996 annual budget, which exceeded $100 million, reflected the economic progress made by the Seminole Tribe of Florida, Inc.[2] The tribe continues to expand its economic horizons, and in 2007 it appeared to be on the verge of creating even greater economic success.

The overall functioning of tribal economic activities, centered in the large, modern government headquarters in Hollywood, is computerized and more efficient and better organized than in the past. The Constitution of the Seminole Tribe originally established the Tribal Council as the chief governing body (composed of a chairman, a vice-chairman, and council representatives from each reservation), and the council currently administers the Seminole Police Department, the Human Resources program, the tribal gaming enterprises, citrus groves, the Billie Swamp Safari, the Ah-Tah-Thi-Ki Museum, and the majority of the cigarette-related industries. The tribe's Legal Services Department supervises a public defender's office, the Water Resource Management, and the Utilities Department. The tribe does not operate a court system; legal and criminal matters not resolved at the local level are referred to the proper state or federal authorities. The Seminoles' drive for economic independence has been aided by the fact that the tribal government is exempt from all state and federal taxes. Individual tribal members are liable for the same state and federal taxes as any other citizen.[3]

The economic changes from 1945 to the present have been slow in coming, but are dramatic nonetheless. Joe Dan Osceola recalled that "prior to 1957 . . . there wasn't any kind of activities or jobs for the Indians on the reservation—none whatsoever. It was a typical Indian reservation. That is the most depressed oppressed area that you can imagine. So now what you see today, is the difference between day and night."[4]

After World War II the Seminoles primarily worked in unskilled jobs, were isolated from mainstream Florida, and still lived in chikees. Seminoles earned a living in various ways, but few held high-paying jobs. Many worked in truck farms and at cattle ranches, and some made craft items to be sold to tourists. Others worked at the BIA in Hollywood and in various tribal enterprises. Still others worked as teacher's aides, aides to social workers, and in flood control projects. As late as 1973, 60 percent of the families had incomes of less than $3,000 per year, and in 1981 the unemployment rate reached 40 percent at Big Cypress and 25 percent at Brighton. Of those employed, 75 percent worked for a federal or state program designed to aid Seminoles or drew paychecks directly from the tribe.

Over a period of some thirty years, Seminole families moved from chikees into frame or concrete-block houses, purchased the latest home appliances—stoves, refrigerators, washing machines, televisions—and adopted white dress. By the 1990s virtually all Seminole families owned a car or a truck. These changes lessened their sense of isolation but also put them into more frequent contact with the outside world. In order to survive and function within the white world of business, the Seminoles had to adopt certain manifestations of white culture. The prevailing cultural attitudes forced the tribe to conform to a Western sense of time, to accept a more rigid structure to their lives, and to understand non-Indian values and traditions. This transition and bridging of cultures was not easy, but with better education and more business experience, the tribe adapted successfully.

In the early 1970s the Seminoles had a life expectancy of forty-four years and had high rates of infant mortality, tuberculosis, and alcoholism. With increased financial resources and the expanded availability of clinics, doctors, and medicine, Seminoles health and life expectancy improved markedly. Children are now born in hospitals and families can get birth control pills, immunizations, and insulin to treat diabetes.[5]

Older Seminoles talked candidly about economic hardships and the difficulties of reservation life in the 1970s. Carl Baxley, a prominent cattle owner, thought of the Seminoles "in the same class as black people. They [Seminoles] worked out in the fields, were looked down upon by the white people. I guess in today's society you would look at them as migrant workers . . . but probably with more disadvantages . . . not having an education and having to deal with the government on different issues." There was also "racial discrimination back then, which still exists today, to a certain extent, it is just called a different word. But yes, it was rough being on the reservation, rough trying to survive out there and not having any skills or education, because back in the early days it was forbidden for a lot of kids to go to school." Seminole parents did not want their kids to go to white schools, and "the white people did not want the Indians coming to their schools." Baxley thought that whites viewed Seminoles as poor because they were "recipients of free lunches through the government programs. . . . And hell, everybody knew you came up from the reservation, which was a poverty stricken place."[6]

Louise Jumper described how life had changed in economic terms since the 1970s. "There have been lots of changes, some for good and some for bad. I can remember my family was poor all the time. We were always hungry. . . . So we have come a long way from being poor. . . . Through the dividend program we have a home, whereas [otherwise] we would not have a home. . . . My husband and I work very hard to provide for the children. . . . And we make sure they get experiences, like going to the movies, going to town . . . , which we never did because we never could. . . . I only went to town about once a year for a long while, if I was lucky enough." Now, said Jumper, they are working and the dividends are helping out and "I hope we are part of the group that puts that money to good use and not buy drugs and just throw it away."[7]

James Billie, in a 1973 interview, said that he did not think of himself as poor or his tribe in a state of poverty, but changed his mind when in contact with whites. "I saw a lot of non-Indians had money and they had this and that and I couldn't afford it." Billie learned to "stand on my own two feet" and to fight for economic equality.[8] Marie Phillips, a forty-two-year-old in 1999, lamented the fact that some family unity had been lost with the newfound wealth. "Yes, it is very different today than what I grew up with because . . . your grandparents, your father and mother, all of your aunts and uncles your brothers and sisters, everybody lived in one camp." All this changed when "they started living away from the extended family and . . . having to work to provide for themselves."[9]

In the late 1940s the main sources of work and income, other than the government subsidies, were cattle raising and vegetable farming. Several families earned a living in the cattle industry, which had been initiated under federal government auspices. The Seminoles have always exhibited a certain pride in herding cattle, their first real capitalistic enterprise. "The cattle business has always been and always will be a mainstay in this tribe," noted Carl Baxley. "It is there for life, it has been one of the things that got us to where we are today. We are recognized throughout the cattle industry as one of the five largest producers in the United States—certainly one of the best pro-

ducers in the state of Florida. Our cattle are second to none."[10]
By the 1960s, aided and trained by state agricultural agents, the
Seminole cattlemen quickly learned the business, expanded their
herds, and improved the quality of their beef.

As early as 1740, Indians established permanent grazing ter-
ritories with large numbers of cattle. The Seminole leader, Cow-
keeper, was reputed to have a fine herd of cattle numbering between seven and ten thousand head grazing on the Alachua
Prairie basin.[11] Acquiring grazing ranges for cattle was one major reason why the Seminoles moved to Florida in the eighteenth century, but they had largely given this up when they
moved deeper into the swamps to avoid contacts and conflicts
with the whites.

The modern Seminole cattle business, however, began around
1935. The regional director of the Resettlement Administration
decided to save the lives of some cattle and transferred the beef
from the drought-stricken "dust bowl" to the Brighton Reservation. The federal government offered a start-up herd of some
twelve hundred, but most of the initial shipment died because
the stock arrived in a half-starved condition. Nonetheless, the
survivors provided a nucleus for a growing herd, and within
four years the operation was "one of the most successful exper-
iments on large-scale irrigated pasturage ever attempted by the
Bureau of Indian Affairs."[12] The common herd was subsequently
sold to individual owners. Since cattle were distributed only to
those who lived on the reservation, some tribal members saw
this as an attempt to persuade reluctant Seminoles to settle on
the newly designated federal reservations. The cattle industry
had significant social, economic, and political consequences—
perhaps most important was the Seminoles' greater reliance
upon and involvement with the federal government.

According to anthropologist Jessica Cattelino, the cattle business changed the Seminole social structure by facilitating the development of class distinctions; that is, those who were more

successful in the industry had a higher status in the community. Because cattle were initially distributed only to men, cattle ownership also changed the concept of property ownership, since previously, in this matrilineal society, women had been the primary property owners. Thus the cattle industry increased the "economic differential between men and women."[13] Eventually, through inheritance and changing social mores, women became successful cattle owners.

The cattle industry became self-sufficient primarily because of the professional assistance of Fred Montesdeoca, the agricultural agent for Okeechobee County. He encouraged the Indians to learn the proper care and treatment of cattle and helped them with range control, improved grass, and trained them to work as ranch hands. In 1939 the Brighton Indians elected three trustees to supervise the program. In 1940 the earnings from the sale of bull calves and steers came to nearly $5,000—a sum sufficient to cover operating expenses and to purchase an additional herd of forty-six Hereford heifers. By 1953, having averaged a net profit of $19,000 a year, the Seminoles repaid the U.S. government for the original allotment of cattle.[14]

Mary Jene Coppedge, one of the younger interviewees at age thirty-three in 1999, recalled that "the Brighton people were the first to receive cattle. . . . Cattle were shipped from another place that were starving and put on trains and shipped out here and supposedly given to the Indians. But they were not given to the Indians. In the long run they were purchased."[15] Stanlo Johns remembered that "there were 450 head of cattle that were shipped out of Black Mountain, Apache country [White Mountain Apache Reservation]. When they came, half of them were dead; they were starved to death."

Johns thought that the gift of cattle was an attempt to force the Seminoles to live on the reservation. Some Seminoles began tending to the cattle and others started coming to the ranch to help out. "See, that is what they [the federal government] were coaching them to do, bring them on the res [reservation] and say, well we are going to sell you five head or ten head. These will be yours; you can pasture over there. . . . That went on and the guys borrowed money to get into business and most of them were successful at it." The money they borrowed, continued Johns, "was paid back in less [time] than they anticipated" and the cattlemen "began to become sort of a business [man] instead of just a Florida cow farmer."

Johns expanded on his view that the cattle program began because "the only way they [the federal government] could put them on the reservation was to start some kind of project, because the Indians back then would not work. . . . I mean, literally, would not work." He knew that federal officials "did not know how to coax people onto the reservation, because they [Seminoles] did not want to be on the reservation. I remember when I was just a kid, we used to talk about this and they would say, well, it is just a way of tricking us in there where they can capture all of us and then they are going to send us off. This was a thought that I guess their grandfathers had taught them way back. . . . Eventually, as Indians began to move on the reservations . . . they began to pick up some type . . . of work habits of some sort, . . . and then eventually we were where we are now. But it did not come to us in that quick of a fashion. It took us probably forty years or longer."

In the beginning, lamented Johns, no Seminole tribal organization existed and "we were just a bunch of wild Indians running around out here chasing cows for pretty close to twenty years." When the tribe became incorporated in 1957, "the first organization that we ever had was the cattle program."[16] Richard Bowers corroborated Johns's story and explained that the cattle industry was "an experiment to keep the Indians from going here and going there. The cattle would make them stay in one place, to raise the cattle. The United States gave them so many head to take care of [just] to keep them on the reservation."[17]

For many members of the tribe, raising cattle was appealing not only as a way to increase their income but also as a way to build equity. As Joe Frank explained: "At that time [in the 1960s] the cattle program really took off. It was something that an individual tribal member could build on and, at that time, the cattle program was the only way a tribal member could really build any equity out here. Off the reservation, most people view homes as a way of building equity, of building their estate. Here on the reservation, where the land is tribally owned and you really can't sell a house, a house doesn't have that much value. It is just shelter. The cattle program gave tribal members a chance to build equity on the land."[18]

From the 1950s to the 1990s, the cattle industry improved dramatically in terms of quality of product, new technology, and efficiency in the raising of the cattle. As Carl Baxley explained in 1999, "one of the things is that we have more improved land. We have a better quality of cattle. We participate in a lot of state programs. As far as brucellosis [an infectious disease of human beings caused by pathogenic aerobic bacteria, transmitted by contact with infectious animals] goes . . . , all cattle on the reservation are certified cattle. That means they are free and clear of brucellosis." Baxley noted that the Seminoles were becoming more self-sufficient in their work. "We have had all kinds of people come in and give us suggestions on how to improve our herds and . . . what the market is calling for. But I guess in the last five to six years we have taken it upon ourselves to do our own legwork and go out there and get our own hands dirty."[19]

The tribe responded to the challenge of becoming more competitive in the cattle business by upgrading its operating procedures. Don Robertson said that the tribe changed "our operation, our cattle breeding. . . . Now we are in the process of changing to get more genetics into our herd and get what the packer wants and what the consumer wants, the type of cattle that do well in the feed yards and do well when you slaughter them at the end product, so that the meat is more palatable, it has a more consistent taste to it." Thus they switched to Black Brangus bulls, a mix of Angus and Brahma bulls.[20] Mary Jene Coppedge explained that they moved to cross-breeding because "you have got to have the Brahman influence within this type of area because of the heat, the humidity, and the insects. Brahman has a natural insect defense. Brahmans can sweat and they are more heat tolerant than most breeds are, so a lot of Florida and the hot climate areas have crossbred a lot of their cattle."[21] In 2001 the tribe purchased the controlling interest in the HK Cattle Company, one of the oldest Brahman cattle operations in the United States.[22]

The Seminoles also embraced new technology. "Today . . . we have cow pens for just about every cattle owner, which means we can take the cows in faster, work them faster," recalled Richard Bowers. "A lot of advancement in medicine, techniques, machinery, and everything has advanced so much, to a point where we even sell our cattle on video sales. People all over the country don't have to move anywhere, they can see it on video. . . . I would never go back thirty years ago. Everything is just so much easier and more convenient now." In addition, the cattle industry has "a natural resource program which . . . makes sure that the land resources or any type of resources are not depleted. It is just like keeping things right so that nothing gets depleted or overused where you don't abuse the natural resources."[23]

As of 2000, the tribe focused on breeding, growing, and fattening up heifers for sale. The tribe had 5,500 two-year-old and yearling heifers at Brighton and 3,500 head at Big Cypress, not including the bulls, which numbered around 380.[24] The Seminole cattle industry was ranked twelfth in the United States as cow-calf producers, and Seminoles were among the largest cattle owners in Florida. Despite years of success, some Seminoles saw a difficult future for the cattle business. "Cattle has never been a profitable program here because it seems like the prices keep going down while other things are going up, like the medicine, the fertilizer," said Polly Osceola Hayes.[25] Andy Buster agreed that "the cow business is kind of fading out because there is not that much money in beef. A lot of them, like my wife's relatives, are going into the sugarcane business because that is up at this time."[26] Although the tribe continues to lose money on cattle, some individual owners prosper. Also, raising cattle provided employment and gave the tribe a sense of operating independently of federal government control. Despite the loss of income, cattle have become a reminder of "Seminole belonging and community identity" as well as an essential part of Seminole heritage.[27]

The cattle industry, despite initial discrimination against women, served as an experimental environment for a most dramatic change in gender roles. Initially, although a few wives had inherited cattle, many women were involved in the cattle business primarily to prepare meals for the cowboys. All of that changed when more women inherited or purchased cattle. They became proficient at raising cattle and at running the business.

According to Betty Mae Jumper, some women had cattle as early as the 1920s. "I told the people that my mother had over 500 [head] when I was a little girl, and people did not believe it." An investigation "found out I was telling the truth, that she did have over 500. Because her two brothers died and she was the only one left with the cattle, and it was all hers. She sold some, but did not sell it all."[28]

Not until recently have women owned a significant number of cattle and been accepted as capable owners. Mary Jene Coppedge succinctly presented the current female view of cattle ownership. "I do not see myself any different than a man cattle owner. It is a business."[29] Lorene Gopher commented on the influence of women in Seminole society in general and her attitude toward the cattle business: "Whatever goes on in my family or in a Seminole family, it seems like it has to be initiated by a woman. . . . We all kind of work together. When we start marking them [the cows], I know I go out there and mark the cows myself . . . Somebody has to throw it [the cow] down and I go out there . . . cutting the ears. I do it myself."

When asked if the status of women in the Seminole tribe has changed, Lorene replied: "I believe so. I think we realize now that, I always want to say that we run everything. . . . We run everything, because in our tradition, our place is ours. My house is mine. . . . It was not his. He was the provider. So, now, like if they get divorced, he wants the house and all that. No, that is not going to work with me. That is my house. If I get divorced, he is gone. That is just the way it is with me. . . . And the cattle I would keep them, too. The laws are not written that way: but *my* law is." Lorene increased her influence by becoming a member of the Cattlemen's Association. "They did not want women sitting on the cattle committee: it should be the men. I used to hear them say that. I sit on the cattle committee now because they know who has a big mouth and they know who knows what is going on."[30] Seminole women wanted to retain a matrilineal society, but they also wanted to be on the cattle committee and have influence in the political and economic decisions of the tribe.

Nancy Shore also commented on the difference in how men and women worked with cattle. "It does not matter. I think it is just like the men do what they have to do. But the women, especially if they are cattle owners, they always want to go out there and see what is going on." Shore added laughingly that "one thing that men do not do is they do not cook. . . . They know how, but they are cowboys so they are going on to the cows while the women do the cooking." In the end, concluded Shore, women "do anything and everything."[31]

Many young girls grew up working cattle, riding, hunting, and fishing like the men although the traditional Seminole division of labor would normally have discouraged them from doing so. Marie Phillips recalled going hunting with her father: "We would work cattle with him, we would do just about anything a boy would do."[32] Polly Osceola Hayes remembered that since her older brother was away and her younger brother was too small, "I was their only cowboy. I got to where I could rope and ride with my Dad."[33] Daisi Jumper, when asked if women did the same kinds of things as men, said: "If they are able, they do. They ride horses and round up cows. If they are not able, they provide the lunch and the refreshments and drinks for the people that work on their cattle. If they want to go ride a horse, they do."[34]

The male tribal members' opinion of women in the cattle business varied from a traditional view of women's place in society to an acceptance of women's equality. Paul Bowers saw women in their historical role: "We have some who are cattle owners. Most of them, if the men are the owners, their wives bring food, fix the lunches for the cattlemen at work, and keep the food up there. That's what they do."[35] Paul Buster supported Bowers. "Just kind of like keeping the home fires going, meeting the needs, such as cooking, and seeing to it that the husband or the people that were working in cows had something to eat during lunch or supper, and taking care of the children, taking care of the wash, things like that."[36]

Richard Bowers, however, had a different opinion and thought that opportunities existed for everyone. "I have seen a girl do just about anything that the cowboys do out there. Not all, but I don't see any difference. If they want to do it, they will do it, and if they don't want to, they will sit back. A lot of the older people cook the meals during the lunchtime for the cowboys."[37] Don Robertson generally concurred: "Well, there are probably way more men that work in the cattle industry than there are women, but I do know some pretty good women who ranch. . . . It is a little dangerous . . . to get in the pens with cattle and move them around and work them, give them all their health

shots and de-worm them and stuff like we do. . . . Women have
to be careful because men are stronger and they can move around
better. But there are some good women cowboys that I know.
Or cowgirls, I should say [laughter]. I know some that can rope
just as good as men. Maybe better."[38]

One offshoot of the cattle industry was the development
and growth of rodeos and rodeo clubs. Many Seminoles participate in rodeo events, as they see the rodeo as an essential part
of their culture and a significant form of entertainment. Richard
Bowers remembered when Brighton started the first rodeo club
and built their first arena. "That was to get people interested in
it. If you knew how to ride a horse, such as working with cattle
. . . , you had a little step ahead. . . . It helps out getting to know
how horses work, how cattle work, and of course, the bull-
riding . . . what kind and how big they are or how mean they
can be. . . . As a matter of fact, the rodeo became an event because of ranch work."[39]

A lot of Indian kids have become involved in the rodeo, and
all four of Paul Bowers's children participated. "I have a daughter . . . and she is a team roper and a bare racer and a breakaway.
I have a daughter in high school and she does breakaway, bar-
rels, poles, and team roping. I have a son, and he is a bull-rider
and a saddle bronc rider. I have a younger son and he is a junior bull rider."[40] Don Robertson claimed that the rodeo business has "gotten way bigger. There is a lot more money nowadays than there used to be, and it is more organized. There are
lots more rodeos over the United States and even in Florida. . . .
[There is] the Eastern Indian Rodeo Association and there are
some good Indian cowboys that rodeo. . . . And it is pretty big
in the Seminole tribe, I mean it has been here a long time."[41]
Robertson conveys an interesting change in terminology. He
eschews the common usage of the phrase "cowboys and Indians" and instead refers to "Indian cowboys." Surely that is progress over the old stereotypical image of the savage Indian who

only stole cattle. Now Indians engage in the profitable enterprise of raising cattle.

While the cattle industry has more recently been a economic mainstay of the tribe, the Seminole Tribe survived over
the years by hunting, fishing, and farming. "Most of the livelihood for the Seminole Indians was farming, maybe not on a big
scale or anything, but farming or gardening around the villages
and living off of the land. Also, the women were gatherers. . . .
The men were mostly providers, hunters, and minded their
own business of livelihood." Over time their economic practices changed very slowly. "Back in the 1950s and 1960s," said
Paul Buster, "some of us did not go to civilization, to town . . .
[except] maybe once every two months . . . , to get the neces-
sities that we could not get ourselves, like salt, flour and those
kinds of needs. . . . But pretty much of the survival that we did
was that we grew all our own vegetables, and we had our own
pigs and chickens and things like that. If we needed a deer, we
would get that."[42] At Brighton Reservation, each family was al-
lotted a five-acre field where they could grow pumpkins, potatoes, corn, and sugarcane. Almost every family owned wild hogs,
and hog raising became a profitable enterprise.[43]

Joe Frank agreed with Paul Buster. "The economic practices
one hundred years ago were just to survive, plant some food to
eat, hide from the military, and survive. Sixty, fifty years ago, with
the advent of truck farming here in south Florida, the opportunity arose within the tribe for single mothers to rear families."[44]
Life, however, proved to be very difficult for single mothers who
were trying to raise a family by working in the fields and following the crops. "My mother was around," Marie Phillips remembered, "but she worked a lot because she was a single mother,
my Dad had left us when we were little. She was raising us, but
with the help of our grandparents she could go off the res and
go work somewhere. She would work ten to twelve hours a day
out in the vegetable fields somewhere. . . . She never went to

school so she did not know how to read and write so she would
go out and . . . she would pick tomatoes or cucumbers or peppers or whatever was in season at that time." All the children
had to work in the fields to make ends meet. "I was eight at the
time and I think my younger brother was six. We would go out
there and we would earn about twelve dollars a day. We would
give all our money to our mom so she could pay the bills and
we would have a vehicle to ride in and food to eat."[45] Alice Johns
Sweat had the same experience as a young girl. "Mostly, back
then, it was fieldwork, farmwork. Even when I was old enough
to work, I was out there on a farm."[46] Jeannette Cypress "ended
up quitting high school, tenth grade and I went to work [while
five months pregnant]. . . . I ended up working in the fields—
they picked bell peppers."[47]

Many Seminoles shared similar stories about the vicissitudes
of life as farmworkers and the lack of economic opportunity.
Victor Billie's father "started working in farming, like tomatoes,
picking, for seasons. So, we had to move around. We had to go
to . . . Fort Myers, Naples, Sarasota, all that. My mother started
working then in the fields."[48] Jacob Osceola's parents worked in
agricultural pursuits, his mother in the Immokalee area and his
father near Brighton working with cattle. His family was thus
separated—a "broken family" as he termed it.[49] Paul Bowers's
father "did not have any education. In those days, they did not
go to school. They were just, you know, whatever they could
find to do . . . maybe picking tomatoes, . . . string beans, or whatever. They went out, farmed and worked."[50]

Over time, truck farming and working in the fields died
out as a major source of income. "With the prosperity that the
tribe has with the . . . gaming, there is more opportunity. . . .
They don't have to go to Immokalee or they don't have to go
to Okeechobee. They don't have to go follow the crops. They
can find the jobs here. They can find work at above the minimum wage, where parents can set a role model for their kids."[51]

Jacob Osceola had the same view: "The tribe started to come into additional revenues in their budget . . . coming from bingo and cigarettes, so . . . dividends were given out, and more jobs were given in terms of programs. . . . People more or less filtered into those job positions so I think farming for their own needs probably phased out."[52]

Some tribal members expressed regret over the end to a self-sufficient way of life and the loss of family gardens. "I remember my grandma, we always had corn and pumpkin, and squash and tomatoes, and just different varieties of vegetables. And it was always that way, as far back as I can remember," said Mary Jene Coppedge. She also thought it unfortunate that there were fewer gardens than in the past and lamented the end of the strong sense of a shared community. "If they could find any rich soil, they always . . . would plant a lot, and it did not matter if one family planted it, it was for everybody. So, if anybody wanted pumpkin, they would come and get it. But my grandmother was always like that, too. She always shared."[53]

Louise Gopher complained that the young people in the tribe did not understand or appreciate the difficult times their parents and grandparents experienced. "Our people were brought up the hard way; . . . my parents worked in the tomato fields and did hard work. And I did, too. People my age were out picking tomatoes and picking up roots on . . . week-ends for money. And now it is just handed [out], money every month, and so it has kind of messed up our motivation. But we are working on that. We do special programs with our kids and talk to them and make them understand."[54] Joe Frank commented on the fact that the farming base of the tribal members was dying out and with it, an essential part of the Seminole culture. "Most of the elders knew how to raise food. They knew which foods to raise. Those elders have passed away, and they are passing away now. There is a conscious effort to teach the young, but it is really tough, going out and hoeing a patch of ground, to compete against M T V."[55]

While most worked in vegetables and truck farming, other jobs were available to tribal members during the 1950s and 1960s. Lorene Gopher's aunt worked with Lykes Brothers, a huge land and cattle corporation, for a long time,[56] others worked for the tribal textile plant in Brighton in the 1960s,[57] or planted hay for ranchers,[58] while others learned to operate bulldozers or took employment as a mechanic or a welder.[59]

Since 1999, as income from the cattle industry diminished, the tribe changed its views and economic goals and branched out into new farming ventures. "They did not grow sugarcane thirty years ago, and [now] we are into sugarcane," said Don Robertson. "We also have some citrus groves and we have close to a thousand acres of sugarcane now, which we will probably increase a little bit each year. . . . But we are advancing and getting diversified, which is one of the things I thought we should have done and which we have done. . . . A lot of people were against it [the shift to sugarcane] to start with, but now they have seen the profitability that is going to come off of it and the future of it looks real good."[60]

Stanlo Johns talked about those who opposed his decision to grow sugarcane. "I was not making any money on the cattle, I was just getting by, just floating, I knew that all my friends on the outside were all in sugarcane. . . . So I jumped into it, and, of course, it made a lot of people mad, and I am talking about local people." Johns had to appear before the cattle committee for approval, since they controlled the land. He thought the land was best suited for cane and eventually prevailed. "But you know talk behind your back, and all that. I knew that was going to be, I knew that before I started. . . . So, with the help of several of the cane growers and associating with U.S. Sugar, I went in and said, I am going to farm this. And they said, well, it is going to be work. And I told them, that is okay, I have worked all my life and never gotten anywhere. I said maybe with this I will do something. It is an uphill struggle because I have not harvested any of it yet."[61]

By 2004, citrus growing became less profitable for the tribe. The four hurricanes in 2004 destroyed 50 percent of the orange crop at Brighton and reduced production to the lowest level in a decade. Jim Talik, executive administrator for the Seminole Tribe, Inc., admitted in 2004 that "we have been losing money in citrus." He recommended that farmers turn to organic citrus or diversify their crops.[62]

At the end of the 1970s the main source of new income for the tribe came from radically non-Indian enterprises. In 1971, when Howard Tommie became chairman of the Tribal Council, he supported the Nixon administration's policy of self-determination for American Indians and introduced several free-enterprise programs. In 1975 Tommie learned from other tribes about the profitable tax-free cigarette stores known as "smoke shops." In 1977, Marcellus Osceola opened the first small cigarette sales store on the Hollywood Reservation, a wise choice since the shop was located within a short drive of large populations in the Fort Lauderdale–Miami metroplex. When the shop opened with cigarettes bought from an Alabama firm, long lines of cars formed along U.S. 441 to purchase a carton of cigarettes for $5.50, without having to pay the Florida tax of $2.10. Despite competition from tax-free sales on military reservations and veterans hospitals, the stores were an instant success.

Because the Florida Division of Alcoholic Beverages and Tobacco did not collect taxes from the Seminole smoke-shops, the Broward County sheriff and a cigarette vending company filed suit in county court to force the collection of state taxes on all Seminole cigarette sales. The state authorities ultimately did not intervene, probably because they did not feel comfortable challenging federal reservation law or believed that Florida law was inadequate to allow them to enforce collection of the tax.

The Seminoles won a signal victory in the court case in March, 1978 when the Florida District Court of Appeals reaffirmed the original decision, ruling that under Florida law, the tax on cigarettes could not be collected on the Seminole reservation. The wholesaler, the firm in Alabama, had the responsibility of collecting the tax, but since the firm was out of state, Florida had no jurisdiction. Aware of the conflicting opinions on this issue in other federal courts, the Seminole tribe launched an effective campaign in the state legislature which led to the passage of a law guaranteeing the tribe the right to continue tax-free sales.

Emboldened by their success in the courts, the tribe opened "smoke shops" on other reservations and built a new drive-through facility in Hollywood. The early shops were located in rather dingy buildings or converted mobile homes with a drive-up window. The income from these sales allowed the tribe to provide jobs for unemployed Seminoles, and quickly improved the financial condition of the people.[63] Carl Baxley "got into the cigarette business back in April of 1983. There had been tribal members selling cigarettes on the reservation tax-free, state tax-free, not federal tax, and it kind of opened the door for a lot of people to take that opportunity, if you could find a piece of land. I was fortunate enough to find a piece of land and get approval from the tribe to put up a cigarette shop." Baxley noted, however, that "at one time it was a great business to get into, but since then it had just kind of dwindled away. . . . You have a lot of non-smoking campaigns going on now. A lot of the elder smokers died off. You have a lot of lawsuits going on. And the price of cigarettes has gone up dramatically in the past year. So there are a lot of factors contributing to it. People are being made more aware that it [smoking] kills you."[64]

Early on the tribe realized that there would have to be some rules and regulation for the "smoke shops" in order to prevent price competition. Joe Dan Osceola understood that "if we didn't have any regulations . . . they [the rival "smoke shops"] would go a little bit lower than the next person . . . and they would get all of the customers. . . . If you are going to start a cigarette shop, then we had the council [tribal] to approve that. We have these laws and regulations, rules and ordinances, that everybody sells cigarettes at the same price."[65] Some shop owners, like Jacob Osceola, appreciated the job opportunity but recognized the limitations of his work. "One of the changes, I think, is in terms of employment, where I am able to receive a pretty good salary. . . . I have learned how to run a cigarette shop, I will not say a business, because built-in profits for a certain venture is not really a business, that is regulated by the tribe. . . . It actually does not induce the entrepreneurship, to go out and do the best you can to make more money. It is just the best location that is going to achieve a better realizing of the income from that product. I think in the last thirty years the tribe has helped individuals to get into business, and [it] may not be business per se, but it gives them a step in that entrepreneurship."[66]

The opening of the first "smoke shop" gave the Seminoles a stable enterprise that continues to bring substantial income into the tribal treasury. Gaming, however, is the number one economic enterprise for the Seminole Indians. In December 1979, the Seminoles, under the leadership of James Billie, the new tribal chairman, opened a high-stakes, unregulated bingo hall in Hollywood—the first of its kind in the country. The upscale, $900,000 hall accommodated fifteen hundred players and featured closed-circuit television, a large tote board, valet parking, climate control, and security guards. The BIA would not lend money for bingo halls, and banks were also reluctant to do so since they could not foreclose on bad loans if the business were on federal property; so the Seminoles were forced to turn to outside investors to build their new facility. The profits were split 45 percent to the backers and 55 percent to the tribe. The venture proved to be an immediate success with customers arriving from Tampa, Orlando, and Jacksonville by the busload.

Buoyed by the initial response and the large profits, although
Florida law limited bingo prizes to $100, the high-stakes bingo
games had the nightly super jackpot run as high as $19,000. In
November 1980 the tribe opened a smaller bingo hall in the Brighton Reservation.

The success of the high-stakes, high-profit bingo halls led
to several legal challenges. In 1980, Bob Butterworth, the sheriff of Broward County and later the attorney general of Florida,
brought suit to close the bingo facility in Hollywood. He charged
that the hall violated state regulations which restricted both the
hours of operation and the size of the jackpots in bingo halls.
The tribe sought injunctive relief, once again invoking its sovereignty and claiming immunity from state laws regulating bingo.
Under the doctrine of tribal sovereignty, states do not have civil
or regulatory jurisdiction (that is, they cannot levy taxes) on federal Indian reservations. In *Seminole Tribe of Florida v. Butterworth*
(1980), the U.S. District Court for the Southern District of Florida held that the tribe could continue to operate the bingo halls
because the state's bingo statute was civil and regulatory (rather
than criminal and prohibitory) and that Congress had never au-
thorized the states to impose general regulatory schemes on Indian lands. This favorable decision was affirmed by the U.S. Fifth
Circuit Court of Appeals in 1981.

The tribe worked hard for several years for the right to open
a gambling casino on the reservation. A federal appeals court
decision allowed the Seminoles to ask the secretary of the interior for permission to open a gambling casino under the provisions of the Indian Gaming Regulatory Act of 1988. The act
gave the tribes exclusive authority to operate bingo and other
"traditional" games common to all charity events. The tribes
could use slot machines only in states that permitted them. The
act further directed states to negotiate in good faith to devise
"tribal-state compacts" to regulate Class III (casino) gambling
and allowed federal courts to hear any opposition to the com-

pacts. The state of Florida stymied the Seminoles' request for casino gambling by using a provision in the state constitution that prohibited casino gambling.

Following the provisions of the Indian Gaming Regulatory Act of 1988, the tribe brought suit to force the state to negotiate a compact, and the case worked its way to the U.S. Supreme Court. In *Seminole Tribe of Florida v. Florida* (1996), the Court held that Congress does not have the power to force states to negotiate compacts with the tribes.[67]

Although thwarted in pursuit of a compact with the state of Florida, the Seminole Tribe continued its gaming operations. The U.S. Supreme Court ruled that the states had no authority over gambling on Indian reservations, but the state of Florida disagreed with that decision. The state has, for years, tried to shut down what it considers to be the Seminoles' "illegal gambling operations," but the tribe has refused to comply. The state argued that the Department of the Interior does not have the right to set a policy that is opposed by the people of the state. The Department of the Interior claims it does have jurisdiction over tribal reservations, and Bruce Rogow, an attorney for the tribe, insisted that Indian tribes, under federal law, are entitled to gaming.

The state of Florida fears that the federal government will soon authorize the Seminoles to engage in full-scale, Las Vegas–style gambling with roulette wheels and blackjack tables. When Lawton Chiles was governor, James Billie offered to give the state half of any profits the tribe gained from gambling. Chiles refused, turning down an estimated $100 million per year. He argued that the state's voters had defeated a constitutional amendment to legalize gambling and said that he would not negotiate with the tribe over casino gambling. Governor Jeb Bush also took a hard stance against gambling.

The tribe ignored the opposition of the state and continued to expand its gaming operations. In 1991 the Seminole Casino Hollywood, which was the first high-stakes operation in the country, became a twenty-four-hour-a-day facility with bingo, tournament poker, and 770 employees.

In 1994 the tribe opened the Seminole Casino Immokalee with a bar, restaurant, gaming machines, poker, and a Seminole Native Arts and Crafts shop. Next came the Brighton Seminole Gaming Casino, and then in March 2000 the Coconut Creek Casino began operations, with plans to develop Las Vegas–style gaming and entertainment.

By 1997 the Hollywood casino had become the tribe's biggest moneymaker. According to a series of articles by the *St. Petersburg Times*, the tribe paid $24.2 million in management fees to the Seminole Management Company (SMA), a private company that financed and built the casino. The tribe eventually paid $60 million to buy out SMA's contract. Howard Tommie, who did not run for reelection in 1979 as Seminole chairman, signed a deal for a share of the Hollywood hall's profits. In 1992, for example, Tommie received $2.4 million from the casino profits. Michael Cox, formerly general counsel for the National Indian Gaming Commission, criticized Tommie for taking money from the tribe: "This isn't the first tribe where leadership has benefitted." Despite the success of the casinos and an increase in the dividend paid to each tribal member, the *St. Petersburg Times* stated that unemployment and school dropouts remained high.[68] In July 2000, however, the *Times* reported that the tribe's annual budget had reached $203 million.[69]

In July 2003 the Seminole Tribe, Inc., opened the $100 million Hard Rock Hotel and Casino in Tampa. Because the Seminole tribe is a sovereign nation and is exempt from local building requirements, they built the twelve-story hotel-casino-restaurant complex without comprehensive site planning, impact fee requirements, citizen input, or local government oversight. The complex features 250 distinctly designed hotel rooms, a sports bar, a music venue and nightclub, a Hard Rock retail store, and a pool-spa complex in addition to 1,500 video gambling machines, 55 poker tables, and a bingo gallery serving up to 800 patrons. At the opening ceremonies, featuring fireworks and a concert by Huey Lewis and the News, the ribbon cutting unleashed a huge crowd and within minutes all of the electronic machines were being used. The tribe praised the new venture as one of their greatest accomplishments and explained that the new hotel-casino would be a great asset to the economy as it would bring in a large number of tourists and new jobs.[70]

Shortly thereafter, in May 2004, the Seminoles opened another Hard Rock Hotel and Casino, this time in Hollywood, Florida. The latest property had 500 hotel rooms, 130,000 square feet of casino space, an arena with 6,000 seats, twenty-four-hour dining, a 22,000-square-foot health spa, and a Seminole Village and Museum. The tribe anticipated that the facility would bring in 20,000 customers a day with a $1.25 billion economic impact on the south Florida economy. James Allen, chief executive officer of the gaming operations, declared that "this facility is going to change the way the tribe, entertainment and hospitality are perceived in south Florida. There is truly nothing like it." Tribal Council member Max Osceola Jr. proudly explained that the new project raised the level of the tribe's sophistication in the business world and made a "positive economic statement for the tribe." As of 2003, income from the gaming operations accounted for more than 90 percent of the tribe's cash flow and thus funded more than 90 percent of the tribe's expenditures on health care, education, housing, economic development and social services.[71] The agreement with the developers of the Hard Rock properties required that the Seminole Tribe pay them 17 percent of the gross revenue from the two casinos. In 2001 that gross revenue was around $218 million.[72]

In 2002 and 2003, charges from the *St. Petersburg Times* alleging misuse of both tribal gambling funds and U.S. government grants forced the Seminole Tribe of Florida to provide a

response. At the center of the dispute was the longtime chairman of the Tribal Council, James Billie. Billie, a charismatic
leader and the public face of the tribe, had, according to some,
ruled with an iron hand.

During his life, Billie had been a Vietnam infantryman, an
alligator wrestler, a dropout from Lake City Community College, a hairdresser, a landscaper, and a country singer. Now he
managed a business empire with annual revenues of half a bil-
lion dollars—making it one of the top fifty corporations in Florida. According to the *St. Petersburg Times*, "Billie rules like a be-
nevolent dictator. He bails out tribal members who get arrested,
treats the tribe's newspaper as 'part of my weapons' and forgives
tribal loans to those he favors if they can't repay." While tending
to his duties as chairman, Billie lived a life of luxury. He drove a
fancy Mercedes sedan, owned a forty-seven-foot yacht, had priority use of a $9 million Falcon 50 jet (which formerly belonged
to Philippine president Ferdinand Marcos) and three helicopters,
and owned twenty acres of land in Oklahoma.[73]

In their exposé of Billie and the tribe's gambling enterprises,
two *Times* writers, Brad Goldstein and Jeff Testerman, charged
that there were suspicious payouts at the casino and that not
enough of the gambling profits had been returned to the tribal
members. When Howard Tommie left as chairman of the Tribal
Council, according to the paper, he received an extraordinary
payout of $12.5 million for the interest he owned in SMA. Ac-
cording to Goldstein and Testerman, the scarcity of information about the tribe's finances had led to the criticism that excess
funds had been funneled to Howard Tommie and James Billie.
Billie rejected the charges and defended the use of the jet as being necessary for him to travel to various business meetings and
further stated that buying the plane was a good investment, as
it had appreciated in value.

The *Times* also claimed that the tribe had misused federal
funds. Although gambling had been intended to reduce the Sem-

inoles' reliance on federal aid, the estimated take from both federal and state sources in 1995 was $39.2 million—funds primarily expended for education, health care, law enforcement, and water management. Housing and Urban Development auditors concluded that the tribe had squandered federal tax money, and other government auditors charged that the tribe had exaggerated the number of children eligible for Head Start funds.[74]

Billie's internal critics were reluctant to challenge him for fear they might lose their dividend checks or suffer the loss of children's tuition. Billie fought the indictments and increased the pressure on the tribe when he offered a $5,000 reward for the names of those who had supplied information to the *St. Petersburg Times*. In the *Seminole Tribune*, Billie accused the *Times* of resorting to questionable, illegal, and unethical tactics in a "tabloid style" investigation of the Seminole Tribe: "The *St. Petersburg Times* has pried into the most intimate sectors of an entire American Indian culture—searching from bedrooms to boardrooms and harassing Tribal members and employees in a manner not seen in this part of Indian Country since the U.S. cavalry rode horses and swatted the Indians to walk faster on the Trail of Tears." Billie said that the tribe had nothing to hide, but the charges had damaged the reputation of the tribe and he was considering legal action.[75]

In February 1999 the Seminole Tribe sued the *St. Petersburg Times* and the two reporters, charging the paper with racism, violation of civil and criminal law, and failing to properly supervise the two reporters who wrote the story. The suit sought the sources and documents used in publishing the series and also sought to restrict the paper from future reporting on the tribe. The suit alleged that the exposés "were racially motivated" and sought "to ascribe to the Seminole Tribe and its leadership racist stereotypes regarding Indians as savage, uncivilized and corrupt." The tribe argued that the paper had violated journalistic ethics by targeting tribal employees and encouraging them to "violate and breach their fiduciary duties to the tribe" to covertly furnish confidential and secret information to the reporters. *Times* attorney George Rahdert denied that the reporting was racially motivated and said that the lawsuit tried "to silence news coverage about a gambling enterprise which has separated a lot of money from a lot of people in Florida."[76]

In April 2001 the Fourth District Court of Appeals affirmed a lower court decision and dismissed the tribe's lawsuit against the *St. Petersburg Times*. The court decided for the paper on the basis of First Amendment rights and determined that the articles constituted an appropriate attempt to gather information. The decision did not please the *Seminole Tribune*. The paper believed the articles were intended to hurt the tribe and were not intended to enlighten its readership. They kept referring to "a basement level of journalism" and the "scary intimidation of a reckless press."[77]

The tribe soon became involved in another contentious lawsuit, this one an internal struggle. In *The Seminole Tribe v. James Billie*, the tribe alleged that Billie and former tribal administrator Tim Cox had destroyed and falsified records in order to pay $169,000 to Christine O'Donnell. Billie, although suspended as chairman by the tribe, agreed to be "financially accountable" for the $169,000 and would repay the amount in full. According to the tribal attorney, this decision had nothing to do with the sexual harassment suit filed by O'Donnell or the separate forensic audit of tribal finances.[78]

In April 2003 the Tribal Council, after assessing the results of the outside audit, decided to remove James Billie as chairman. They based their decision on Billie's "admission of guilt" during a March 13 hearing to answer the council's statement of charges. The council found Billie guilty on nine counts as he either answered "guilty" or did not dispute the charges. The former chairman claimed that the conduct of which he had been accused "was done with the tribe's best interest in mind."

The charges and findings of the Tribal Council amounted to a serious indictment of Billie's tenure as chairman. Count 1 stated that Billie "lied, deceived and misrepresented crucial information to the Tribal Council" about the tribal investment accounts. He secretly transferred money into investment accounts resulting in losses of over $200 million in tribal funds. Count 2 charged that Billie had established a secret, offshore, illegal internet gambling venture and concealed the undertaking from the Tribal Council. In count 3, Billie admitted to authorizing hundreds of thousands of dollars to purchase Legends Hotel in Nicaragua. Later, as indicated in Count 7, with the ownership of the Legends Hotel in dispute, Billie paid two friends $80,000 to try to steal the hotel from the tribe. Other charges divulged that Billie created false documents to justify the illegal spending of millions of dollars, that he tried to undermine the authority of the council when suspended, and that he disregarded the restraints placed on him by the Constitution of the Seminole Tribe. Under oath in a federal trial, Chairman Billie stated that he "regarded the Tribe's investment account as his money to do with as he pleased."[79]

In May 2003 the Seminoles overwhelmingly elected Mitchell Cypress as the new tribal chairman. As Cypress and the other new leaders took their oath of office, they celebrated a "new beginning" after some "turbulent times."[80]

Although the Seminoles made huge sums from their gaming activities, the tribe ran into trouble when it came to how those earnings were used. The head of the National Indian Gaming Commission, Philip Hogen, warned that the federal government would shut down all Seminole casinos unless the tribe stopped using illegal gaming devices and ended an unsupervised spending program that pumped millions into luxury cars and gifts for cronies of the council members. The discretionary spending plan allocated $5 million to $10 million annually to each member of the Tribal Council to spend as they wished. These spending excesses had been documented in a 2002 federal conspiracy, embezzlement, and money-laundering trial involving three employees of the Seminole Tribe. David Cypress, Mitchell Cypress's younger brother, admitted that he spent $57 million in less than four years. He bought so many luxury cars for friends that he lost track of who got what. He also spent $350,000 for a friend's boxing gym and $5.8 million for another friend's landscaping business.

This excessive spending violated the Indian Gaming Regulatory Act of 1988, which specified that money from tribal gaming must be used to finance tribal government operations, to provide for the general welfare of the tribe and its members, to promote economic development, and to make charitable donations. Hogen, who had the power to close gaming activities and levy fines for failure to follow the rules, met with the Seminoles in 2004. They decided, wisely, to work on financial reform by increasing the monthly dividend, curtailing arbitrary expenditures such as travel, and earmarking more funds for tribal education programs.[81]

Despite some attempts at financial reform, the Seminole tribe had to confront additional fiscal abuses. According to the *South Florida Sun-Sentinel*, a handful of tribal leaders continued to benefit at the expense of other tribal members and handed out millions of dollars to themselves, their families, and their friends. David Cypress, reported the *Sun-Sentinel*, continued his exorbitant spending: "From David Cypress' fund, 945 tribal members received assistance totaling $13.6 million. Of those, 30 people got more than half the money, including Cypress' three daughters, his ex-wife and brother Mitchell Cypress."[82]

Several members of the tribe complained that they were not getting their fair share of the funds, and this led to a grassroots recall of the 2004 budget. Subsequently, the Tribal Council began holding open budget meetings, implementing new budgetary procedures and agreeing to greater transparency. After numerous interviews with tribal members, Jessica Cattelino learned that their "primary concern about officials' discretionary spending was not the fact or the size of the allocations but the equity with which they were (or were not) distributed." While press reports focused on the large sums of money spent and on possible corruption, many Seminoles did not see the problem as one of too much money or tainted money from gambling. They instead blamed "leadership failure, interpersonal tensions and personalized greed." A few saw their elected official's greed as an assimilation of the white man's values. Cattelino noted that tribal skepticism about spending remained high. There are continued calls for constitutional reform that would reduce the power of the Tribal Council members and eliminate their edge in elections based on a high expenditure of funds right before voting takes place.[83]

On the positive side, the Seminole Tribe of Florida, Inc., used its newfound wealth to increase its charitable contributions by a considerable amount. The tribe has sponsored scholarships for needy students and has contributed to neighborhood community programs for health care, education, and the Little League. It pledged $3 million toward the creation of a historical park in Fort Lauderdale and gave a large sum to the Broward County Red Cross. The Seminoles also like to point out the dramatic ripple effect that tribal spending has on the local economy. In 1997, partly to counter some local resentment about their wealthy status, the tribe took out an advertisement in several non-Indian newspapers: "Which Floridians employed over 2,200 other Floridians, paid over $3.5 million in federal payroll taxes and purchased more than $24 million worth of Florida goods and services last year." The answer: "The same Floridians who operate citrus groves, manage one of America's largest cattle herds and have acted as stewards of the Everglades for over 200 years." The ad concluded with the seal of the tribe: "100% Seminole. 100% American."[84]

In January 2006 the tribe purchased land in Osceola County and filed a request for a casino license from the Department of the Interior. The Osceola County Commission has hired a political consultant to lead the fight against the casino, and local citizens have organized a group called Stop Indian Gambling Now (SIGN). Their fear is that gambling will bring in unsavory characters and undermine family values in the community.[85]

In December 2006 the Seminole Tribe shocked the business world by purchasing the famed Hard Rock International, the music-themed chain of restaurants, hotels, and casinos. The tribe paid $965 million to the Rand Group of Britain, one of the largest purchases ever by an American Indian tribe. Founded in 1971 in London, in 2006 Hard Rock employed about 7,000 workers at 124 restaurants in twenty-four countries and operated seven hotels, two casinos, and two concert venues. The company also owned one of the world's largest collections of rock memorabilia—including items from Elvis Presley, Bob Dylan, and Madonna. It is perhaps ironic that the tribe now owns artifacts revered by white culture. The Seminoles planned to finance the deal through equity from the tribe and debt issued by a new operating company, which would control Hard Rock. One consultant estimated that the new assets could generate as much as $900 million in gross receipts for the tribe. The Seminoles held the announcement ceremony in the Hard Rock Café in Times Square. Bobby Henry, a Seminole medicine man in traditional regalia, delivered a blessing in the Mikasuki language. Max Osceola Jr. proclaimed a special day in Seminole history. "Our ancestors sold Manhattan for trinkets. We're going to buy Manhattan back, one burger at a time."[86]

Widely recognized as the ones who originally tested the legal issues with high-stakes bingo, the Seminoles have been a model for Indian gaming since. They have been in the forefront of tribes who developed successful gaming properties, and with the purchase of Hard Rock they became major players in the gambling and hospitality industry. Although not all gambling activities are highly profitable, gambling did become a bonanza for 220 tribes in twenty-eight states who have gaming operations. In 2005, all of these operations brought in gross revenues of $22.6 billion.[87]

As of 2006, the Seminole Tribe, Inc., was taking in more than $300 million per year, and each of the approximately 3,240 tribal members was receiving a yearly dividend of $42,000. In 2007 the *South Florida Sun-Sentinel* updated the figure to $120,000 per year per tribal member.[88]

On November 13, 2007, Florida governor Charlie Crist and Tribal Chairman Mitchell Cypress signed a historic compact that would allow blackjack, slot machines, and baccarat at seven Seminole casinos. In return for allowing Class III gambling, the state would receive $500 million upon federal approval of the deal, at least $100 million during the first year of implementation and a guaranteed minimum of $150 million by the third year of operations.

State legislators from both political parties threatened to sue Crist, arguing not only that the state was getting the "short end of the financial stick" but also that any compact with the Seminoles required legislative approval. Eventually, House Speaker Mario Rubio filed suit. The governor responded by explaining that the U.S. Department of the Interior had set a deadline of November 13 for the state and tribe to reach a deal and thus had forced his hand. If the state did not make the agreement, Crist said, then the federal government could have done so, and the state would have received no money. Crist wanted the funds from the twenty-five-year agreement to support education in the state.

The agreement also included a clause that would allow the Seminoles to drop out of the deal if lawmakers approved the expansion of gambling in any counties other than Broward or Miami-Dade. The compact thus made the state a partner with the Seminoles in an effort to prevent gambling from spreading beyond the reservations. The state would lose the revenue from legal gambling if any expansion were allowed. The tribe enthusiastically welcomed the agreement, stating that they would increase their payroll from 7,000 to 17,000 in three to four years and that the casinos would soon become national and international destinations.[89]

On November 18, 2007, the *St. Petersburg Times*, in a persuasive editorial, complained that Governor Crist had exceed his authority. State law allowed for only high-stakes slot machines and forbade all other forms of Class III gambling, including blackjack and baccarat. Also, the Indian Gaming Regulatory Act, in discussing tribal compacts, referred only to the need for approval by the state and did not use the word "governor." Thus nothing in current law or the Florida constitution specifically gave Crist such authority.[90]

The Florida Supreme Court agreed. In a unanimous opinion on July 2, 2008, the court ruled that the governor had no authority to change state law and thus could not allow the Seminoles to expand to Class III gambling when these activities were illegal in the state. The power to make such compacts fell exclusively to the legislature, which could authorize its own agreement with the tribe. The tribe and Crist appealed the decision, but their request for a new hearing was denied by the Florida Supreme Court in a 6–1 decision.[91] Despite the legal uncertainty, by May 8, 2008, the Seminole Tribe had begun the process of instituting Class III gambling in all of its casinos.[92]

Nonetheless, the once impoverished, racially segregated tribe, persecuted and forced into uninhabitable swampland, now had turned the tables by achieving wealth that would have been unimaginable in 1979. A few tribal members insisted on being self-sufficient, partly because they thought that gambling might not last, but also because they wanted economic independence and control of their future. The Indians' desire for economic self-reliance stemmed from their larger conception of being "unconquered and also because of long simmering resentment of the Bureau of Indian Affairs and their paternalistic attitude." Finally, the Seminoles had been cheated repeatedly by racist and shady investors and now they had control of their main—and for many, the only—option for success: the gaming industry.[93]

The ultimate question is how the large influx of money from gambling will affect the tribe's values and culture. Some individuals criticized gambling as a practice that preys on the weakness of others and argued that they were sacrificing their values in the pursuit of the almighty dollar. According to Jessica Cattelino, however, most tribal members saw no moral peril to the tribe from gambling. She further indicated that financial security did not translate into a loss of tradition, culture, or identity for any minority group. "There is no reason to assume that wealth, more than poverty, would lead to cultural loss."[94]

The tribe's newfound freedom and monetary largesse came after many years of extreme hardship, and most tribal members are grateful for their hard-won wealth. For example, Mary Jene Coppedge has always been grateful for the benefits derived from gaming and concluded that bingo was the most important economic activity. "Bingo has done a lot for my tribe. I can remember going to school and wondering if I would ever get a chance to go to college and wondering how I was going to pay for that. Since bingo has come . . . it has given us an opportunity to have more and be able to do more, not just by having some money and going and spending it the way you want to, but to be able to send your children to whatever college they want to go to, to be able to have the health care that we have now, the facilities, the school, it has just been an economic boost for my people."[95] Cleve Baker served as an example of a Seminole economic success story fueled by gaming profits. He took his tribal stipend, studied to become a chef, and opened his own restaurant, the Renegade Barbeque Company. The restaurant is an upscale steak and barbecue restaurant at the Seminole Hard Rock Hotel and Casino in Hollywood. It serves Native dishes such as alligator and Indian corn soup. Baker pursued the American Dream, but did so on Native American terms: he achieved success while preserving the heritage and sovereignty of the tribe. "I owe everything I have achieved to the tribe."[96]

Joe Dan Osceola appreciated the importance of Seminole gaming but was troubled by white attitudes toward Indian gaming, especially when whites "tried to put an injunction on us and tried to stop us. They tried to close down the gaming. The white people unfortunately, the majority of white people, they do not have power, but there are a very few people that are in power that we have a lot of problem with. You cannot make a judgment of all of the white people, of course, because people in power are the ones that make your life miserable, if they vote against your best interests. You want to take care of your people on the reservation, but they [whites] are happy as long as you do not make money, as long as you sell the trinkets, beads, beside the road, as long as you are not in competition with anything they do. In education, it is hard to send your child to a private school by just selling trinkets and beads by the side of the road. You cannot even drive a fairly good car . . . without having that kind of support [money from gaming] from the Tribe."[97]

Tribal members are of two minds when considering the impact of the gaming industry. No one disputes the financial benefit, but some did not want to rely solely on gaming and saw gambling as a threat to traditional values. Jim Shore, the tribe's legal counsel, argued that "there are no two ways about it; gaming has gotten us to where we are. I think back to 1979–1980, when we first started the bingo hall here. . . . The one here was the first of its kind across the whole country . . . and it took off elsewhere." Shore understood that "it has always been a risky thing with gambling, and I think, maybe, while we have a chance with the money, we ought to diversify into other things, just in case gaming is ever knocked out from under us. . . . It may not be a big, quick money-making business, but at least something that will be ongoing."[98]

Richard Bowers concurred. "I am going to say, right off hand, gambling has changed and advanced the tribe leaps and bounds because of the money or the economy that the reservation has. We had no economy back thirty years ago. . . . I remember when we were going to school . . . that the Christian organizations would come and give us secondhand clothes for us to go to school in. That would be a big thing for us because we wanted the best clothes. . . . We were too young to know that it was charity. We don't have to rely on charity anymore, and these people here today can go out to the best stores and buy their clothes, whatever they want. . . . Everything is just so much better, so convenient and easier than it was. To get back to the gambling, I think it does help a lot of people and it makes sure that we do what we want to do and not limit us to how much it would cost."[99]

Joe Frank also agreed that "the most lucrative economic endeavor they [the Seminoles] have is gaming." Frank said that the Seminoles, like everyone else in America, want to "provide for their kids. I think every race of people wants their kids to have it a little bit better than they did, to enjoy a few more things of life. A lot of the tribal members are getting to enjoy some of that expectation that we are led to believe is available to every middle-class American."[100]

Tribal members understood explicitly the influence that increased wealth had on their lives. Paul Bowers pointed out the effect that additional funds had on employment. The gaming, bingo halls, sugarcane, cattle, and swamp safari brought in revenue that the tribe could use "to make all of these other jobs available for the tribal members and the non-tribal members."[101] With computers and the newfound wealth, Paul Buster found the reservation "entirely different from when I was a kid growing up. . . .

Nowadays people have four-door air-conditioned trucks with a twenty-foot trailer they can put four, five, or six horses in and be over there in ten minutes."[102] Joe Dan Osceola appreciated the fact that the tribe's wealth allowed them to build the Ah-Tah-Thi-Ki Museum to preserve Seminole history and culture. "So, that is something good for the public to know. . . . I would think it is good for the public and good for the tribe."[103]

Other members of the tribe worried about the negative impact on their traditional values due to a heavy emphasis on gambling and an increased commitment to capitalism. Samuel Tommie philosophized about the duality of views: "I feel that the economic practices kind of jeopardize, kind of steps on people's rights as it goes along. In some cases, our economic system and our government system is based on the United States [system] and it becomes totally useless when it comes to human rights. So I think some of the things we practice do a lot of damage to the environment. . . . The money does help out the people, but what is the process? The process is, if we are doing gambling, then there are people being addicted to gambling and it might be bad for their families. So economy is a very funny thing. . . . I wish things were different. I guess it is a big rat race or else we would not be in gambling. I mean, this gambling brings in a lot of money, yes, but it hurts a lot of people. It is the good old American way." Tommie thought the economy's impact on Seminole values depended on the individual's point of view. "If they are more Americanized, then maybe it does not matter to them. If they are more in touch with their traditional values, then they will say, hey, this does not feel too good."[104]

Older Seminoles believed that the affluent lifestyle affected young people's attitudes, making them less motivated to work and provide for themselves. Louise Gopher, age fifty-four, continually warned young people about dependence on handouts from the tribe and federal and state governments as well as expressing the Seminole's long-standing distrust of the state and federal government. "It has made people less motivated to do for themselves. . . . We try to tell them that the government is always after us. They are always trying to pass legislation to cut anything that we have like that."[105]

Betty Mae Jumper, age seventy-seven, concluded that "a lot of this money is ruining them [young people]. When we did not have money, we did not have any drinking and problems going on as bad as we have now. If they [the Tribal Council] had thought the other way and did not give them money all at the same time and just maybe divided it in two or three ways, maybe that would have been better. But they get the whole amount of money and then they get drunk, a lot of them do. Some of them do not. . . . But, young people, we lost a lot of them . . . with accidents, drinking and driving." Jumper continued: "It is good that they get money, that they can support themselves and build new homes and all of that. Some of them do that. Some of them do not. Some of them just . . . stand out in the front, from day to day, until the dividend time. They come and borrow . . . money . . . and go drinking. And then, by the dividend time, some of them do not have any [money]. So, they borrow it for next month. and that is the way they go. That is what I do not like because it is really hurting them."[106]

The younger Seminoles have had difficulty resisting the temptations that wealth has brought, and some have experimented with drugs and alcohol. A large sign on the Brighton Reservation warns: "We fought too long to die by our own hands. Stop drugs, alcohol and violence." As a result, the tribe began putting 75 percent of the dividends for minors into trust funds that cannot be accessed until they are eighteen. By that time, the leaders hope, the children have been taught the proper values.

Many tribal members use their money to travel and buy houses off the reservation. They spend more and more time away from the reservation and begin losing touch with each other and their heritage. One elder lamented the situation. "You drive around [the reservation] but don't know who to wave to because everyone has these new cars and you don't recognize them. . . . Will they continue to know each other? Will the tribe hold together? Who knows? We shall see."[107]

The Tribal Council used gaming proceeds as seed money for businesses such as contracting firms, a limousine service, detailing emporiums, and a company that owns and hires out stage equipment to promoters. In the last few years, however, partly due to the availability of higher-paying jobs, an interest in craft work has died out. The Seminoles still make dolls and baskets, carve canoes, and do beadwork for sale in the museum, but there is limited revenue from these sources. Sadie Cypress regretted that "nobody hardly makes stuff anymore now and the kids are not learning. Before too long, I do not think we will have baskets and dolls. But, a few of the younger ones are learning now how to make baskets and dolls. I do not know if they will keep it up."[108] Some single mothers used money from craft sales to buy groceries and pay bills. When Marie Phillips's children were "old enough to thread a needle, I taught them how to do it [crafts]. I told them it is always something good to have, even if you have an education. It is something to fall back on, or just something to know so that one day you can teach your kids. And just so that something is not lost along the way. Preservation is more of what I was trying to teach them, to keep it so that they do not lose it. That is how I feel about the language. Teaching my grand-daughter."[109]

For much of the twentieth century, tourism has been essential for the economic well-being of the Seminoles. The tribe promoted a crafts market and alligator wrestling as integral parts of the tourist trade. The Seminoles became involved with tourism early in the twentieth century when their trading income was in decline, when farmers and developers drained the Everglades for agriculture and new towns, and when inundated by an influx of new settlers. By 1930 the new economy of tourism employed more than half of the tribe, and many others worked to supply goods to the emerging markets.

By 1911, the Seminoles had located a camp on the Miami River on Musa Isle where Willie Willie established the Musa Isle Indian Village. Although by 1930 hunting still accounted for two-thirds of Seminole income, Musa Isle and Willie Willie had begun to make a profit. Musa Isle ultimately fell into the hands of businessman and promoter Bert Lasher, who also developed Osceola's Gardens and Osceola's Indian Village in Miami. The Seminoles set up villages at Coppinger's Pirate's Cove and at Silver Springs near Ocala. By the mid-1930s the Seminole villages had become one of the leading tourist attractions in the state, partly due to the city of Miami's active promotion of the sites. The villages featured alligator wrestling; tribal members living in chikees while performing daily chores such as cooking; Seminole weddings; and the sale of hides and crafts, such as cypress dugout canoes, dolls, drums, and patchwork goods. Seminoles earned other income from posing for pictures with tourists, and the attractions provided the Indians with a constant seasonal income.[110]

Tourism has remained an important and typical part of Seminole economic activity to the present and has remained consistent with the early villages in both form and function. Historian Patsy West concluded that, despite criticism from whites and government agencies that the exhibits degraded the Seminoles, tourism provided both a steady income and a cultural identity for a people proud of their heritage. West's research showed that the cultural life in the Indian villages did not deviate significantly from traditional practices; in fact, they strictly followed traditional customs. The experience did not degrade Seminole culture, but rather created a greater appreciation for what their ancestors had wrought.[111]

Since 1970, the tribe has expanded tourism significantly. In addition to the full-scale Ah-Tah-Thi-Ki Museum on the Big

Cypress Reservation, the tribe also has the Billie Swamp Safari, an attraction that allows visitors to skim across the water in an airboat or a "swamp buggy," sleep in a Seminole chikee, and listen to Indian folklore around a campfire. Originally the tribe used the site's eighteen hundred acres as an exotic hunting preserve, but eventually they changed it to an ecotourism attraction. They advertised the safari as an opportunity "to witness first hand the delicate ecosystem of a land on the edge of civilization and the solitary beauty of tropical hardwood hammock [and] cypress domes." Visitors could also see a traditional Indian village, watch alligator wrestling, observe unusual wildlife, and have a snack (gator tail nuggets and Seminole fry bread) at the Swamp Water Café.

If they desired, they could stay overnight in a chikee at the Seminole Camping Village, go on a Big Cypress Hunting Adventure, or spend the night at the Big Cypress RV Resort. The safari realized immediate success, as the number of visitors at the end of the 1990s averaged about 150,000 per year. Buoyed by an increase in tourism, the tribe worked with the state on improving advertising to attract a larger number of tourist, especially foreign tourists.[112]

In spite of the increased emphasis on tourism and culture, the tribe found it nearly impossible to get experts to demonstrate their skills in the traditional crafts. Henry John Billie was the last of the old canoe makers, and they had difficulty finding alligator wrestlers. For decades the Seminoles entertained visitors with alligator wrestling—an idea first introduced by white promoters. Moreover, saurians ran deep into Seminole history as they once hunted them as a source of hides and food. Michael Osceola, as of 2000 the only Seminole still wrestling, warned of the great danger of alligators. "You can't domesticate them. They don't know you and they definitely will never love you. . . . They have a brain the size of a sweet pea." The gators, continued Osceola, can move across dry land faster than a human and if they attack in the water, they are even more deadly. Anything they eat they swallow whole." Despite insurance, decent pay, and benefits, the tribe could not find wrestlers. Most young Seminoles took other employment or left the community. Desperate, the Seminoles decided to advertise in the *South Florida Sun-Sentinel*: "WANTED: Alligator wrestlers. Must be brave and a risk taker. Males and females o.k. No experience needed." Surprisingly, they did not get many applicants; after all, Tribal Chairman James Billie had lost a finger in 2000 while wrestling an alligator.[113]

Despite some criticism that those in the tourist trade were being exploited and had somehow lost their dignity by appearing before gawking tourists, those who participated in the industry from the 1920s through the 1960s were not negative or apologetic about their experience. In fact, they were proud to show whites their history and culture. Jeannette Cypress remembered: "I think tourism has always been a part of life for us. That is probably how we survived before we got gaming and other things. I remember going, as a youngster, to this village in Miami. My parents had to go there and sew and do things in front of tourists. I did not think of it as being bad. And then I worked at a village . . . I was like a tour guide. I always felt like I was out there promoting the tribe in a positive way. I did not want people to stereotype us, like, oh, drunk Indians. You know, you hear that all the time. So, I guess it was a way for me to tell people. I had kids asking me, can you see in the dark? Where are your feathers? It was one way to tell them who we really were. I never thought anything bad [about it]."

Cypress also commented favorably on the establishment of the Billie Swamp Safari. "I think it is a good public image, too. I do not want everybody to think, all they do is casinos and gambling and bingo. They do not realize that we have citrus and cattle and we are normal like everybody else. I have had people think that we do not pay taxes, that everything is for free, and they are in shock to know that we have to pay for everything. I even had a person ask me one time, . . . because you are on the reservation like this, if you kill somebody, they will not do anything to you, right? And I am like, where have you been? . . . [P]eople think that just because people are different colors on the outside that everything is so different, but really it is not. We might have the cultural things that are a little different, but still, basically, we all have the same problems."[114]

Other tribal members also argued that the museum and tourism were effective ways to explain the tribe's history and culture. "I think it is a good way of disseminating information on what the Indian tribes are about," said Jacob Osceola. "I think that sometimes the dominant society has this Hollywood sort of vision as to what an Indian is, and the museum and the Swamp Safari shows them a different light, other than Tonto and [the] Lone Ranger and 'Hi-Ho Silver, away,' that sort of thing."[115]

When asked if tourism had changed much over the years, Joe Frank answered: "I don't think it has changed that much. In the last fifty years the only change has been in the amount available to tourists. The tourism that we have available now has always been there, going back into the 1940s and 1950s, probably when [the] Tamiami Trail was just completed. What we have today is just an extension of that." The only change, mused Frank, was that there were a "lot more opportunities for tribal members to be directly in charge of their own little piece of the tourism pie."[116]

Carl Baxley approved of the economic motivation behind tourism, as it forced the tribe to safeguard their cultural heritage. "I think tourism makes you preserve your heritage and tradition by trying to market it. Now, if you are not going to market it, then you would probably have no reason [to preserve it], other than some medicine guy saying we need to save it. But by trying to market it as a tourism attraction, it makes you preserve it because it makes you talk about it, it makes you relive it, it makes you think about it." Baxley also saw tourism as valuable for helping young Seminoles understand their past: "You see people walking around looking at our culture, how we used to eat and live back in the old days. One hundred years has not been that long—well, twenty years in our case. I was raised in a chikee hut . . . with a dirt floor; that is where I slept. I took a bath in the ditch. So I am from the old-timers school. . . . We ate a lot of turtles. People went and picked tomatoes and peppers and they always brought some home and we ate off of that. I think it is a heck of a good position to be in because I can go back and forth. And there are very few of us that can do that. My kids have no concept of how it used to be, no concept."[117]

Daisi Jumper agreed that tourism was critical in saving Seminole culture because "we have to know what we are talking about to tell the tourists. So, we have to find out more about what we are telling them and that makes us go to our elders and learn. And the younger people that do not really know too much about Seminole history or culture, it gives them a chance to hear about it while the others are telling the tourists."[118] Victor Billie, however, worried that there was more of an interest in making money than in preserving the culture: "They preserve, but in time they are going to change it again to try to make more money, trying to make it interesting. Sometimes it is heading the wrong way."[119]

Recently, the tribe has taken the lead in developing ecoheritage tourism in Big Cypress. Lee Tiger, a Miccosukee, defined and described the purpose and benefits of ecotourism: "Ecology tours; that is learning about the nature of the surroundings: plant life, wildlife, and human life. The heritage side of the tourism is the heritage of the Florida Indian people, who have been here and have adapted to the Everglades and found a way to exist and the lifestyle of what they went through many years ago. So what has basically been created in Big Cypress is an opportunity for people to experience, for a day and overnight, or a multi-day arrangement, an eco-heritage experience. They have hiking, they have swamp buggy tours, and they also have air-boating, which people love to do. . . . And then we have, at night, folklore, around the campfire, storytelling, beadwork, woodcarving, and various different activities that one could observe and be a part of."[120]

Andy Buster elaborated on the heritage experience by citing a "tracking project in which you go out and track the animals as well as the[ir] spirituality." Then "we have a gathering in the circle . . . we will talk while we sit down, and each morning we share different dreams that we had dreamed the night before . . . or what we plan to do or something that is bothering us that we want to bring out. . . . We mostly work with the spiritual part of the people because that is where the healing comes from. Also we invite people who represent the big companies, like Du Pont and like Shell Oil Company, that drain the earth or use from the earth whatever the earth provides. . . . We invite those people to see what really lives within nature. The whole idea is for them to see what they are doing to nature when they are draining it out for chemicals and stuff."[121]

Lee Tiger worked vigorously to expand ecotourism by trying "to partner with . . . the tourism people in greater Fort Lauderdale [to] create a relationship . . . with the Convention Visitor's Bureau. Not only that, we have now partnered with the state of Florida, the new tourism department, is it called . . . 'Visit Florida.' And I also have a seat on the [state] tourist board." Tiger served on the state board so that Indian people would have representation and because he wanted the ecotourism packages "recognized by the state and the country and also the world. They [the Seminoles] have taken a leading role in doing that and deserve to have the product out there because it is the best. It is a very fine product."[122]

In addition to sharing their views of life with others, Seminoles saw ecotourism as important because it enabled the tribe to preserve their land and the environment. "I know my grandpa used to say, you just cannot go traipsing through the woods and just tear things up," said Mary Jene Coppedge. "If you keep constantly tearing things up, it is not going to be there. The ecotourism that we have here, and are able to share with other people, the non-Indian population has gone out and destroyed theirs, and I think because ours is still intact, it is fortunate that it is still intact, now we will be able to share it with someone else and teach them what was once there."[123]

Environmentally sensitive Seminoles regretted the draining of the Everglades and the building of roads, houses, and other infrastructure that had changed and disrupted their native environment forever. They longed for the rather simple and pristine life they shared in the 1960s. "We lived in chikees," recalled Marie Phillips, "and they did not have any big canals like they do now, and if it rained hard, we slept on platforms . . . and it was just a couple of inches before the water was touching the platform. There would be snakes and stuff swimming around. I guess we thought it was just part of life. Sometimes you would hear things just a foot away, just fighting in the water, and you did not know what it was but you just went on about your business."[124] Daisi Jumper remembered that "the land was very wet and there was a lot of water. You could find fish anywhere. You never starved. You could just go out there and get alligator or turtle or deer. . . . [S]ometimes we had to walk around in the water, [it was] even under our chikees. That was all right. That was our life. But then they made those canals and that is where all the water went. So, the land got to be very dry. I guess it was good but it was not how we lived, it was different . . . we did not have very many fish anymore. . . . There became more roads and more people coming in and coming through and the place got busier and busier. It used to be very peaceful and there were not many cars around, and then even our houses changed. I grew up living in a chikee. . . . My oldest son grew up in a chikee and then we had to start living in houses. That was different."[125]

Samuel Tommie lauded the Everglades as a beautiful and unique place and deplored the damage done by the Army Corps of Engineers and developers. "The flood control system that was put out here to dry out the Everglades in south Florida has totally interrupted the plant life, the animal life, and changed the whole environment. . . . There is no other place in the world that is like this. Down where the Everglades and the river of grass runs into the saltwater, where the fresh and saltwater mix, that is probably the only place on this planet where the different types of fish can be found. It is a pretty amazing place." Tommie denounced the continual building whereby developers took swampland, dredged up the muck, built houses, and replaced some of the water with a man-made lake. "They are willing to do this because these people can buy permits from the authorities to go ahead and do this. At the same time, they cannot replace what they are taking. It might be muck to them, but it is something that took millions of years for it to happen. They . . . continue to do a lot more damage. . . . It is a serious impact." Interstate 75, which runs from Naples to Fort Lauderdale, served as a dam so the water could not move naturally. "Because of the unnatural flow of things, it has caused a lot of damage. All in the name of economy and progress."

While recognizing the need for progress and development, Tommie understood the powerful influence that the drive for wealth had on individuals. "[I] try not to get too comfortable with the money, the material stuff, now that I have more than I need. It becomes a psychological thing, money is always dangerous. There are people who have a poor outlook on their lives because they do not have enough money, and there are people with a lot of money and they have the worst outlook on life and the worst treatment of their fellow people. It is always a dangerous thing and I try to keep perspective on that."[126]

Seminoles consistently blame whites and big business for polluting their tribal land. Victor Billie argued that the sugar companies were responsible for pollution in the area because they came in and drained the Everglades, used the water over and over, and then dumped chemicals into the water. Billie said it was good to try to learn about whites and live among them, but "it is not good to try to be like them, to destroy your land, to destroy the air you breathe, to destroy the water you drink. Those are the things that are very important on this land. If you go to school and learn this technology, it teaches you to hurt and destroy. We have survived on this land for a million years and the Europeans have been here five or six hundred years and look how much they destroy each day. They are not going to see the beauty of Florida and the United States in about twenty or thirty years. . . . And that is a waste."[127]

There is little dispute that the economic changes between 1970 and 2000 have had a dramatic impact on the Seminoles' values, culture, and lifestyle. The increased income from bingo, cigarettes, cattle, citrus, and other successful programs has enhanced the quality of life for the tribe. They have better homes, new cars, televisions, better health care (fully paid by the tribe), a new school and money for anyone who desires a college education, a new museum, much higher employment, dividends from the tribe, and increased economic opportunities offered by the tribe, whether it is working in Billie Swamp Safari or on the new Micco airplanes.

There are those who, however much they appreciate the advantages of a higher standard of living, see the love of materialism as threatening to their values and as lessening the drive for an education and hard work. This was especially true for the younger generation, which did not undergo or understand the hard times their parents experienced. Helene Johns Buster recognized that opportunities were very different for the young people in 2000. She recalls being very poor, but "today, every kid, just about, has their own vehicle. . . . The opportunities they have are so different now. Even in sports and things like that; when my cousins and my brothers . . . wanted to be in sports, they had to have somebody [transport them]—because we were very poor back then and we did not have transportation and things like that. So the school, in order to have the Indians play ball, which they wanted them to because they were very good ball players, they would have to have transportation from school, from practice . . . and back home for them, every day." Buster lamented the fact that since most young people now have their own cars, "they do not play in sports and things like that because they have so much more material things that that stuff is not important anymore." [128]

Mary Jene Coppedge took the opposite point of view. She felt that the economic changes had not affected Seminole values as much as many people claimed. "The values that were instilled in us are still there. I do not think it is so much just because we are Seminoles that our values are diminishing, just because there is better economics or better living, the values are still there." Coppedge made an insightful observation in regard to Seminole values. All of society's values are changing, as many Americans have become more materialistic, more interested in wealth and status. In fact, on a comparative basis, the Seminoles exhibit fewer of these characteristics than the society at large. This is especially true if compared with their wealthy neighbors in Palm Beach and Boca Raton.

Coppedge taught her children "the same values that I was taught . . . and I can see my daughter teaching her son the things that I taught her. . . . So the values are there, the teachings are still there, and you can see that by just the way the young people react and the way they are teaching their children. So, it has not really diminished. I think a lot of people think it has and that we have no values or that we are becoming money hungry . . . but I really feel in my heart that it is not. . . . And when you live here and you see things every day, it is different than a non-Indian person coming in and they say, well, golly, he drives a $50,000 car, or she has got Tommy Hilfiger clothes on so they just must be dishing out money. . . . I think . . . we may have $50,000 vehicles or wear Tommy Hilfigers, but that is not all of it. They do not see what I do every day. They do not see the teachings that are passed on or are being taught to me by my elders every day. So, they really do not have the right to say a lot of the things they do. And my values, to me, are still there."[129]

2. Seminole Education

By the late 1960s the Seminole Tribe of Florida had made only modest strides in having its children attend K–12 schooling; very few members of the tribe had graduated from high school or attained a postsecondary education. Although Indian children from the Hollywood and Brighton reservations attended the local public schools, this was arranged after prolonged negotiations with local school authorities. The public schools in Broward County did not accept Seminole students until after World War II; shortly thereafter, Glades County admitted children from the Brighton Reservation. However, youngsters living on the very isolated Big Cypress Reservation, located almost at the geographical center of the lower peninsula, continued to attend a government-operated day school through the elementary grades until they were eventually accepted into the Hendry County schools.

In none of these settings did young Seminoles make significant educational advancements that would be necessary if the tribe were to escape the poverty and lack of economic opportunity that marked its existence in the days before gaming came to the reservations. Nor were they being prepared to handle the sudden affluence that would come with bingo and other tribal business enterprises. It would take aggressive tribal leaders who placed a greater emphasis on education to turn things around over the ensuing three decades. In essence, tribal authorities initiated a Seminole educational renaissance that resonates within the tribe to this day.

Unlike other tribes of the southeastern United States, such as the Cherokees, Chickasaws, Creeks, and Choctaws, the Florida Seminoles had no tradition of literacy in either English or the native languages. Throughout much of the late nineteenth century, the tribal remnant that had avoided removal to Indian Territory following the Seminole wars eschewed contact with outsiders. They rarely ventured from their camps deep in the Everglades and Big Cypress except to trade at frontier villages such as Fort Myers, Fort Lauderdale, or Miami. A few Indian men learned just enough English to facilitate trade, but for the most part the elders wanted nothing to do with the white man or his ways and ordered that children not learn English on penalty of death.[1]

Hunters and traders occasionally visited the Seminoles' widely dispersed settlements, but they did not welcome missionaries until a delegation of western Indians, primarily Baptist Seminoles and Creeks from Oklahoma, visited in 1907. Thus young Seminoles had neither the interest nor the opportunity to learn to read and write. The rare exception was young Billy Conapatachee, a Mikasuki-speaking Seminole from the Big Cypress region, who went to live with Captain F. A. Hendry of Fort Myers in 1879.

Hendry, the largest cattle owner in Florida at that time, had taken a liking to the young Seminole boy. Billy lived in Fort Myers for three years and attended the local "academy" with Hendry's children. Billy also served as an interpreter for ethnologist Clay MacCauley when he conducted a survey of the Florida Indians for the Smithsonian Institution in 1880. The elders did not want Billy to learn to read and write English, however, and threatened to kill the young Indian because he had learned the white man's ways. But Captain Hendry intervened and sent word that if anything happened to Billy, the tribal leaders would have to answer to him. Billy's father also prevailed upon the elders to spare his son. He argued it was much better that the tribe have at least one man who could read and write English and Billy could learn what the white were doing and could then inform the tribe.[2]

By 1883 Billy had returned to his home at the Big Cypress

region, and for a long time no other Indian came to the whites seeking an education. At least into the 1950s, some tribal elders forbade anyone from getting a white education, using whipping, ostracism, and ridicule to enforce their edict. After the Seminole wars, explained Billy Cypress, the Seminoles kept to themselves and had their own way of life and education, which was fine for them. Why should they go out to a foreign country to go to school? "That was their school for their children, we have our own school for our culture, too. So white man's school was taboo and there were tribal punishments for people."[3]

Mary Frances Johns held that a strange tale that circulated in the early 1950s was one reason the Seminoles feared the white man's education. The story claimed that if you were educated by the whites and spoke English, then when the "communists" came to the United States "they would cut off your tongue to keep you from speaking, voicing your opinions or speaking of other people. If you didn't speak nothing but your own language, and your language was not written, then they wouldn't worry about it."[4] Billy Cypress corroborated Mary Frances's story and revealed that when the communists or Russians (meaning any alien group that would come to conquer the whites—the context provided by the Cold War in the 1950s) came, whoever had been "educated would be killed first," and if the Indians wore pants like the whites (that is, if they displayed white culture), they would also be killed.[5] Even into the early 1960s, some parents still feared white education. When the school bus came, they would tell their kids that the bus driver "might want to kill you, so you might as well run to the woods" and hide until the bus was gone.[6]

In 1899, when Ivy Julia Cromartie, at eighteen years of age, arrived to become the Fort Lauderdale settlement's first schoolteacher, none of her students were Indians. The following year she married merchant Frank Stranahan and offered informal instruction for Seminole children who accompanied their parents who traded at her husband's store on the New River. For several decades she also drove to nearby Indian camps and made contact with the children, but not the parents, most of whom remained suspicious of whites. The children, very curious about their white visitor, would watch her from the bushes. She recalled that it took six months to a year for them to become acquainted. Mrs. Stranahan "thought it was terrible for these beautiful young boys and girls not to have any education and to be against the government," so she took it upon herself to begin rudimentary education. Although the parents continued to oppose white education, she helped some of the children learn their ABC's, and a few learned to read and spell.[7] But her sporadic efforts were no substitute for regular government schooling for Indians. Mrs. Stranahan urged federal officials to open a reservation on land west of Fort Lauderdale and to provide adequate educational facilities.

The first effort to have Seminoles attend a government school came in 1926 when BIA officials established the Dania Reservation—renamed Hollywood in 1966—as a home for sick and indigent Seminoles from the east coast of Florida.[8] The Indian agent, Lucien Spencer, also wanted a number of Indian families living near Lake Okeechobee to move to Dania and enter their children in the newly constructed day school there. When tribal elders resisted, Spencer cut off their rations; "at the end of three weeks starvation they moved here and placed their children in the school," he later reported. The day school opened in 1927 with instruction in English. At first the school employed only one teacher, suffered from a lack of supplies, and attracted just three students. Enrollment grew slowly. Because of a lack of parental support, children attended infrequently and were unruly, but the school functioned until 1936, when it was closed ostensibly due to financial difficulties during the Great Depression.

The racially segregated Florida public schools of that day did not admit Indians, so the only alternative for Seminole youngsters who wished to continue their education was to attend the Cherokee Indian School in Cherokee, North Carolina. The first group of Seminoles went in 1937, and by 1938 five had enrolled: Betty Mae Tiger (now Jumper), Moses Jumper, Howard Tiger, George Huff, and Agnes Parker. Agnes Parker and Betty Mae Tiger were the first Seminoles to graduate from high school. It would not be until 1957 that a Seminole, Joe Dan Osceola, graduated from a Florida public high school. The Cherokee school closed its residential unit in the 1960s, but a few Seminole students attended other federal Indian residential schools in the western states.[9]

Today it is instructive to look back on the modest beginnings of what became a Seminole educational renaissance and realize how difficult life must have been for those who were sent to the early no-frills reservation schools, especially in the 1920s and 1930s. Their only alternative to advanced education was the Cherokee Indian School and other federal institutions. Two venerated tribal elders from that generation, Betty Mae Jumper and Jimmy O'Toole Osceola, shared some of their early recollections about the first schools and how they viewed boarding schools as a positive alternative.

Betty Mae Jumper, a child of six when her family came to the Dania Reservation, entered the white man's school. Her grandmother and other Seminole elders strongly opposed her decision, but her mother supported her efforts and Betty Mae eventually developed a love of schooling. "Some of them [parents] sent their children to school. We weren't forced to go. We could go if we want[ed] to go, but we didn't have to go. They didn't tell us to go. But once in a while the curiosity got us so that we would get there. I think we were pretty loud or mean or something that they didn't stay too long, the teachers didn't. In those days we didn't know what school was and we just won't cooperate, that's all. . . . None of us didn't stay too long. We come and spend a few hours, and we would just walk out when we feel like it. I went to school all right, but it is just that I didn't stay long enough to know what it was all about. That's why I didn't know nothing until I went to [boarding] school on my own."[10]

After the Dania day school closed in 1936, Betty Mae "told my great uncle that I wanted to go to school and my mother and they told me they would try to get me into Dania. But they would not allow it, so the superintendent said that maybe we could go to boarding school. And so we went and called the government boarding school. One [Haskell] was in Oklahoma and one was in North Carolina. They said they would take us anytime and for us to come up. The government said they would pay our way if we wanted to go. My great-uncle and my mother knew that I wanted to go to school and they told them to go ahead and make the arrangements for us to go. But my grandmother, she was against school and she said that books are for the white people, not for the Indians. But I went anyway; my cousin Mary and I went and my brother. We chose to go to Cherokee, North Carolina. That is where I stayed and graduated from high school."[11]

Billy Cypress explained why some Seminoles went off to boarding schools like Cherokee and Haskell. "There are several reasons why kids go to boarding schools. Some of them are social reasons and academic reasons. Some students may not be able to make it in public schools, or they have problems that were insurmountable in public schools—both academic and social—and they might have had home conditions that warrant that they go to boarding schools away from home. But not every kid that goes there has all these problems. Some kids go there because it is an all Indian school, but it's a little different from a public school. You have more Indian contacts, it's an all Indian student body."[12]

Betty Mae Jumper and her cousin Agnes Parker not only became the first Seminoles to graduate with high school diplomas, but they also received training as a public health nurses at the Kiowa Hospital in Oklahoma. Agnes relocated to Colorado, but Betty Mae returned to Florida and married her classmate Moses Jumper, then settled into a lifetime of service to her people. She served many years in tribal government and in 1967 became the first—and to date the only—woman elected chairman of the Seminole Tribe.

Mike Osceola, who claimed direct descent from Chief Osceola, had an experience similar to Betty Mae Jumper's. Mike was born and raised in the Musa Isle Indian Village, a commercial camp on the banks of the Miami River, and his father had encouraged him to learn the white man's customs and language. His father, William McKinley Osceola, taught Mike to count, add, and subtract, and Mike also learned to recognize some English words that appeared under photos in the Sears Roebuck catalog. By age sixteen, Mike recognized some English words, but he did not know the alphabet and could not read English.

Nonetheless, Mike was eager to go to the white school to expand his knowledge of the white language and culture. His father agreed, but since Mike was too large and too old at sixteen for elementary school, the authorities allowed him to attend high school. He entered Miami Senior High in September 1937, and his teachers were helpful and cooperative. Mike could not read, and the school had a difficult time deciding on what courses he could take. The English teacher stayed after school and taught him the fundamentals of grammar, but other than counting, he knew nothing of math or any other subject. Eventually the school allowed Mike to take business arithmetic, biology, English, mechanical drawing, and manual training. Despite the cultural differences, Mike got along well with his classmates, although he was shy around girls. After Mike completed two years of school, his principal concluded that Mike would never graduate from high school, but praised him for showing remarkable adaptation and amazing progress in such a short time.[13] Mike played on the football team with George A. Smathers, later a U.S.

senator from Florida and a strong supporter of the Seminoles in their struggle to avoid termination in the 1950s.

The success achieved by Agnes Parker, Betty Mae Jumper, and (to some degree) Mike Osceola indicated that the Seminoles possessed the ability to perform effectively in the classroom if their parents would allow them to attend school and if they had a strong support system at the school.

Although the public schools had denied Betty Mae and her classmates access to education in the 1930s, by 1946 Seminole youngsters were attending classes in Broward County. "The DAR [Daughters of the American Revolution] and Friends of the Seminoles [a Fort Lauderdale group headed by Mrs. Stranahan] fought to have the door opened for the Indian kids to go to Dania. . . . So, that is the way it started."[14] Since that time Seminole children from the Hollywood Reservation have continued to attend public schools and graduate in relatively larger numbers than those from the outlying reservations.

Vivian Crooks, a non-Indian education specialist for the tribe, recalled going to public school with Indian children from the Dania Reservation. She was sure that her experience with Indians made it easier for her to work with them as an adult. "Billy Cypress used to run down to the house on Stirling [Road] . . . and Pat Gopher. We would sit on the front of the bus, and the rest of them would sit in the back because they were very rowdy. We were the students, the three of us. It was natural."[15] Crooks confirmed that Indians were involved in many activities at McArthur High School in Hollywood. An old yearbook revealed that she and James Billie (later a tribal chairman) were in the band together. "I have a yearbook with him; he was in track. I think it was in 1955. . . . It was just curious because Billy Cypress was president of the class. . . . We had a lot of Seminoles on the football team."[16]

Seminole youngsters frequently shifted from school to school as their parents moved around the reservations seeking employ-

ment, or occasionally school authorities moved them for political reasons. Richard Bowers explained how these decisions affected his education: "I went to Dania elementary school for
my first three years. Then I was transferred to Okeechobee,
and I stayed there until I got to be in ninth grade. Then I was
transferred to Moore Haven because they said Brighton was in
Glades County and not Okeechobee County. They wanted the
school kids to go to Glades County, so we went to Moore Haven. I went to Moore Haven and graduated out of there." Bowers continued his education when he "went to Junior College
in Lawrence, Kansas for about one and three-quarter years. I
played football there. . . . After the football seasons were over—
it was only two years—I felt like I was not needed over there
anymore, so I joined the service, stayed in the service, went to
Vietnam, and came back."[17]

Although the Dania school closed during the Depression,
the government opened another small day school on the Big Cypress Reservation in 1938. Little more than a thatched-roof chikee partly enclosed with plywood walls, the school had few at-
tendees and no regular teacher for years. The tribe built a new
frame classroom building after World War II, but the school
struggled because of the physical isolation and the traditional
apathy toward new ways. As a result, the inhabitants of Big Cypress were the least acculturated of the tribe and remained adamantly opposed to white education.

In 1966 the BIA constructed a modern elementary school at
Big Cypress Reservation. The Commissioner of Indian Affairs
Robert Bennett came from Washington DC to inaugurate the facility, which was called the Ahfachkee School. *Ahfachkee* means
"happy" in the Mikasuki language. Indeed, it had all the physical trappings of a happy place where learning could take place.
Set in a large grassy play area next to a cypress stand, the con-
crete-and-glass structure contained two air-conditioned class-
rooms, a kitchen and cafeteria / assembly room, as well as an

office and workspace for teachers. The tribe opened an Indian Health Service clinic in the same complex, making it a center for community activities.

Many members of the tribe had vivid memories of the evolution of tribal education. Jimmy O'Toole Osceola recalled the modest beginning of education at Big Cypress Reservation, where in 1938 "they had a school going on for small children. I was too big for that so I did not go. I hung around because they were my friends. Different teachers would come and teach the children. . . . The first schoolhouse was a chikee. It had a floor above ground and it had [plywood] sides halfway up. The other half had screens, screened all around, except both ends of the chikee were walled, because you would have to have a door to lock it. At the end you had blackboards or stuff up there. . . . There was no school for my age at that time and the other boys and girls my age."

Osceola recalled that in 1943 "the agency was inviting other young Seminoles who would like to go to . . . boarding school in North Carolina. I wanted to go so bad and my father would never have signed the papers for me to go. But I had my sister agree and she did not know how to write her name. She fingerprinted for me. He wouldn't sign because . . . he was a medicine man's helper and he wanted his children to live the way he lived. But he was glad after I learned a little to help him." While grateful for the educational experience, Osceola felt it alienated him from some aspects of tribal culture, especially the Green Corn Dance.[18]

Paul Buster remembered the old school before Ahfachkee was built. "I went to school here, on the reservation, one little room, one little old wooden house. There were, I guess, first grade through fourth or fifth grade, something like that. It was just one room, one teacher. We had most of our activities in that one little room schoolhouse. We had our lunches in there. We had different things in there except during recess we would go out. That is where I got my start in education. I think I was a little bit older when I started school, too. I was probably seven or eight years old, something like that."[19]

For many years Big Cypress residents harbored ambivalent feelings about the Ahfachkee School. They questioned whether it was a good school and whether it was preserving their culture. Mary Jene Coppedge guessed that "at the time my children were going I did not think it was [a good school]. . . . It was not so much the school as the administrators that they had there and some of the teachers. That was before the staff they have now. I feel like Dr. [Sharon] Gaffney now has come a long way to do and implement a lot of things in the school. I have three nephews that go there now—two nephews, now one is in military school, but I think it could be better. To me, I always think that things could be better."[20]

Mitchell Cypress, on the other hand, believed that dramatic improvements had been made. "When the tribe took over we wanted to go ahead and get state-certified teachers, so we got Florida state-certified teachers. And they always get recertified yearly, or every two years, or every five years. So now we are at the level of competing with the Clewiston school [in Clewiston, Florida, about forty-five miles away]. But if the kids are not learning, it is not the system's fault. It might be discipline. Or it could be whatever. Maybe they need to evaluate more. . . . I think now we are doing a hell of a lot better than the bureau school, but it is an opinion of mine."[21]

While the Brighton and Hollywood parents generally accepted sending their children to public school, at Big Cypress there remained a greater fear of going to off-reservation schools. When asked how she felt about sending her grandchild to public school, Marie Phillips responded: "My husband is very protective of her. I wanted to send her to Clewiston school after kindergarten, to send her there for first grade, and he said there are a lot of crazy people that are off this reservation; we do not

need to send her where they are. You see a lot of these shoot-
ings and stuff at schools and all these other crazy things going
on, thinking that would be in the outside world and they get to
mingle with other students that are there. If they lived on the
reservation and went to school they would not have that opportunity."[22] Part of Phillips's reluctance to put a young child
on the bus to Clewiston stemmed from the experiences she and
other Big Cypress children had decades earlier. She knew firsthand that it was a long, wearing day for children. Even though
her grandparents "were both very encouraging," she "had to
get up at four thirty or five o'clock every morning to catch the
bus [to Clewiston]."[23]

Many complained about difficulties with the bus. For Daisi
Jumper "it was riding that bus and being enclosed. We did not get
the best of treatment in the outside world, but that was not the
reason that I quit. I really did not care. I had to be there and I was
there. If they did not like me, so what. I did not really care. . . .
I guess I just got too lazy riding that bus. Back then, thirty years
ago, it was over an hour and a half. One way. Because we had an
old raggedy school bus that did not make it half the time. It was
always breaking [down] and I think that was when we were still
under the government, I guess, because we had an old gray bus
that the government supplied and we had to ride that thing and
it was not a very good bus. In the winter it was cold, and then
it was hot, and it was always breaking down and it was slow. I
guess I did not like the traveling part."[24]

For the 1969–70 school year, the federal day school consisted
of four grades taught by a qualified husband-and-wife team and
a bilingual teacher's aide. The school provided both breakfast
and lunch for the forty pupils—twenty-seven boys and thirteen
girls. Students were not required to attend the school, and because most parents were apathetic about education, attendance
varied widely. At school, the teachers taught the children personal hygiene, table manners, and other life skills, leaving less

time for academic instruction. As a result, the Big Cypress children had poor reading and language arts skills.

Unfortunately, the Ahfachkee School suffered from many of the same deficiencies that marked Indian schooling elsewhere. The federal government provided teachers who taught a κ–8 curriculum utilizing standardized materials that were not adapted for use with Seminole students. Moreover, the school found it difficult to retain teachers, who had to live in government quarters next to the school and interact with a very isolated and traditional Indian community. The program was plagued by erratic attendance, frequent turnover of teaching staff, and limited achievement by Indian students on standardized tests. In addition to the language handicap, Indian children exhibited poor study habits, had no books or reading in the home, received little encouragement from their parents, and found little relevance or application of their studies to the Seminoles' lives. They could see no connection between school and employment.[25]

Those who wanted to go beyond the fourth grade were sent to the public school in Clewiston. Rather than face the one and one-half hour long early-morning bus ride and late-afternoon return, a large number of Seminoles dropped out. Those who stayed at Clewiston had a difficult time adjusting, remaining shy and withdrawn. They could not participate in after-school activities due to the bus ride home, and they usually performed several grades below their classmates.[26] These dismal results would not change until the tribe took charge of education in 1982.

At the Brighton Reservation northwest of Lake Okeechobee, the federal government also opened an elementary day school in late 1938. It operated for sixteen years with the same teacher, William Boehmer. Boehmer described what it was like in 1938 when he was the only teacher and did double duty as the bus driver. At that point very few Seminoles had ever gone to school, and no effort was made to enforce compulsory schooling—they came if they wanted to and stayed if they liked it. In the first year there were thirteen students, ranging in age from six to fifteen years. Very few spoke any English, and attendance was erratic, especially during the winter vegetable season when the children worked with their parents in the fields. Boehmer emphasized reading, writing, and arithmetic but had a difficult time communicating with those who could not speak English.[27]

The Brighton school closed in 1954 because the Brighton people wanted their children to attend public schools. The youngsters now had a somewhat different experience—school districts competed for the Brighton students because of increased federal funding to the schools and because they learned that Seminoles were excellent athletes. The competition for Indian students was complicated by the fact that Brighton Reservation is located in the extreme northern section of Glades County, closer to Okeechobee City in neighboring Okeechobee County than to Moore Haven in Glades County. Naturally, school officials in Glades County were unwilling to have "their Indians" attend a neighboring county's schools and were certainly not going to transport them there. They also objected to Okeechobee County school buses using their county roads to transport Brighton students to Okeechobee City.

Hendry County, to the south of the reservation, did not want Indian students at all—they viewed them as the responsibility of the federal government, not the county. Lottie Baxley said that Hendry County "had a hard time accepting Indians in public school. . . . [T]hey said they didn't want no savages in their school."[28]

Joe Dan Osceola recalled that the reservation day school offered only a limited educational opportunity. He, too, might have gone to the Cherokee School, but instead his group was the first to attend public school in Okeechobee City in the early 1950s. "I remember one year I was going to go to Cherokee, North Carolina, because that is where all of my friends were going and I was in school at Brighton Reservation day school. . . . I was like in the top, what I mean [is that I was among the] older students over there. One teacher covered the first five grades by himself and he would spend a lot of time with the younger children, so it was obvious that they needed more help in the formal education starting off. But then the older students were kind of neglected. . . . My cousin Dorothy Osceola . . . [and] Polly Osceola . . . , we were the first three students enrolled in Okeechobee. We toughed it out because there was no bus service, and we had to go about twenty-five or twenty-six miles one way, but we toughed it out for the first year. Then the second year, as luck would have it, in a good way, the students who used to go to North Carolina for boarding school and everything, they had to revert then to going to school in Okeechobee. . . . It did some good because the children were able to stay with their parents and still go to school. The bus was sent to the reservation and we started going to school."[29]

Osceola remembered that one reason he succeeded in school was that he had a lot of encouragement from his parents: "They never had any schooling so they worked out in the field—they know what it's like not to have an education and they didn't want us to be like that. And so they encouraged us to go to school and so I'm happy that they did encourage us because . . . us coming from the reservation had a better record attending the school [although] we have to travel twenty-five miles one way, better than a person living five blocks from the school, because education means something to us and still, it means something to me."[30]

Lorene Gopher attended the Brighton day school: "I remember . . . 1954 was when we went to Okeechobee school. I mean that is when I went over there in the fourth grade, the 1954–55 school year I think. . . . We went to the day school then they were going to close it down. So then we went over to Okeechobee school."[31]

Youngsters from the Brighton Reservation apparently had little difficulty assimilating at the Okeechobee school. When asked if they suffered discrimination, Joe Dan Osceola responded: "None whatsoever. As a matter of fact, we are fortunate that we had athletic skill on the reservation. We started playing ball— football, basketball, and baseball. We were treated much better than the other students who were playing ball. As a matter of fact, I was captain of my basketball and football teams in my last year of high school."[32] Stanlo Johns echoed this sentiment. He attended Cherokee for a couple of years, but "by that time they saw that the Indian kids were such good athletes that the local schools started picking them up. They said hey, how about you all going to school here? From that we started going to school here in Okeechobee."[33]

Unfortunately, few Indian students who attended the Okeechobee school in the early years were adequately prepared if they chose to pursue higher education. Joe Dan Osceola noted: "I was going to Florida State [University] but they did not see it that way because I did not pass the entrance test. I missed by a couple of points and I took the test twice. . . . Reverend [Genus] Crenshaw . . . had talked to me about going to college, the college where he had been before, which was Georgetown College in [Georgetown] Kentucky. He got me a scholarship, so that is where I went for four years; two years straight, and I spent a year out, and then another two years. So, I spent four years up there in Georgetown College in Kentucky. But I did not receive my degree."[34]

Many adult Seminoles remembered the long dispute over the busing of Indian children to the public schools, which did not seem to upset Indian children as much as the adults. Some parents preferred the Glades County schools to the Okeechobee County schools and continued to send their children to schools they knew and trusted. Helene Johns Buster recalled that "the first school I went to was Okeechobee. I went to the Okeechobee system for the first two years, and then the Glades County system said we had to come over there because we were in their county, because you get all the assistance of subsistence for the amount of students that are there. So they transferred all of the Seminole kids from Okeechobee to Glades County; they said we had to go there because we lived in Glades County. . . . Well, I was in third grade, so whatever age that is six, seven or eight years old. So I went to school there until my eleventh grade." When asked if changing schools made any difference, she replied: "No, because everybody that you went to school with and all that, they all went over there too. It was just the white kids that didn't go over there, but all the Indians went. Everybody that you rode the bus with and all that stuff, the people that were in your same grade, they were all there, too, it was not like you were just thrown into a place with all strangers."

Nevertheless, some Seminoles were upset that while they were being bused to Moore Haven, white children who also lived on the county line and had cars were allowed to remain at the Okeechobee school. As Buster explained, "Way over on the side where Buckhead Ridge is those people lived right on the county line, so they took their kids to Okeechobee. They had to drive their kids there; the bus did not come to them. That was our big thing, you see; we could have gone to school in Okeechobee, but Glades County would not allow Okeechobee buses to cross their line to pick us up. . . . But then it was years later . . . the Seminole Tribe found out, the Brighton community found out, that we did not have to go to Moore Haven [Glades County] schools. The money would go to whatever school we decided to go to. So from that point, [Brighton kids went to Okeechobee] because Okeechobee was a better school—which I totally did not agree with. They had more to offer, but being a better school? I sent my kids to Moore Haven because it was a smaller school, and the teachers were my old classmates. They knew me and if they had a problem with my daughters, they did not have one problem calling me, whereas Okeechobee was a bigger system. They did not know me, they did not know who my daughters were, or anything like that. To me, that made a difference. Both of my daughters graduated from the Glades County, Moore Haven, system."[35]

Nancy Shore came from a very traditional family, but they wanted her to go to school. Her experience in changing to the Glades County schools was not quite so positive, and she did not want her own children there. She recounted how the Brighton families fought to have the children returned to Okeechobee schools. "I was up to ninth grade in Okeechobee, and then I graduated in Moore Haven when they transferred us. . . . Back in 1980 or maybe 1982, the parents got enough education that they wanted to switch back to Okeechobee. So they went back to Okeechobee school. They did not like the school system in Glades County, and they did not think that school was big enough to offer things that the kids needed. . . . I really did not like it. There were really not that many choices that you could take. You just had to take what they gave you. . . . So when one parent said, why don't we see if we can get our kids back over to Okeechobee schools, there is a bigger school and maybe they have bigger classes or [more] subjects that they can offer, we started working on that."

As Nancy recalled, "We left and went to Okeechobee, then after that Glades County still wanted us. . . . And we said, no, we just do not want to stay over there. I think at that time we got tired of people telling us what to do so we had to go to court and everything, get the commissioner of education from Tallahassee to come and sit in on the hearing for us, with Glades County and Okeechobee County and the Seminole Tribe. But the Seminole Tribe was all prepared because they had their own court reporter and they had all of the things to back them up, like the reading program and psychological testing. We had a psychiatrist there to speak on our behalf, for us to go to Okeechobee, and Glades County did not have anything, they did not have anything to offer. . . . So, Betty Castor, she was commissioner of education at that time, said the Seminoles can choose any school that they want to."[36]

The educational opportunities available to Joe Dan Osceola's children in the 1990s stand in striking contrast with the difficulties Brighton children faced in the 1950s. Osceola's children attended private schools. "The school [Sheridan Hills Baptist School] is probably about three miles from here but it is a private school," he stated. "We have been fortunate where our tribe picks up the tab for us but we pay part of that. The tribe, one of their main goals is school and higher education. The tribe has been really lenient towards my family for children to attend school. As a matter of fact, all five of them are in private school now. We are the first families to start private school at this school we are at now. . . . A lot of them from the Hollywood Reservation are going to school there now."[37]

By the 1990s the Seminole Tribal Council had made a strong commitment to educating the tribe's children. Utilizing funds derived from their enormous gambling revenues and with assistance from the BIA, the tribe built, at Big Cypress, a new Ahfachkee School, a state-of-the-art educational facility that rivaled anything in the state. One of the few accredited tribal-run schools in North America, Ahfachkee took on the responsibility of educating Seminole children. There is probably no school in the state so remotely located and also no school with more special programs, field trips, and special events.

The new buildings, dedicated in 1991, housed classes for kindergarten, elementary, and middle school grades, as well as a high school program for those who did not wish to attend public high school. The school provided every child with a computer at home as well as at school. In addition, the school offered a broad array of counseling and vocational services. In an attempt to preserve tribal traditions so important to the identity and the future of the tribe, all Ahfachkee students were given intensive cultural education. "The school maintains an intimate contact with Seminole tribal elders, medicine men and women, tribal cultural leaders, storytellers, craft artists, native language experts, historians and current government officials." To that end, there is a Grandparents Day and the Gathering of the Clans when Betty Mae Jumper might come to tell stories and legends and Sonny Billie would speak on Seminole medicine. The students would also learn how to make pumpkin bread, baskets, and canoes.

According to the *Seminole Tribune*, the school also gave students knowledge of society outside of the reservation by sponsoring field trips to historical museums and to Washington DC to see the federal government in action. The school provided a new building and the technical equipment for a sound educational environment, but the school succeeded because of a dedicated staff, significant community support, and generous funding by the Seminole Tribe.[38]

The Ahfachkee School seemed to prosper until 1997, when the tribe encountered trouble with the school's acting principal and some other employees. The Ahfachkee Parent Advisory Committee (PAC), an organization that tried to get more parents involved in the school, complained that the acting principal arrived at work late and left early, that she played favorites among the teachers, that she failed to communicate with both teachers and parents, and that she did not act in a professional manner. Because the school would lose its accreditation if it did not function properly, the PAC requested that her contract not be renewed. Betty Mae Jumper weighed in with an editorial and joined in the complaints about the school: "We refuse to let others come in from the outside to walk all over us. We fought for a long time to have things up to date, so you all either work or get out and let those who can do the job right, do so." Eventually the tribe did remove the acting principal and hired more-qualified administrators.[39]

The tribe quickly got the school back to a high standard. In 2000 an Associated Press story pointed out that the school had earned a Title I Distinguished School award, the only Indian school to be so honored. The number of students had increased from 88 to 142, and tribal funding from gambling revenues (supplemented by $800,000 from the BIA) had increased its education budget of $1 million—a sum that worked out to more than $12,600 per pupil. The average spending on a national level for students from kindergarten through the twelfth grade, was $6,251—half of the Seminole expenditures. The school had a student-teacher ratio of 8–1 when most similar schools had a ratio of 20–25 students per teacher.

From the time in 1997 when federal officials had considered taking over running of the school due to low test scores and a high dropout rate, attendance shot up 21 percent, the dropout rate fell by 18 percent, and the proficiency scores in reading, writing, and math soared. Dr. Sharon Byrd-Gaffney, director of school operations, explained that the school's goal was "to be a Seminole prep school, where the Seminole children are sent to prepare them to go off to the better colleges in this country" and to provide them with a mainstream curriculum while at the same time promoting their indigenous culture.[40]

The tribe provided buses to ensure that the children from the reservations had access to their schools of choice. A scholarship program provided admission into private and parochial schools, while a college education would be underwritten for those who qualified academically and maintained an acceptable grade point average. Gradually the number of Seminole high school graduates increased and college enrollments grew. Some continued on for postgraduate and professional degrees. A striking number of these educated Indians have opted to return and work for the Seminole Tribe in various capacities.

Dr. Sharon Byrd-Gaffney, the assistant principal of Ahfach-kee School in 1999, offered insights into the problems of the school and how she tried to rectify them and build a meaning-ful instructional program. From her account one can see why the Seminole parents in 1997 had reservations concerning the school. "In a nutshell, my husband [Pat] was here 1991–1992 and had a nice quiet school year and everything was fine. Then he left and went to teach in a university. The man they hired was a very, very bright man, Harvard educated, and had great ideas; but, as with a lot of idea people, he was not able to carry them through and do these things. I think that progressively over the years he became frustrated that he had the wonderful ideas and thought he had solutions but just could not do anything. He began to withdraw, stay in his office a lot. The whole program just went to pot.

"Parents began to say, well, if you are not going to run the school, we are going to have to step in and take over. And very literally, Leslie [Billie], the tribal chairman's wife, and Missy [Me-lissa Arlene] Sanders, our parent involvement coordinator . . . began to step in as the leadership of the Parent Advisory Com-mittee and start to take over the school and try to run it. They had to step in; they had to do mundane, everyday things like textbook orders. It was a mess. And the Parent Advisory Com-mittee, and the community meetings, and they finally drove him out, the principal, at about Christmas time. The 1997–1998 school year. And they just did not renew his contract at the end of the year.

"So about this time, about two years ago they started look-ing for a principal and they said, well, we are going to contact Dr. Gaffney and see if he would be interested in coming back, and for a long time he said no, he was not. And finally into the summer he said yes, maybe . . . and they hired him. But he asked me—I was on an eleven-month contract with Broward schools— if I would spend my month off out here helping him look things over, get an assessment of what was happening, do basically an audit of the program, the accreditation, where we stood with our grants, and that sort of thing. So I spent four weeks out here with him and at the end of that time I said, you are in real trouble. You have bitten off probably more than you can chew. Good luck. So he said would you consider coming out here with me? I said okay, all right; let's think about it. So we did. . . . They created a position, advertised it, interviewed, and hired me. And it was a long process because this school was in one mess."

Byrd-Gaffney continued, "When we came out here, the status of accreditation was in real trouble. See, there is a five-year cycle with the Southern Association of Colleges and Schools, and every five years you have to have a site review. We knew we were two years away. There were staff who were not properly certified, there were people doing jobs that were not necessary to keep the accreditation, or the jobs that were needed were not filled. There was no real library here. I cannot even call it a library; it was an old collection of really old books. They had them in the smallest classroom. They had bookshelves stacked on top of bookshelves going all the way up to the ceiling. . . . An elementary school child could not reach a book way up there. It was really a mess. And it had no librarian since my husband left here in 1992. So as far as I am concerned, they did not have one.

"I went back and the paperwork was a shambles. They had either shredded everything or had just thrown it to the winds. We had to gather up all the records from the pile, and that pile, and that drawer, and we were missing a big gap of information. I had to do things like call Washington and ask for different grants. I had to call [the] Southern Association and ask for copies of reports and annual reviews and such. I pieced it together and basically they were sadly out of compliance with a lot of things. So, we began to rebuild it. In talking to the people in Washington about where we were with the grants, and can you send us more copies of things, and such, they told us that because of our lack of compliance with the consolidated school reform plan they were going to fund us one more year and it was a wait and see thing. Can you guys pull it together? The only reason they continued to fund the school one more year is because of the new administration. The prior administration, had they continued on, they would have pulled the funding that year."[41]

Byrd-Gaffney went on to explain the relationship between the federal government and Seminole tribal government for funding the Ahfachkee School. "About 40 percent of our funding comes from the Bureau of Indian Affairs through what they call the Indian school equalization program. It is like any other state. Every state has a base student allocation. We give you X amount for every child who comes through the door and then we will give you increments on that for different services that that child needs, like special education and such. We have the same setup with the BIA. We are covered by the fifty-first state, which is the federal government. We are not part of the State of Florida, as far as schooling goes. All of the bureau-funded schools are considered to be in that fifty-first state.

"We set about writing a new school reform plan using the National Study of School evaluation guidelines for doing it, which is a very introspective look at what the school does—the work of the school, so they say, and I like that term. We look at who the community is, who it is serving, look at the mission of our school, and then make sure that the mission of the school is still what we want it to be. We rewrote our mission after we studied who we were serving. Then you take a look at what you want the students to be. We visualized, our mental image was, what do we want the students to look like, feel like, be like, act like, do, when they walk across the stage at graduation.

"The mission is to provide, bottom line, the best education possible, provide what they call the white man's education within the culturally sensitive environment here, to bring them up with the same quality education and then some, but also to

retain their Native ways. To honor that culture, to teach and restore the language."

The very traditional Big Cypress community expects a heavy
emphasis to be placed on preserving the language and culture of
children attending Ahfachkee. When asked if members of her
faculty had the expertise to do this, Byrd-Gaffney replied, "Yes,
Theresa Jumper, who is a trained cultural arts specialist. She is
not a trained teacher or a certified teacher but is trained as a cultural arts specialist and she is just a natural teacher. . . . Then we
have a language program that we have devised that the classroom aides implement, who are all Seminole-speakers or Seminole tribal members. So, they have daily infusion of the language
and the culture in the classroom through the aides and twice a
week they go to a cultural specialist. One is the culture and one
is the language. They are learning the Mikasuki [language]. This
is, in fact, the brand, more or less, of the Mikasuki language that
is unique to this area, too, because if you went to Brighton there
is more of the Creek influence. And if you went to Hollywood,
or any of the other reservations, you would have a bit different
flavor, I think. This is more the local version."[42]

The tribal education specialist, Vivian Crooks, praised the
curriculum at Ahfachkee and how it had helped cut down on the
dropout rate. "It is a role-model school, now, for all of the Native
American schools. They are adhering to the Goals 2000 from Florida school system state requirements. We have eighteen children,
probably less now, going to the Clewiston schools, by choice—
it is a choice of the families and we have 115–120, depending on
the day, going to Ahfachkee. Years past it was flipped."

Crooks explained that Ahfachkee now had an alternative
high school. "Years ago before the high school and before all the
choices available to our students, you went to Ahfachkee until
sixth grade, and you had two choices: get on the bus at six o'clock
in the morning and go to Clewiston, to a totally different atmo-
sphere that maybe wasn't your choice, or go to a Native Amer-

ican boarding school in Oklahoma. That was it. If you didn't fit in those two molds, you dropped out. Now we have an alternative school here—it is competency-based learning . . . in front of the computer . . . and when you learn the skills, you get the credit. It is not time based; it is competency based."[43]

Despite the money and effort expended to improve educational opportunities for students attending Ahfachkee School, the results have been disappointing according to Dr. Sharon Byrd-Gaffney. When queried about how well children had made the transition from Ahfachkee to other schools, she responded, "Not well. We have a very, very high incidence of failure when they get out of there. That is why Vivian [Crooks] is working really, really hard to get better and better at matching the situation to students. I do not understand it, but traditionally Indian children do not adapt well to other situations outside their home. To take them to another community, they do not do well. Even in situations where they go away to an intertribal school, [as] they call it, with several tribes represented there, they go away maybe to a school that is all cultures, predominantly white, a lot of them, they just do not like it. They do not fit in; they do not adjust well. A lot of them come back. We wish they did not. We wish they could stay, as we have one young lady doing right now. She will be a success story. She finished her high school here, now she is away at Haskell Indian Nation University majoring in elementary education. This is nearing the end of her first year and she is doing wonderfully. . . . They [her parents] took these children all over the country to rodeos and competitions and they viewed that outside world very differently."[44]

Jeannette Cypress is typical of many Seminole mothers who themselves had a modicum of schooling and want better for their children. Her own educational career was spotty, but she persevered and recognized the value of an education. She noted that the income derived from gaming dividends allowed her to send her children wherever she thought the schooling was best for them. "I worked with the WIC [Women, Infants and Children] program for pregnant women, and transported patients to hospitals and interpreted. I even took an EMT [emergency medical technician course] and did different things. It is kind of hard for me to remember the years, but along the way they told me about this program that some students were going to at the University of Miami. It was called the HEP [High School Equivalency] program. It was for different people, like Spanish [Hispanic], black, Indian, white people who wanted to go back and get a GED [General Equivalency Diploma]."

Cypress remembered that the University of Miami "offered [it] where you could apply and you stayed on campus, and they provided the meals and everything. You worked with computers and you could get a high school diploma. I applied for that program. I got in there and I got my diploma in six months. From there I continued to work. I have worked for the social service program in different departments of the tribe. I went to college a little bit at BCC, Broward Community College, just picked up some courses. . . .

"My little girl goes to Head Start and the preschool program, and my little boy goes to kindergarten and my two sons go to private school in Belle Glade called Glades Day. One is a tenth grader and one is in the eleventh grade. My daughter goes to Clewiston High School, she is in the tenth grade. My nephew goes to Vanguard in Lake Wales; it is a boarding school and it is private. . . . My daughter went to the reservation school until the eighth grade, my two boys went here for a while then went to middle school in Clewiston. . . . They went to Clewiston High School for a while but I guess they felt they were not getting a fair shake in sports, so they wanted to try Glades Day. So that is where they go. The seventeen-year-old has a car and he drives, so they ride together. They are happy there and so they will probably graduate. And my daughter chooses to stay where she is;

she is playing sports there [Clewiston High School]. She is going to stay there."[45]

Paralleling the dramatic development of Seminole education K–12 since the early 1970s was the number of individuals who secured a postsecondary education. As Joe Frank noted in 1999, this is due in large part to changed parental expectations: "In the twenty-seven-year period you are talking about, the attitude on higher education has really opened up. I think there was some interest back in the early 1970s, but there were just not too many opportunities. Today there is quite a bit of opportunity for students to go, and a lot of the parents out here now have at least a high school or GED or something. I think that a lot more parents expect their kids to go, whereas back in the late 1960s and early 1970s the education level of parents just was not there, and they didn't really push." When asked if this motivation should also apply to vocational and technical education, he replied, "I like it because when I got into my field that is what I attended, a technical training program at Lake City Community College. I pursued it, and I think it is beneficial. Any type of training for any type of vocation is needed."[46]

Louise Gopher became the first Seminole woman to get a university education, but it was not an easy task. "I graduated from Indian River Community College in Fort Pierce in 1965, then I graduated from Florida Atlantic University in 1970. I got a B.Sc. Degree in Business Administration. Then I said that is it. I did not even go for graduation. I was just so glad to finish. Mail it to me. Now, I have a daughter who graduated from Florida State about two years ago. She is trying to twist my arm into going to a master's program with her somewhere. I do not think so."[47]

In 1999, Louise Gopher served as educational counselor at the Big Cypress Reservation. Perhaps reflecting on her own success in coping with white schooling, she is an eloquent exponent of having Indian youngsters in public school. Although mindful of parental concerns, she stated, "I think going to the pub-

lic schools from kindergarten on up helps us to be able to mix
with the outside world. And Big Cypress, I believe, has the same
choice. They can ride the bus and go to Clewiston, or they can
stay on the reservation and go to Ahfachkee. So, I guess they
choose to go to Ahfachkee School, and then at Ahfachkee School
they are only mingling with the reservation kids that they have
grown up with. . . . They do not go to the outside area until they
have finished school."[48]

Seminoles have attended a variety of postsecondary programs over the years. Initially many of them went to BIA schools
in western states. Typical was Lorene Gopher, who graduated
from Okeechobee High School in 1963. "After that, I went on
to, they called it business school at the time, but I think it is a
college now, Haskell [Haskell Indian Nations University]. They
called it Haskell Institute. . . . [It is] a four-year program now
[in] Lawrence, Kansas. [I attended] two years, because I already
knew what I was going to do. I was doing the office work. So, I
did that and I came back, and I went to work for the Bureau of
Indian Affairs, the Seminole Agency, with Billy Cypress, who is
the museum person now, I worked for him. I worked there and
lived in Hollywood from probably 1966 to 1974. . . . It was with
the education program."[49]

Nancy Shore attended Miami-Dade Community College; she
then received her bachelor's and master's degrees in social work
from Barry University in Miami.[50] Billy Cypress was the first Seminole male to complete college. He graduated from high school
while living on the Hollywood Reservation. Billy explained that
he was treated pretty well by whites while in high school. "Of
course, you are always an Indian and you're a little different, but
as far as the treatment went, it was very good in the local high
schools." In fact, Billy was in several clubs and was elected president of the student council. He then graduated from Stetson
University, served as an officer in the U.S. Army, and later received his master's degree at Arizona State University.

Despite his excellent educational record, Billy Cypress knew that the tribe still had great progress to make in promoting education. "We're newcomers to the education scene, much less the college scene. And first we had to build slowly and get a group of college grads . . . and we had to sell education to the whole tribe. One time education was bad, you know, it was a white man's school. So they [the tribe] have come a long way from the last twenty or thirty years to the point where we can start being selective and trying to get more education beyond high school." Billy continued by saying that as the Seminole Tribe progressed, they wanted to go into new fields and they needed qualified people for these positions. The tribe generally had to go outside to find the teachers, lawyers, and experts they need, but Cypress indicated that even as early as 1972 the tribe was encouraging young people to get professional degrees and that the attitude toward education in the tribe had improved significantly.[51]

Perhaps the most compelling story of a Seminole's struggle to acquire an education and overcome a major physical disability is that of the Seminole Tribe's general counsel, Jim Shore. The son of Frank Shore, a famous Seminole medicine man, Jim grew up on the Brighton Reservation and attended both Okeechobee High School and federal Indian boarding school. "I think I got back from high school, the boarding school, in 1965, and I think between 1965 and 1970 I was doing cowboying and everything else. Then I think it was 1970 when I had the car accident that took my sight. That is when I decided to go to college, and I spent about two years playing around with doctors, 1970, 1971, and 1972. I started junior college in 1973. Then I graduated from law school in 1980, so I went full time for seven years. But I did not have a big sit-down and decide that I should go to law school.

"The only thing that kept me moving [was] that I was, let's see, twenty-five when that happened; I was twenty-seven when I finally started junior college. I guess I could have just lay around there and maybe died of a heart attack by now, just lying around and eating, or whatever. But some people in my family have grown to be old people, [in their] nineties and over one hundred. So, I figured, hell, I might live forever. I might as well start doing something just in case. That is when I decided to try junior college. I always just took it one semester at a time. If I make it, well and good, if not, the hell with it. I guess I did well enough that I stuck with it until I finished law school. Even when I was in my last semester of undergraduate—I was a history major— I did not know what I was going to do with a history degree except teach, and I did not want to be in a classroom. So, at the last minute, I decided to try law school over at Stetson. One of my classmate's father's partners was on the Board of Trustees, or something, so we tried to see if he could get me in there, and they did. I think they were hoping I would flunk out so they would not have to deal with me.

"So, I started in the summer. I think I only took one course in the summer because back then law school was a whole different ball game than undergraduate stuff. I survived the summer. I always took the minimum hours, twelve hours a semester, or something. I went through the summer sessions. It was either 1976 or 1977, and then I graduated in 1980. I think I came on with the tribe in 1981. The general counsel they had then left in either 1982 or 1983, and then they put me in his position. I have been there ever since. . . .

"When you are about to graduate from law school, just like everybody else, you will send out résumés. The reply you always get back is that they will keep your application on file. But when I shipped one out to the tribe, James [Billie] was the chairman then, he said, whenever you get ready just come down here and we will talk money. And that was it." When asked if college graduates like himself were returning to work for the tribe and would there be enough jobs in the future, Shore responded, "I think some do but according to the chairman, that is not a requirement. The tribe will assist an individual to go through college and pay for most of their expenses, and they can come back if they want. But if not, then that is, according to him [James Billie], one less person he will have to worry about anyhow."[52]

Virtually unlimited access to schooling at all levels for those who qualify has undoubtedly improved social and economic opportunities for Seminoles. Most tribal members are rightfully proud of this accomplishment. Carl Baxley, a successful businessman despite his limited formal education, expressed high regard for the achievements of those Seminoles who pursued an education. "I think I read an article in the magazine yesterday where the chairman had made a statement that 75 percent of our people are educated now. Seventy-five percent of our people, which is probably true, maybe even more than that. But that statement was not true twenty-five years ago. So we have come a long way, as far as being educated, and a lot of our tribal members are out there in the nursing field, and we have people that have been to the University of Florida for cattle and veterinary and agriculture. We have tribal members that are attorneys. We have tribal members that possess PhDs. Twenty years ago that was unheard of; you would be lucky if you had a tribal member that graduated from high school. So education plays a very important role here and it trickles all the way down to the cattle, citrus and sugarcane that we are now involved in. We have diversified a lot and it is due to education, because the lack of education will only hinder your ability to move forward. I am forty-three years old and know that now. When I was fifteen or sixteen, I knew everything then too—at least I thought."

When asked if this new Seminole eagerness to take advantage of educational opportunities extended to his own family, Baxley answered: "Absolutely. And both of my kids graduated from high school. They do not have a GED; they graduated from high school because GED was not acceptable to me. And I expect both of my kids to go to college. It is mandatory that they go to college. You would think that coming from a high school dropout that would not be a priority to me, but it is. I have learned the hard way, that I should have taken advantage of it back then."[53]

However, a number of Seminoles question whether today's youth will pursue higher education when they are already financially secure. Although she lauded the fact that education was available to Seminoles and was pleased that many had taken advantage of it, Helene Johns Buster expressed concern that the newfound affluence of the tribe was also a hindrance. The motivation to study hard and get ahead in school, she felt, is vitiated by the glut of cash pouring into the Seminole community today. "It makes it accessible, but harder for them to get to because they have so many other things. . . . It is more accessible because the parents have their own vehicles and the kids have their own vehicles and the money and the money is there for gas to go back and forth. It is more accessible that way. But because of the materialistic things that our children are more involved in today, it makes it harder for them to get to school. They have other things going on in their like that are more important than school.

"It is just not there. The whole motivation for going to school that I remember was that because you did not want to work out in the tomato fields and you did not want to be a field hand and be in the sun forever. You had to get an education so that you were out of that and that you had some kind of profession. That was the motivation to get you out. But our kids never worked in the tomato fields. They never had to harvest any kind of food or anything. So they do not know what really hard work is and having to work for your clothes or anything. Everything is given to them.

"Yes, our kids have dividends [income derived from tribal enterprises], and from what I see today the majority of the kids have the control over their dividends, whether they are eigh-

teen or not. They have the control, or that is the hold they have
over their parents, their dividends. They have the kind of clothes
they want, I mean they wear the $200 tennis shoes and what-
ever is in style and all this. We were doing good to have tennis
shoes from the dollar store. And when we had a Saturday and
Sunday off, we were in the tomato fields working for $8 a day
so we could help pay the bills at home so we would have electricity and things like that. When the prom and things came up,
I remember my mother going to the tribal government to get
a loan so that we could have prom dresses and the guys could
have tuxedos to wear. Now, those boys wear them and the girls
wear those things, all of the time now—and things cost twice
as much as those kinds of things.

"I mean, the thing to go to school was so you could learn
how to make money and have a job. Hell, when you have money
coming in that is probably more than what your teacher is making in a month, what is the motivation to go to school—for just
being Seminole. Hopefully, it changes one day. . . . It is kind of
like newfound money. You get all of your playthings and all of
the things you always wanted with that. And then after you get
all of that stuff you realize, hey, there is still a life, I still have to
live a life, even with all of my toys I still have to go and make a
life for myself. Hopefully we are going to get, as a tribe, into that
place where we say, oh, okay, we still have our toys now. Now
I need to learn how to invest the money. I need to think about
my future. We are not at that point yet."[54]

The Seminole Tribe is entering into yet another stage of its
educational renaissance. As it continues to expand its economic
base in the twenty-first century, there will be less and less motivation for youngsters to pursue education as a means to financial security. One challenge for tribal leaders therefore will be
to cultivate the value of schooling for self-development, that
is, education for its own sake to improve the general quality of
life on the reservations. Current Seminoles would do well to

heed the words of Virgil Harrington, the former superintendent of the Seminole agency. Harrington, in 1971, said: "I don't
think that we can overlook the fact that education, whether it
is gained through experience or through academic training . . .
sticks out most in experiences that I had, that improved the social and economic conditions of the Seminoles."[55]

3. Transformations in Religion and Medicine

Beginning in the mid-twentieth century, the Seminole people began to experience fundamental transformations in both their spiritual life and the way they tended to health needs. Historically there has been a close connection between spiritual beliefs and the physical medicine practiced by the shamans or medicine men of the tribe. The Green Corn Dance was the fundamental ritual that fused these two spheres. It received its name because the ceremony takes place in late spring to coincide with the ripening of the new corn crop. As developed among the Florida Indians, the Green Corn Dance—actually a series of dances and related functions held over a period of several days—is a variant of the busk (fasting) ritual practiced for centuries in towns (*italwa*—which signified a "square ground town," the ceremonial and political center of a Creek community) of the Muskogee or Creek Nation, where the Seminoles and Miccosukees originated before migrating to Spanish Territory on the southernmost peninsula.

The busk or Green Corn Dance renewed respect for the gods and was a vital part of Seminole culture. The dance marked the beginning of a new year and usually occurred during a full moon in July or August. According to early reports, the annual festival started with a two-day fast. The Seminoles then purified the sacred ground by cleaning and refurbishing the square where the ceremony took place. Each side of the square had a rectangular cabin with benches, where, based on protocol, the chiefs and members took their places. The participants then purged themselves with the black drink, purified themselves in the sweat lodge, and abstained from sex.

At the close of the third day, the celebrants extinguished the home fires and lit a new ceremonial fire in the raised square. The presiding priest then spoke to the men and women separately, criticizing their behavior and exhorting them to live cleaner, purer, and more virtuous lives. The priests broke old pottery, extinguished old fires, dissolved marriages, and gave each participant a new start. On the fourth day the men and women began fasting and dancing. In the grand finale, all members of the tribe ate the first ears of new corn and enjoyed a ritual cleansing bath in a stream.

Some corn dances lasted four days, others lasted eight. The beliefs and practices varied from tribe to tribe, but the essential element remained tribal unity. The new fire purified the community before the spirit world, while individuals purified themselves by fasting, with the black drink, and in the sweat lodges. By atonement, purification, and dancing, the Seminoles tried to achieve balance with the spiritual, social, and physical worlds. The Florida Seminole Green Corn Dance, a distilled version of the early busk ceremony, was carried into the twentieth century with its core elements intact.[1]

The Green Corn Dance changed over the years, but it continued to reinforce several important ritual elements that ensured social stability as well as cultural continuity and cohesiveness. First, it affirmed the people's belief in the Breathmaker and other supernatural beings that controlled their destiny by mediating between the upper, middle and lower worlds of the Indian cosmos. Second, the ceremony provided for both individual and corporate purification prior to the start of a new year as determined by the agricultural cycle. The medicine man, in his capacity as spiritual leader, prepared the spiritual medicine. Third, during this period the council of elders also held a court session to adjudicate old individual and group grievances. It was also a time when young men coming of age received their adult names and the tribe affirmed marriage unions. Lastly, and perhaps most important, the ritual served as a form of cultural revitalization in which the group reaffirmed its unity of beliefs and oneness as a people. The breaking of the fast by feasting on the new corn crop confirmed personal and tribal renewal. The lighting of the new fire on the dance ground and the fire's distribution to the various clans and households symbolized that renewal.

Indian culture in Florida underwent radical dislocations engendered by two major armed conflicts with the United States from 1835 to 1842 and again from 1855 to 1858. Virtually all Seminole towns were destroyed, most of the Indian population was killed or sent west to Indian Territory in present-day Oklahoma, and only a remnant remained secluded in the vastness of the Everglades. While most of the chiefs were killed or deported and town governance structures destroyed, a number of medicine men survived and emerged as strong spiritual and political leaders. Not all of the pre-removal elements survived in the Florida version of the Green Corn Dance, but enough of the original structure remained to make it the linchpin of the Seminoles' attenuated religious practices.

The 208 Seminoles reportedly found by Smithsonian ethnologist Clay MacCauley during his 1880–81 survey (most likely an inaccurate number) belonged to one of three busk groups. These groups were still functioning in the 1950s when Louis Capron and anthropologist William Sturtevant, based on personal observation of the ceremonies, wrote their classic descriptions of the medicine bundles and busks of the Florida Seminoles and Miccosukees.[2] However, from these reports and other observations it became clear that the Green Corn Dance was rapidly losing prominence as the Florida Indians' central religious focus.[3]

The introduction of Christianity had a major impact in transforming Seminole society, accelerating the decline, but not the demise, of the Green Corn Dance. The Episcopal Church had established a mission station near Immokalee at the end of the nineteenth century, but it closed in 1913. The Baptist Church's early attempt to convert the Indians also met with little success. The arrival of Christian Indian missionaries from the Seminole-Creek Baptist Church of Wewoka, Oklahoma, in 1907 eventually opened the door for effective proselytizing among the Florida Indians. Joe Frank recalled that the Episcopalians "came at the turn of the 1900s and they had a pretty big impact at the time. They set the stage for the Baptists who came during the 1940s and 1950s." Frank also noted that the Episcopalians were non-Indian and that, since the tribe did not trust them, they made no converts.[4]

Ivy Stranahan, wife of the trader Frank Stranahan, remembered driving out to the reservation every weekend to teach Sunday school, using religious material supplied by the Presbyterian Church. Mrs. Stranahan noted the coming of the Baptist missionaries in 1907 which led to more tribal members attending religious services. She recalled that the Baptists loved to sing, and although the minister preached in the Indian dialect, the congregation sang the hymns in English.[5]

A group of Oklahoma Indians seeking converts returned each winter for several years and sent a permanent missionary, Willie King, in 1936. King proved to be effective because he spoke both Muskogee and English and managed to convert a few women and children. One of them, Betty Mae Jumper, recalled that King "used to teach us about God and that is where I learned that [if] you live under his ruling, that you will not be scared of anything because he will protect you."[6] Despite King's best efforts, Christianity made limited headway among the Seminoles.

Attitudes changed when a dynamic young Creek-Seminole preacher, Stanley Smith, arrived in 1943. When Smith first preached at the newly established First Seminole Baptist Church there were seven members, all women. Joe Bowers, the first male member, was baptized in 1944, and when Josie Billie, an important medicine man, converted in 1945, many others joined the church as well. On the Big Cypress Reservation it is alleged that some individuals became Christians out of a desire to improve their social status and to gain some influence as either preachers or members of the church council.

Bob Mitchell, who was part Mohawk Indian and a trusted friend of the Seminoles since 1916, noted that Smith also had some less-than-admirable personal qualities that placed him at odds with both church authorities (the Southern Baptist Convention) and conservative Seminoles on the reservation. Mitchell thought Willie King was a fine man, but he referred to Reverend Smith as a "holy terror" who "did more damage than anybody ever has since." Mitchell claimed that Smith had come to Florida with no money and ended up with $20,000 in his bank account. Smith, according to Mitchell, charged members a dollar a month baptismal fee. "You know, the guy used his religion as a whip." In addition, Mitchell recounted that Smith sent several of the young men in the church, limited to those with good-looking wives, off the reservation to work. "He told them he was a prophet of God and if they didn't go, he would have them severely punished." The men were superstitious enough to go, and then "he [Smith] proceeded to get their wives pregnant." Although the Southern Baptists had originally sent and supported him, eventually "they disowned him."[7]

After losing his financial and ecclesiastical support from the Southern Baptist Convention, the charismatic Smith led his followers to open a competing Independent Mekesuky Baptist Church with sanctuaries at both Hollywood and Big Cypress reservations. This schism among the Christian Seminoles caused great stress in the community, although the animosities abated significantly after Smith suddenly, and somewhat mysteriously, disappeared. He reportedly returned to Oklahoma.

One story circulated claiming that the Seminole elders at the Green Corn Dance had passed a decree that would have ended his life and Smith departed posthaste. Bob Mitchell declared the medicine men and council "finally decided to knock him off.

And as far as I'm concerned, I would never have lost any sleep over it at all. . . . I went by and I warned him, simply because I felt it was my Christian duty."[8] There were other tales, mostly unverifiable, that Smith had a criminal record that was about to be exposed. In any case, his departure brought relative calm to the community. In 1946 the Southern Baptist Convention built a handsome church and parsonage at the Hollywood Reservation and sent a non-Indian pastor to tend to the flock.

By 1945, 182 out of the 600 tribal members had committed to Christianity, and by 1970 there were seven Baptist churches. The increased power and influence of the church tended to undermine the authority of the medicine men.[9] One of the early converts was Billy Osceola, a Creek-speaker from the Brighton Reservation who became a Christian at twenty-five years of age. He provided eloquent testimony on how he became a Christian, attended the Florida Bible Institute in Lakeland, and became a leader of his people. "At that time, one missionary [Stanley Smith] was sent down to Florida from Oklahoma and he started preaching among the Indians at Big Cypress. . . . There's no church building or nothing, so he [Smith] went [and] hold the service in home[s] and in Josie Billie's [the former medicine man] camp, and about thirty, thirty-two people came that night for service. Josie Billie [was] accepting Christ for his personal savior and twenty-two Seminoles were [to] follow him. . . . [I]t was about twenty-five, twenty-six years ago, I think, when I became a Christian.

"So, since I accepted Christ as my personal savior . . . my life was changed. I still want[ed] to work, but the Lord got a hold of my life and changed it. I was changing my ways and so I had a great desire to go to school and learn . . . more Bible. So, at that time, the Baptist Home Mission Board had a scholarship for any Indians that want to go to school for training. . . . Sam Tommie, Josie Billie, Junior Buster, and Barfield Johns, the five of us, went [at that] time and then, I was told that, well, I am not graduate completely, but they give me a diploma. I just want[ed] to come back and preach [to] the Indians in Florida. So I came back in 1952, this was my old home, and my people live here. . . . At that time, another old Indian missionary [was here, but] he's not doing much. [H]e visit and talking to people and helping the sick ones and carrying [them] to doctor[s] and talk[ing] to them about the Christ, [as] personal savior. That's Willie King."[10]

When Billy Osceola returned to the Brighton Reservation in 1952 there was no church, and the only place he could preach was in homes. The First Seminole Baptist Church on the Hollywood Reservation received all of its funding from the Baptist Home Mission Board. "They give me fifteen dollars a month to buy groceries for the people and invite them to come and I feed them and preach [to] them at the same time. So, we had a good start and a large congregation." With the help of Christian Seminoles from Big Cypress and Hollywood, the small congregation grew steadily. However, due to strong opposition from non-Christian Indians to having a church on the reservation, the Lykes Brothers Corporation provided a small tract of land just off the reservation.

Osceola recalled that "when we had afternoon meeting and they [those opposing the church] said, we are not Christian Indians on this reservation and we don't care about the church you are talking about. If you like to go to church, why don't you go to Okeechobee or Moore Haven or somewhere else and join the white people's church? We don't want a church. . . . So they said that and I told the Southside Baptist Church in Lakeland. They said, okay. We just gonna find some land outside, maybe adjacent to the Indian reservation, and so they did. They talking to Lykes Brothers and Lykes Brothers give us the land, about two acres of land, and then later enlarge that, about almost five acres now over there. So, that's why we build a church outside."[11]

By midcentury most Seminoles living on the federal reservations were nominally Christian, and the preachers became dominant figures in the community. When the Seminole Tribe was formally organized with a constitution in 1957, its first elected tribal leaders, Bill Osceola and Billy Osceola (not related), were both lay preachers. The emergence of a new group of Christian political leaders further eroded the power of the medicine men.[12]

The rift between Christian Indians and those who still followed the medicine men became more pronounced over the next few decades. Paul Buster attended the First Seminole Baptist Church in Hollywood. Unlike some in the tribe, Buster believed "that you cannot really walk the fence. . . . Either God is dominant in your life or traditions and paganism, or whatever it is called, . . . dominates your life."[13]

Many members, while acknowledging that there was some good in learning both Christianity and the old ways, wanted, as Victor Billie said, "to keep my Indian ways stronger than English or non-Indian ways." Billie was not a Christian and did not want to be. He had his "own belief, our own God. Our God, we call him the . . . Breathgiver. We do not want to kill our God and his teaching and his laws that were given to us, to satisfy someone else's law and God. I do not want to go in a church and kneel down and pray. God is everywhere to me. God is the water, God is the land. God is the sky and the universe. . . . All I need is God with me and inside of me to survive."[14]

On the other hand, the staunch Indian Baptists—of both churches—were strongly opposed to holding the Green Corn Dance on reservation land and, having grown in number, exerted enough political power to have it banned. Until recent years the Green Corn Dance was held on private land away from the reservations. The main reason for the remote location was to move the pagan practices off the reservation. By contrast, members of the more culturally traditional Miccosukee Tribe continued to hold their annual Green Corn Dance on tribal land under the auspices of the tribal government, and it was generally open to Seminoles who wished to attend with their clans.

It should be understood that when most Seminoles refer to "Indian medicine" they often use the concepts of spiritual beliefs and associated physical curative practices interchangeably. For many Indians the two ideas cannot be separated—physical medicine works only if one believes in the overarching spiritual realm that gives the medicine power. They are opposite sides of the same coin, and to separate them is an arbitrary distinction imposed by outsiders. However, as we will see, the practice of herbal healing—separate from spiritual medicine—has been retained by many. Therefore, for the purpose of bringing greater clarity to this study, we have grouped what Seminoles discuss in the spiritual realm separately from what they disclose about curative practices. Even so, the two spheres often overlap in Indian narratives and culture.

There has been a significant amount of discourse on whether Christian beliefs can coexist alongside traditional spiritual beliefs of the Seminole Tribe. Lorene Gopher understood that the missionaries "came to save us or help us or something," but they ended up confusing many Seminoles. The Baptists told the tribe "you cannot do your medicine and you cannot do your corn dances because that is not the way to get to heaven. The only way was to go to [the Christian] church and . . . read the Bible. . . . Since our elders could not read, they had to rely on what these people told them." Gopher understood that in the early days of the missionaries the tribal members had a difficult time accepting the new beliefs, and while many gave up old practices, some went back to using the medicine and following the cultural and spiritual connections to their past.[15]

Joe Dan Osceola understood the dilemma that many tribal members faced. He pointed out that the Southern Baptist missionaries converted many of the leaders. They went to a Christian church and spoke only one language, English. The Seminoles began losing their traditional culture as well as their language, and this led to indecision among the tribal members. Because of their uncertainty and confusion about the new Christian beliefs, many Indians never lost faith in the healing power of the medicine men. Osceola had great praise for the ability of Josie Billie, "the last, great Indian medicine man that the Seminoles ever had." Osceola knew of several cases where white doctors concluded that Indian patients needed surgery. The patients would go back to the reservation and see Josie Billie, and he "would use some kind of herbs and chant and he would make it happen." In effect, the patient was cured and no longer needed the operation. The white doctors knew about Josie, admired him, and wanted to meet him to discover his secret.[16]

Around 50 percent of the Seminoles were thought to be Christian, with the majority of those members of the Baptist Church. Many, like Paul Buster, were born into the church. His parents were Christians, and "I was raised all my life going to church." He first attended the Big Cypress Baptist Church, and then he moved to the Hollywood Reservation, where he attended the First Seminole Baptist Church. While there were differences in beliefs between Christians and traditionalists, Buster did not accept the notion that there was a social division between those who are Christians and those who believe in traditional spiritualism. Everyone, he held, got along without conflicts.[17]

Interestingly, some Seminoles see little conflict between Christianity and their Native beliefs. Many Indians do, in fact, straddle the fence and participate in both Christianity and their traditional religion. Helene Johns Buster was typical of this group. She had been baptized and was a Christian, "but I really do not attend a church." She remembered that in the 1960s and 1970s the church was the center of everything, but in the 1980s things changed and people often returned to the old ways.[18]

Alice Johns Sweat discussed the conflict between various religious beliefs on the reservation and the difficulty of understanding the position of the Baptist Church, which consistently discouraged participation in the "pagan" Green Corn Dance. Sweat understood that Christians "depend on God, he meets your needs, [and] you pray to him, whereas at the Corn Dance, you take part in this tradition. This is what you grow up with. This is part of me. Why are you saying I cannot go there, be a Christian, and take part in it. But, I did. I went anyway. Then, afterwards I would feel guilty because, here I am supposed to be a Christian, yet I was still going over there and taking part in the dances and stuff. But I yearn for that. I want to hear them singing. I grew up with that. It is only so many days out of the year. What is wrong with it? I have a chikee out there today, you know, because that is part of what I grew up with. I do not want to give it up. It is still my roots. That is the way I look at it."

Sweat's views are typical for those Indians who wrestle with the importance of the traditional way of worship and the more recently introduced precepts of Christianity. She, like many other Seminoles, chose her own way. "It is your choice on how you handle it. . . . On the Christian side, you know there is heaven and hell. Then, on the Indian side, you know there is the spirit world. It is the same thing. You just do not interpret it in the same way. I guess it depends on who is telling you . . . what you believe."[19]

Jeannette Cypress praised the openness and tolerance of Seminole society. She attended church and considered herself a believer, but "I believe and respect whatever anybody else wants to worship. I go [to church] and I also believe in the Indian medicine." She took her kids to church, but not all the time. "But if they choose to go on their own, I am not going to say, no, you cannot go. I also teach them about traditional medicine and try to tell them to be open-minded, because in this world you are going to meet a lot of people with different ideas and . . . beliefs and you can't sit there and say, my belief is better than yours. You just have to be open and that is how you learn." She explained that "we all live together and we respect [each other] and do not try to force . . . our views on others." Tribal members' religious beliefs vary according to the individual: "You will have some that go to church and they will feel that Indian medicine is the Devil's way. . . . Then, you will have some that might have been that way at one time but then, because of health reasons, they will come back to the Indian medicine."[20]

Some attitudes toward the church were determined by previous religious experiences. Carl Baxley was "baptized back when I was a young kid. I really probably did not understand the significance of why we were doing it, just that everybody was doing it and I did it, too. Now that I am an adult and make my own decisions, I do not go to church. I believe there is a God. . . . I do ask for forgiveness and I pray for other people." One reason Baxley no longer goes to church is "that when I was a kid, I was made to go, dragged to church, punished for not sitting there and being quiet. And I still have those memories. . . . So, I think it is up to the individual, how they want to pursue it. I do not think it is something that should be rammed down your throat, like it was to me when I was a kid—even though I probably needed it and it probably has influenced my life today. But . . . I have always gone the opposite way that everybody else does. I have the knots on my head to prove it."[21]

Different people hold different interpretations of Indian beliefs versus Christian beliefs. Individual preference is clearly the key, as there is no single, clear-cut view. Today, many Seminoles, including some Christian Indians, attend the Green Corn Dance not for its religious content but because they treasure it as an important part of their cultural heritage. Louise Jumper summed up the contradictory views of the Seminoles. "I think most Christians hardly use the Indian medicine. But some Christians believe that God has given us the ability to do the medicine to help our people out. . . . [Then] there are some people that believe that when they are Christian, they get away from all their Indian ways."[22]

Jacob Osceola effectively explained the dilemma Seminoles face when, in effect, dealing with two religions. He argued that the choices were up to the individual. He knew people were supposed to go to church, but "I have really never darkened those doors so I really cannot expand on it. And also Indian religion, I have never really practiced that the way it should be practiced." In the 1970s, tribal members "might have been gung-ho Baptists. But in the 1980s, then I think maybe after a time, they started poking holes in the concept and some . . . might have seen that it [Christianity] is not all what it is sometimes cracked up to be. The same thing with the Indian religion. . . . So, I think the individual who might have had some kind of open mind might have been able to utilize both and probably be a pretty sound person. . . . I think there has to be a lot of explanation or education in religion in both areas to actually give the people enough vision to try to either take one as whole or even both. I do not see any difference in terms of both areas, they run on the same parallel level. . . .

"You take the old Baptist brimstone, fire, and all that stuff and it has got constraints on how you have to behave yourself or how you have to go to this heaven, and Indian religion is the same way. . . . [T]hey have restraints and they have certain rules and criteria that you have to follow. . . . I understand there are probably over one hundred types of other religions in the world, but there has got to be only one God as far as we are concerned and there has got to be only one heaven. . . . I do not know how you get there . . . but some holy-roller Baptist guy says you are going to be walking on streets of gold [in heaven]. And since we were poor, starving Indians out on the reservations in the 1960s, we said, 'Oh, man, that is what I want.'"

Osceola disliked Christmas and distrusted prayer. One Christmas he desperately wanted a Western Flyer bicycle that was displayed in front of the Christmas tree at church. "I prayed and prayed and, sure enough, somebody else got it. Where did my prayers go? . . . This is . . . some of the misgivings [about] . . . these religions that were expanding throughout the reservations. Maybe it was to give us hope." Jacob Osceola also disparaged the view that if you failed to tithe you would burn in hell. He knew how the tribe had become economically successful, and it was "not because we prayed."[23]

It is difficult to measure Christianity's impact on the daily lives of the tribal members, but Virgil Harrington, the white superintendent of the Seminole Indian Agency from 1958 to 1963, disagreed with Jacob Osceola about the influence of religion on the economics and well-being of the tribe. Harrington believed that the missionaries and Christian leaders "had a tremendous effect on changing the attitude of the Indian people towards being a little more progressive, and to give them a spirit of brotherly love towards their non-Indian neighbors and themselves." The missionaries and the church did "a tremendous service to the welfare and the livelihood of the Seminole Indians. They filled a gap that the federal government and the programs and assistance available from the federal government could not do." The church, concluded Harrington, was the main reason why the Seminoles could work in harmony and forgive and forget personal conflicts.[24]

Christianity also had a marked impact on tribal burial practices and attitudes toward death. Ivy Stranahan observed several Seminole funerals in the early 1900s. The Indians would come to the Stranahans and borrow their horse and wagon to transport the dead to the burial place. The Stranahans, following Seminole custom, always approached from the east and would circle the burial place two or three times. The Seminole family then put all of the dead person's possessions, including clothing, guns, ammunition, and other items, into the coffin to be buried with the deceased. Over time, however, the tribe adopted the white practice of using an undertaker and burying their dead in the cemetery on the reservation.[25]

William D. Boehmer, a teacher at the Brighton Reservation, remarked that once the Seminoles became Christian they "lost this fear of death or fear of being near the dead. Most burials are taken care of through a funeral home and the services are all administered by a Christian minister" although there may "be a few that would still bury in the old Seminole custom and Seminole tradition."[26]

For his book *Wisdom's Daughters: Conversations with Women Elders of Native America*, Steve Wall interviewed Jeannette Cypress; her mother, Agnes Cypress; and her 102-year-old grandmother, Susie Billie. Among other things, the three generations of Seminole women discussed the tribe's changing attitudes toward death and burial. Agnes recalled that "in the old days" they did not buy flowers for the funeral, as they did now, they simply stayed in camp for four days, when they believed the spirit had departed. They also tried to bury the body before the four days were up because "if you don't bury the person before the four days, then it's going to take another spirit with them and there'll be another death soon, right after that one. They'll hang around until you join them." She explained that the tribe used special medicine, usually smoking bay leaves, to send the spirit away to a spirit town or spirit land—a place for spirits where they will join their ancestors and continue their lives the way they did previously. Agnes believed that the body dies, but the soul lives on.

Jeannette described her experience when her husband, Palmer, died. His spirit did not leave like it was supposed to and kept hanging around, and she became ill. The elders gave Jeannette the medicine cure, and his spirit finally left. Agnes noted that the tribe never used to bury Indian people in the ground—they left them above the ground. Now, she lamented, "people are starting to follow more the white ways; we're doing the burial services like them."[27]

In the history of the Christian church among the Seminoles, as well as in their traditional religious practices, women have had a limited role as ministers, medicine people, or political leaders. These roles, with few exceptions, have been specifically reserved for men. In part this can be traced to the Creek or Muskogee cultural origins of the people and the tensions that existed between the need for cohesion within the polity and the potential divisiveness of matrilineal clans, which reckoned descent from the women. Formal leadership roles for females were thus subordinated to affirm the dominance of social and political unity, although women remained the primary conduit of cultural values.[28]

That tradition has carried over into modern times. Mary Jene Coppedge thought the role of women in Seminole religion was "to make sure that the teachings were continuing, that you passed on the culture and that the younger children were being taught and cared for." When asked what roles women played in the modern church and if they were church leaders, Coppedge replied: "Nothing more than they do at home. I mean it is just the same thing." Women are "never the leaders or the ministers. . . . We have been Sunday school teachers and nursery teachers."[29]

Betty Mae Jumper, an elderly member of that first generation of Christian converts, corroborated Coppedge's view and expanded on the topic by saying: "We do not believe in a woman preacher. . . . The men have always led, but today there are lots of women who are working [in the church]." She noted that while there were few problems between Christians and non-Christians, sometimes there were conflicts. "I heard a lady and a daughter fussing because the mother is a Christian and she goes to church and her daughter goes to the Green Corn Dance." The woman told her daughter that she would ruin her two lit-

1. Howard Tommie, who served as chairman of the Seminole Tribe from
1971 to 1979, introduced state tax-free sale of cigarettes at the reservation
"smoke shops." Local officials challenged the tribe's right to such sales,
but court decisions and the Florida Legislature confirmed the tribe's right
to operate these shops. Tommie's vigorous advocacy of tribal sovereignty
paved the way for an unprecedented expansion of tribal business enterprises. Courtesy of the Seminole Tribe of Florida.

DONALD GLENN RENNER

2. James Billie, a flamboyant personality and Vietnam veteran, succeeded
Howard Tommie as tribal chairman in 1979 and served until 2001. He led the
legal struggle that confirmed the tribe's right to operate high-stakes bingo
and opened new casinos in Tampa and Coconut Creek. During his administration, Seminole income and standard of living grew dramatically.
Courtesy of the Seminole Tribe of Florida.

3. (*Opposite top*) Seminole Bingo Hall, Hollywood Reservation. The first Seminole bingo hall opened in 1979. The sheriff of Broward County challenged the
legitimacy of the bingo operation; however, a federal court held that the Seminole Tribe could operate high-stakes bingo on the reservations, thus estab-
lishing a legal precedent for other Indian tribes. Courtesy of Harry A. Kersey.

4. (*Opposite bottom*) A Seminole "smoke shop" at the Hollywood Reservation,
ca. 1980. Courtesy of Harry A. Kersey.

5. (*Opposite top*) One of the original concrete-block structure homes
built at the Big Cypress Reservation, ca. 1970. Federal officials encouraged
Seminoles to move to such reservation communities. Courtesy of Harry A.
Kersey.

6. (*Opposite bottom*) One of the wooden homes constructed at the Big
Cypress Reservation, ca. 1970. The homes were built to simulate a
traditional Seminole camp. The building on the right was a sleeping
area, while the smaller, detached structure on the left was a cooking/
dining area. Courtesy of Harry A. Kersey.

7. (*Above*) Tribal headquarters at Hollywood Reservation, 1970. The rustic
stone-and-timber structures were built in the National Park style. The
building on the left was occupied by Bureau of Indian Affairs offices. The
tribal government offices were located in the building on the right.
Courtesy of Harry A. Kersey.

8. (*Opposite top*) Tribal headquarters at Hollywood Reservation, 1999. This modern multi-story structure, built in 1991, houses most Seminole tribal offices. Note the wind sock for a helipad on the roof. The statue commemorates Abiaka (Sam Jones), a nineteenth-century Seminole War hero. Photo by permission of Jessica Cattelino.

9. (*Opposite bottom*) Ahfachkee School, Big Cypress Reservation, ca. 1970. A modern elementary school—the name means "happy" in Mikasuki—was built by the Bureau of Indian Affairs in 1966. It was occasionally used for community meetings, and part of the facility also functioned as a public health clinic. While under bureau control, the school had a high rate of teacher turnover, poor student attendance, and low achievement scores; few of the students continued to public school, which was an hour's ride from the reservation by school bus. Courtesy of Harry A. Kersey.

10. (*Above*) Ahfachkee School, Big Cypress Reservation, 2008. The Seminole Tribe took control of the Ahfachkee School in 1982. Federal funds for Indian education were funneled directly to the tribe via contracting from Washington DC. A new state-of-the-art school was built utilizing tribal funds and is directed by a board of community members. Today the tribe offers pre-K through twelfth grade education at this reservation educational center. Courtesy of Harry A. Kersey.

11. (*Opposite top*) First Baptist Church, Big Cypress Reservation, ca. 1970. Most community leaders on the Big Cypress Reservation in the 1970s attended this church. Its members generally objected to conducting the Green Corn Dance on reservation land. Courtesy of Harry A. Kersey.

12. (*Opposite bottom*) First Baptist Church, Hollywood Reservation, ca. 1970. This church was built by the Southern Baptist Convention in the late 1940s, and a non-Indian missionary occupied the parsonage. The Southern Baptists also trained a number of Seminole lay ministers who occupied the reservation pulpits. Courtesy of Harry A. Kersey.

13. (*Above*) Seminole Hard Rock Hotel and Casino, Hollywood Reservation. In May 2004 the Seminole Tribe launched its extravagant $400 million Hard Rock venue in Hollywood. By 2007 the tribe was able to purchase Hard Rock International, Inc. for $965 million, thus becoming a major player in the global entertainment industry. Courtesy of the Seminole Tribe of Florida.

14. Joe Dan Osceola, seen here addressing a reservation meeting ca. 1971, was the first Seminole to graduate from a public high school in Florida. He served a term as president of the tribe's board of directors and was later president of United Southeastern Tribes. He is a successful businessman at the Hollywood Reservation. Courtesy of the Samuel Proctor Oral History Program, University of Florida.

tle girls "if you do not keep them in school and keep them in the church, because they are going to go, like a lot of the teenagers do, drinking and going on. She said they are going to follow that if you do not take them back to church instead of going to the Green Corn Dance."[30]

Men's commentary on the role of women in the church varied little from the women's version. Andy Buster explained that women hold different positions "like Sunday school teachers. The main part I see is that they do much of the cooking and providing in that way, as well as the child care. Mostly men are deacons." Buster concluded that women are "well respected in that way as they bear children. In that way, they are the ones who provide life. I am not sure how to put it into words except they are well-respected . . . and they also have much healing knowledge. . . . Pretty much in society . . . they are the ones who make the decisions because they are the ones who make things happen."[31] Joe Frank added that while he had yet to encounter a female preacher on the reservation, "I have encountered many women medicine people. In both facets, Christianity and traditional, women are the fabric that hold the whole thing together."[32] Paul Douglas Buster recalled that when Christianity first came to the reservations, women "were appointed as deaconesses and would help out the preacher, help out with the activities of the church. Nowadays, you do not see too many women as deaconesses. They do have part in the churches, like Sunday school and women on mission programs, cooperative programs. . . . But as far as standing up behind the pulpit or helping the pastor . . . you do see not much of that these days." As time passed, Buster explained, the Seminoles learned more about what God had to say about pastors in the Bible and they wanted to follow God's word, which identified men as the leaders, although it is fine for women to help out.[33]

The perpetuation of Seminole folk medicine and ritual songs was not the exclusive province of medicine men, as medicine women were also skilled in preparing medicines from natural materials that grew in the Everglades and Big Cypress regions. The medicine women pretty much restricted themselves to the practice of curative medicines and steered clear of the spiritual medicine because it might lead to the accusation of witchcraft. Jeannette Cypress is the granddaughter of the renowned medicine woman Susie Billie. Jeannette grew up helping her grandmother and her brother, the esteemed medicine man Buffalo Jim, prepare curative potions. She learned much about the process and saw the perpetuation of her knowledge as essential to the continuation of Seminole culture. However, she admitted that there are significant difficulties in this work, as much of the formulary is contained in an archaic version of the Mikasuki and Creek languages.

Jeannette explained how this great family tradition was passed down from one generation to another. "We grew up in a family where my grandfathers all practiced it. We all used it growing up and I think I am destined, like no matter what you do, you always go back to something. I think it is one of these things with me because . . . my grandmother is determined that I am going to know if whether I want [to] or not. At this age, she always wants to have it done. So, I am the one who has to go get the plants. When I first started, I might pick the wrong plant and she would send me back. I have been going back and now I have learned quite a bit from her. My mom is really knowledgeable and she knows a lot of what to do, how to prepare, and what it is for, but she has had a really hard time with the singing and chant-prayer part because she said her memory just cannot seem to pick that up for some reason. It is like a totally different language. A lot of it is old Mikasuki, and then you have some Creek thrown in.

"Myself, I can understand certain words when she sings, but there are parts where she has to stop and break it down and tell me what she is talking about so I can relate to it. I always tell people, it is like going to medical school; like you have people come and go, [asking] what is this for? If you tell them bay leaves are used for something, they think they can grab a bay leaf and use it. It is not that way. It is a lot of stuff that goes into it. If you really want to learn you have to devote a lot of time. You have to go listen to her and she has to repeat a lot of stuff and break it down and explain [it] to you. And then, when you learn the chant, then you have to know what kind of diet you tell your patient and what they can't eat after they use the medicine. How to use the medicine, whether you bathe in it or drink it. And then, you have to learn the plants that go in it. Because, like my grandmother, she had to go out, pick the plants, prepare it, do everything."[34]

As these interviews indicate, significant differences of opinion remain among Seminoles over the viability and validity of the Green Corn Dance. Some individuals refused to comment on the Green Corn Dance since it was a sacred rite of the tribe and its mysteries were closed to outsiders. However, most of those interviewed, whether Christians or non-Christians, had rather strong opinions about the ceremony.

Some tribal members deplored the fact that the ritual and meaning of the Green Corn Dance had changed. It had become less religious and unifying and is today primarily a source of entertainment. "The reason why I do not go anymore is because of the alcohol and drugs that were out there," said Carl Baxley. "The perception of the Green Corn Dance, it is not what it is supposed to be." Baxley regretted that "a lot of young people in our tribe really do not understand what that [Green Corn Dance] means and the significance of it." He understood that the young people had grown up in a different world with computers and cell phones, but regretted that they did not comprehend or appreciate the old values.[35]

The decline in the Green Corn Dance's importance as a religious experience was signaled by the increasing introduc-

tion of alcohol to the dance ground. Although there were numerous reports of Seminole liquor consumption dating to the
trading post era, it is unclear how much drinking was allowed
at the dance grounds while traditional medicine men were still
in charge. Apparently these prohibitions had broken down significantly by the mid-twentieth century. Jeannette Cypress explained why some people do not want to attend the ceremony:
"It all goes back to the Christianity thing. Sometimes I think they
feel like if you are a Christian, you should not go to those, because some people perceived it as worshiping something else.
And then some people think it is a place where a lot of people
just go out and get drunk . . . and they do not see what it really stands for. They think it is time to get together with your
friends and party."[36]

Betty Mae Jumper explained that the Seminoles did not have
alcohol in the beginning: "The Green Corn Dance . . . meant a
lot to the Indians back in the olden days. It meant thanking the
Great Spirit [for] the good year they had. . . . Today it is nothing
but a playground and drinking, that is all."[37] Mary Johns remembered that "when I was a youngster, these ceremonials used to
be, well, they served a lot of liquor, and they would get drunk
and they would fight, and it would just be a mess. It was hard for
kids to be there because of that."[38] Stanlo Johns gave up on his
Native religious observance because "it got to the point that all
of these kids would go over there and just get drunk. . . . Well,
that is not the idea of the Green Corn Dance. It is a religion. It
has meaning. So I quit going after I saw all that."[39] Despite the
drinking at the dance and the Christian antipathy to what is perceived as a pagan rite, Lorene Gopher insisted that many people still did both. "They will do their church thing and they will
do [Indian] medicine."[40]

Partly as a result of the criticism regarding the degradation
of the ceremony through drinking, drugs, and partying, in the
1990s the elders and tribal government revived a traditional Green

Corn Dance at the Big Cypress Reservation and forbade the use of alcohol. Although she understood the importance of the ritual, Helene Johns Buster had refused for many years to go to a Green Corn Dance because her most vivid memory was of her mother getting drunk at the ceremony: "I appreciated it as part of my heritage and culture and I did not want to disrespect any of it. I should have realized back then, even at that time, just being there drunk was disrespectful." She had recently attended the alcohol-free affair at Big Cypress and got a totally different view of the ceremony: "I . . . was a part of the ceremony—the dances, and the cooking around the campfires, and staying there, and spending time there." She found there were lots of people there "that are not drinking and that are into what they were supposed to be doing with the culture and upholding the traditional part of it. That is what is very appealing to me, because, not growing up with a whole lot of tradition," because "they pushed us more to be white, I felt, so that we would be able to function in this world. We did not learn a whole bunch of our stuff there, so now . . . I am learning more about my history and what we should be doing as Native Americans." Buster learned that the purification was designed to help the participant. "They do different medicines out there that are supposed to help you throughout your life. And they teach women when you are having your menstrual cycles . . . , it [the menstrual cycle] is actually purification, too. . . . The women are purified every month, where men are just purified once each year."[41]

Nancy Shore participated in both the Christian church and the traditional ceremonies. She claimed that views of the Green Corn Dance had changed over the years. The early missionaries told them that, as good Christians, they had to give up the Green Corn Dance. Shore, however, has always believed that there is just one God and that "the Corn Dance . . . is to praise him for all the good things that he has [done] for our health. Especially the planting . . . so we bless the corn . . . that is like a

gift from him. . . . And I like going to the Corn Dance. That has
been part of my life all these years." Also, she wanted her family to learn about the Corn Dance. "They are the ones who are
going to carry it forward when I am gone."[42]

Lorene Gopher expressed a similar point of view. She believed Christianity and the Green Corn Dance "can go hand in
hand. . . . How can you give up being a Seminole because you
want to be this [a Christian]? You are still going to be that [a Sem-
inole] even if you go to church. That is our way. I believe you
can mix it." She explained that the Seminole tradition was not
introduced to the reservation fifty years ago like Christianity, "it
has been here since day one."[43]

For Daisi Jumper, being a Christian was the same as worshiping at the Green Corn Dance. "We believed in a Creator, one
who made life, one who made all things, and it is the same thing
. . . we just have a different name for it. Instead of a nice, beautiful church, we have the Green Corn Dance, and that was mainly
to thank the Creator for all the blessings of the year. That was
a time to get together. And it was like having a church, thanking God, and forgiving people, doing away with the bad things
of the year and starting a whole new year. To me there is not
much difference. . . . We prayed wherever we wanted to. When
we did not have churches, we would go in the swamps and sit
down at a cypress tree and pray."[44]

Andy Buster continued to attend the Green Corn Dance and
provided an excellent description of what happened at the ceremony. Although some aspects of the ceremony have changed,
this account reveals how closely the Seminoles have retained elements of the old Creek busk ritual. The Seminoles would plant
corn in November or December so that the green corn would be
ready to be harvested by July. When they brought the corn to the
ceremony, all of the clans would be gathered in that area. "They
would give the corn to each one of them, and that was their way
of giving thanks for what they had. That included their health

and everything that they had, their children and everything in their camp. . . . It is a beautiful ceremony, a four-day ceremony. On the first day they do the opening. On the second day they do the fire-gathering ceremonies. Then on the third day they would have a feast. All the women cook and all the men would go and hunt. . . . At midnight the tribe would roast the corn. It is believed that when the smoke rises in the creator's face, he looks down and realizes that these people still remember their ceremony. They give him thanks. In that way he would bless them for another year. On the fourth day there would be fasting . . . all day and all night. There would be dancing all night. . . . [O]n the fifth morning they would break the fast." Buster mentioned that "it is believed that if we eat without doing the ceremony or the ritual . . . your spirit will become weak. So we must follow the tradition. If we don't do the ceremony, then we don't eat. It is just self-discipline."

The participants, continued Buster, would learn different songs and dances, and on the fourth night the naming ceremony took place. As noted elsewhere, the Seminoles had both an Indian name and an English name. Thus Mitchell Cypress, president of the Seminole Tribe of Florida, Inc., also has the Indian name *Yahee Chadee*, which means Red Wolf.[45] Jeannette Cypress learned from her grandmother that the Green Corn Dance had important social meaning and helped unify the tribe. It was "a time to get together, to celebrate, see your friends, to be like one big family, and the boys kind of grew up and got their man names. . . . It is a time to be happy and not to argue. . . . It is kind of like a New Year for us. . . . It is a good time to teach your kids certain things because you have all the other relatives there."[46]

It was during the Green Corn Dance that the medicine man revealed the contents of the sacred medicine bundle and reiterated their significance for the group. The contents had great intrinsic worth to the Indians and included both spiritual and medicinal items. William Sturtevant believed that this emphasis on the medicine bundle was unique to Florida Seminoles; bundles were not historically a significant part of the Creek busk ceremony.[47] Louis Capron, who observed many ceremonies in the 1930s, described the medicine bundle as "a collection of 600–700 objects—pieces of horn, stone and the like—ordinary enough to look at but possessing extraordinary powers in the eyes of the Indians."[48]

An important element of the ceremony was Court Day, or the handling of most criminal cases. The adult males met as a council, and any person who was guilty of a transgression against Seminole society could try and atone for his or her actions. In some cases the act was forgiven, while in other cases the transgressor was ostracized. In the distant past, some more serious crimes, such as adultery, were punished by cropping the ears or clipping the nose. Rarely, and only in very extreme cases, did the council order an execution. From the beginning the ceremony was used "as the day of judgment as to the situation that might have happened throughout the year. So, if there were any kind of punishment or rulings that had to be hammered out or if there were some types of problems between families or between clans, then this is the time when they were to bring it up and address it."[49]

Capron concluded that the Seminole theory of crime assumed that "obedience to the law is the price one pays for the privilege of belonging to a society. Thus, any person who commits a crime acts against his own good. He is then outlawed before he can infect others. He can no longer be a tribal member until he is rehabilitated by the medicine man."[50]

Also, as a form of personal purification, all the men (not the women) submitted to scratching, a ritual bloodletting, through the use of sewing needles mounted to a wooden frame. In earlier times the blood was drawn using bird talons or the claws of animals. As Carl Baxley explained, this was done "to let out the old blood and let the new blood in and keep you from getting sick."[51] Andy Buster emphasized a more esoteric spiritual cleansing aspect of scratching: "The blood rises in the heavens for recognition for what you have and what you are willing to give. . . . We will give our blood to the universe . . . the Spirit of the universe will receive it. What returns is health." Buster regretted that the original meaning of scratching had been forgotten. In Seminole society, many parents used scratching as a form of punishment. "They use it as a control thing for the children. . . . When I was a little boy my mother would ask me to do something. I would be playing and not do the chore I was supposed to do. Then, she would say, 'you are going to get some scratches.' Then I would."[52]

After the scratching, the participants would further purify themselves in the sweat lodge, by fasting, and by drinking the purgative black drink, which caused vomiting. In addition, the black drink was expected to cure all the diseases for the new year, and since the ritual of the dance had been completed and their faith had been demonstrated, the healing powers of their medicine had been revived and would bring them good health during the year.[53] One of the younger Indian men interviewed, Joe Frank, illustrated—somewhat facetiously it appears—the dramatic cultural changes that have transpired, taking Seminoles further away from these traditions. When asked about the black drink, he wondered if the interviewer was referring to coffee, and when asked if he had ever used a sweat lodge, he replied: "I love saunas."[54]

Frank, who attended the Green Corn Dance and participated in the scratching and fasting, elaborated further on his views: "This term 'black drink' is something that is carried over from colonial days. . . . During the course of the Corn Dance and during the course of the purification stuff, there are quite a bit of different medicines made, and if you are participating, you use it all. But we don't have a pot boiling that we go by and say, 'This is the black drink.' No. That is a carryover from colonial days.

To us, it is [all] medicine. That is why I asked, 'When you said black drink, are you asking about coffee?'"[55] These statements illustrate the Seminoles' ongoing struggle to retain their culture. Frank's response reveals that many of the old ways, such as the black drink and sweat lodge, are just no longer relevant to many young Seminoles, no more so than the dugout canoe for transportation or the bow and arrow for obtaining sustenance.

Seminoles have adopted much of the material culture and business methods of white society, but they try to maintain their sovereignty, their cultural identity as Indians, and their tribal values. Many still live on the reservation, speak a Native language, and retain their clan affiliation. They promote the traditional arts and crafts and continue to celebrate the Green Corn Dance attended by both traditionalists and Christians. Joe Dan Osceola lamented the difficulty modern Seminoles had respecting and learning from the past: "I encourage my children to wear [Native dress] and keep the culture and the tradition going. . . . All of our children, they take part in the Corn Dance and we encourage them to speak Indian language. It is like fighting a losing battle. It is hard, especially when it is not written down. But you just have to keep talking to them."[56] Betty Mae Jumper, one of the grand dames of Seminole society, stated: "I would like to see the young people, the young generation, keep their culture . . . because when you lose it, it is lost. . . . And if you have an older person around that knows, listen to them and see what they say. We do not have too many older people nowadays. They are all gone, the ones that used to tell things."[57]

The Seminoles' drift away from religious beliefs associated with the Green Corn Dance was also reflected in a growing acceptance of the white man's methods of curing illness. One of the first to depend on white medicine had little choice. Jimmy O'Toole Osceola contracted tuberculosis while attending Indian boarding school. When asked where he went to hospital, the reply was, "Shawnee, Oklahoma. After four years, I was cured and

I was asked if I would continue going to school, the doctor there could arrange it for me. But I missed my family for a long time so I wanted to come home. I told him I wanted to come home. After that, after I came home, the doctor told me I could not work hard. I would not be able to work for some time, so I did not work. I would work a little bit, maybe two or three days at a time. I would keep on going, doing the drifting."[58] This inability to perform hard manual labor sent Osceola along a path to developing his talents as a maker of Seminole arts and crafts.

Many Christian Indians turned away from the use of traditional Seminole medicines, seeing them as being Satanic in origin or at the very least, unbiblical. But like so many aspects of Seminole beliefs about religion and medicine, there is no hard-and-fast rule. Some Christian Indians occasionally resort to traditional medicine, and traditionalists sometimes avail themselves of modern health care. For example, Paul Douglas Buster, a professed Christian, stated that although medicine men and women continued to practice traditional healing, "there are just a few left, I think. Johnny Jim was a good man. He was a medicine man. His sister, Susie Jim [Susie Jim Billie], . . . she is a medicine woman. . . . Buffalo Jim is probably one of the legends among Seminoles as a medicine man." Buster conceded that it was possible for a Christian Indian to be treated using traditional remedies, but "it depends on the shaman or medicine man." As for himself, "I don't even mess with it. As a matter of fact, I don't do anything with custom or traditional medicine. I go to Eckerd [drugstore]."[59]

It was not unusual for Seminoles to consult both types of healers at the same time. Louise Jumper believed it is possible to combine both Indian and white medical practices effectively. "I know I went to both. I was depressed; I was into depression for a while, and I went to both and got healed. . . . But sometimes, I would go to the white man's doctor and not go to the Indian, or go to the Indian medicine and not go to the [white man's doctor].

Sometimes I would do both."[60] Brian Billie demonstrated the lingering influence of the medicine men. Despite being an avowed Christian, Billie had no problem using traditional medicines. "I usually just go to the modern medicine. But if it is something that I just cannot beat, then I have to go to the traditional medicine."[61] Another member of the tribe, Joe Frank, admitted that while he treated most of his health problems the old, traditional way, when he had the flu for two weeks he went and got some antibiotics. "I don't know yet of a medicine man who can cure the common cold," he said. When asked if some ailments were treated best by Western medicine, he replied: "I would say healing is a matter of your mind, and some people may have more confidence in one particular form of treatment than in another. That is not to say it is the best, but for that individual it may be what they believe works best for them."[62]

Helene Johns Buster, a registered nurse, also commented on tribal members' tendency "to still use a lot of the Indian medicine or the Native medicine. Sometimes they use it in conjunction with the Western medicine. Sometimes they want to do that [Western medicine] first. Or, if the medicine we are giving them is not working, they will go to the Indian medicine. And we let them know that is perfectly fine." Buster did not think one system was better than the other. "They were equally good and could also work together."[63] Lorene Gopher, on the other hand, recalled that things were different a generation ago. "If my grandmother got sick, we did not take her to town to a doctor. She went and saw a medicine man, and he did what he had to do. And I guess she got better from it. . . . We were a lot the same way. My grandmother was a medicine person herself, so she would take care of us that way." Gopher learned about medicinal plants from her grandmother, "but I did not learn any medicine songs from her."[64] Many Seminole men and women learned about the healing nature of plants from their elders, but few learned the songs that gave the concoctions their power. For women in particular, this activity trod on dangerous ground, as not so long ago they risked potential accusations of practicing witchcraft or sorcery. Nevertheless, the medicine woman Susie Billie was once captured on film singing a medicine song while conjuring protective spirits from the leaping flames of a campfire.[65]

Further confusing the issue is the fact that some medicine people became Christians. When she was asked if medicine men and women could be Christians, Sadie Cypress said: "Yes. Because Grandma Susie [Susie Jim Billie] over here, she makes medicines. She has been Christian for as long as I remember. . . . She has three brothers. They were all medicine carriers. They made medicine and they went to church. . . . All of those people are Christians, and they made medicine until the day they died." Although Sadie Cypress was a Christian, she openly admitted using Indian medicine as well as the white man's medicine. "My father was a minister. He believed in Indian medicine. He said Indian medicine [is] for your physical body. God made that Indian medicine for you to use it while you are here on this Earth for your physical body. Your physical body is a temple of God, but the Bible tells you to believe in God spiritually. But your physical body is something [else]. When you are hurting, God made Indian medicine, any kind of medicine, for you to use while you are here, alive in this world. That is what my father taught."[66]

Louis Capron was one of the first to note that Indian healers were no longer necessarily spiritual leaders. For more than a quarter century, Capron, a close friend of the Creek-speaking Seminoles who lived on the Brighton Reservation, frequently attended the Green Corn Dance. In 1969 he wrote: "The Indian herb doctor still functions. . . . These doctors are not necessarily 'medicine men.' The medicine man has charge of the sacred medicine on which the non-Christian Seminoles believe their well being—even their existence—depends. He presides at the

Green Corn Dance, the purpose of which is to keep the medicine alive and the Indian healthy and fortunate."[67]

The only practicing medicine man interviewed, Sonny Billie, offered a bleak assessment of what the future holds for training medicine people. Speaking of those who studied with him,
Billie mused, "I got about two groups. But the ones that is really into it . . . as far as I see it, they are not so hot." He claimed
to know little about women who made medicine and implied
that women had a limited role. "As far as ladies, I don't know too
much about it. . . . But some of those ladies came and studied a
lot, as far as like a woman part; like a woman treatment site."[68]

Missionaries and tribal officials constantly reinforced the acceptance of the white man's medicine through the use of Indian
Health Service (IHS) physicians and nurses who staffed clinics
on the reservations. The Seminole tribal government also provided ambulances and EMT services for the isolated reservations. Nevertheless, many of the older Seminoles continued to
utilize both traditional cures and the modern medical prescrip-
tions. Dr. David Hilton, an IHS contract physician who worked
among the Seminoles for many years, saw a value in resorting to
various folk remedies—particularly good advice for elderly patients who had to have faith not only in the medicine prescribed
but also in the individual who was attempting to heal them.
Marie Phillips remembered that Hilton "would say, if I cannot
help you, go to the medicine man or the medicine woman and
maybe she can help you. A lot of people have asthma or upper
respiratory problems. And they would get sassafras tea to calm
the asthma attacks and we use bay leaves like aromatherapy—
just the burning of the bay leaves, itself, has like a calming sense
to it."[69] Hilton once confided that he often conferred with the
medicine man Buffalo Jim concerning their mutual patients, and
he reported they both found the greatest problem was patients
who did not follow their orders.[70]

The ready availability of health care for Seminoles is a relatively recent occurrence. William D. Boehmer, the longtime

government teacher at Brighton, recalled how limited the health care for Indians was during the early 1940s. "One of the things, sort of a side responsibility that we accepted, was doctoring minor ailments of Indian children in school and of the people in the community. We kept a small supply of drugs on hand at the school. Today this would probably not be acceptable at all, but in those days it was. Miss Charlotte Conrad, the [public health] nurse at the time, had been working with the Seminoles for a couple of years prior to our coming to Florida. She had good rapport with the Indians. She could only make it to the reservation, though, once every two weeks or something like that— sometimes only once a month—because she had to cover not only Brighton Reservation but also Big Cypress and the Tamiami Trail. And there being no roads then to Big Cypress, this was a real hardship. So if a child had the sniffles or a headache or diarrhea or some other ailment, why, we had some medicines that were necessary and helpful to them. I recall a few instances where adults came to us for assistance."[71]

Twenty to thirty years earlier, explained Joe Dan Osceola, Seminoles were reluctant to see a white doctor, but now, after being educated in the schools, they are more willing to do so and understand that medicine men have very limited healing power compared to many years ago.[72] Helene Johns Buster recognized that because of the large amount of money earned by gambling, the Seminoles had "a wonderful health care system." The money allowed the tribe to spend money on preventive medicine, in order to avoid greater problems "on down the line." "Now you can do preventive things that will help, like if a kid needs to have his tonsils taken out, you can just do that, it is an elective thing" that the tribe will pay for.[73]

Many of the health problems facing the modern Seminoles are exacerbated by poor dietary habits and an increasingly sedentary lifestyle—the same issues that beset the non-Indian world. The new affluence of Seminole families, with large monthly dividend checks derived primarily from gambling-related tribal enterprises, has had a negative impact on their overall health. The traditional Indian diet has given way to all types of processed foods, which led to the prevalence of obesity, a high incidence of diabetes, as well as high blood pressure and heart problems. There has also been increased usage of alcohol and drugs. The tribal government has established medical and rehabilitation programs to combat these ills, but they remain a major cause of Seminole incapacitation.

When Seminoles were queried as to the greatest health problems they faced as a people, an overwhelming majority replied that diabetes was number one. Hypertension and alcohol and drug abuse were not far behind. Interestingly, many of the respondents said that the Indian people were largely responsible for the diabetes toll because they failed to take their medications and would not follow rigorous dietary restraints. Asked if Seminoles had changed their diet and eating habits to combat these illnesses, Andy Buster replied: "Not as much as I would like to see. Yet, it begins with me, and I have a problem because I am a diabetic as well. That is something that is really hard to work with because it requires a lot of self-discipline. It is very hard because it is food. In that way it is hard to cut back. That is the problem I have."[74]

Jacob Osceola's family also suffered the scourge of diabetes. "I guess it is probably the number one killer of Indian people across the United States. And that is something that has plagued Indian tribes, plagued me and my family, for a long period of time. Through generations I guess they have not come up with what really causes diabetes, and I am a victim of it. Maybe it is genetic, I do not know. . . . Like they say, it may skip an individual. . . . My grandmother lived to be 104 years old; when she died she did not have diabetes. But then again, who is to say that she might have had it and just never was diagnosed. I probably had diabetes three years before I was finally diagnosed. . . . After we started getting dividends, we would run down to McDonald's, and Burger King and Taco Bell. *Yo quiero* Taco Bell [as a popular advertisement states]. The next thing you know, we would go to Taco Bell and we were happy."[75]

Viewing illness from the perspective of a tribal administrator, Jeannette Cypress tried to organize programs to combat a disease rampant on the reservations. "I think the biggest thing that we are working on is probably diabetes," she said. "We have a lot of diabetics and the tribe has really gotten into [assisting]. They have wellness/diabetic day at the clinic where they have an interpreter in case some of the older ones do not understand. They have a diabetic breakfast that morning and they will do screenings and talk about medications, any questions. We have a nutritionist on board; we have a person who does exercises now. We have a real nice gym here equipped with weight machines. We even have Tai Bo and aerobics and that kind of stuff now. . . . I see my grandmother, and then I see my mom. Mom is younger and Mom is already struggling. . . . My mom is diabetic. She has some problems with high blood pressure and she is probably sixty now. . . . My grandmother [over one hundred years of age], she still does really well. I think a lot of it is because of the exercise and work. They did not have all that junk food that we eat today, and she had to work hard."[76]

Women's health has been a major issue for the tribe. In recent years the tribe dramatically increased its assistance with childbirth, contraception, and child care. In the 1940s, Seminole women, as a rule, did not go to the hospital for childbirth. They would build a chikee away from the camp and have their child there. William Boehmer, however, recounted an incident where Pocahontas Jumper began to experience problems after three days in labor. Boehmer agreed to drive her and her husband to the nearest hospital—at that time, sixty miles away. Halfway to the hospital, Pocahontas could wait no longer and "the baby was born by the side of the road." Boehmer took out a small pocket knife and cut the umbilical cord. Both mother and child were fine.[77] During the 1940s and 1950s Seminole women rarely used any methods of contraception or birth control, but now that the tribe provides these services free of charge, more and more women are taking advantage of these opportunities.[78]

The outspoken Joe Dan Osceola emphatically identified the worst enemies of Seminole health: "Bar none, diabetes. The other is alcohol and drug abuse, like in major cities. Sometimes you read about that in the newspaper and some kinds of magazines. That is hitting us right between the eyes, the drug and alcohol abuse. Unfortunately, our bodies are not immune to this kind of abuse given by the drugs. Diabetes, of course, is genetic, it comes from the parents; it is inherited. But I really do not believe that. You might have had that kind of life as a youngster. You have no choice but eat that kind of food—fried food and too much starch—when you are a youngster and carry on, but to me it is not in your genes. It is the way that you are brought up, and it is hard to change after being an adult.

"A lot of people did not change, and they are suffering now. But if they know what it will cause and what it can do, they will do their best to [change] their ways or their eating habits. For the longest time they did not have refrigerators, they did not have stoves. The only thing they were able to eat was fried food all the way through. And because of that, I know that a lot of tribal members, their health is suffering because of that and not enough greens in their system, hardly ever. . . . So I would see that those are the two or three different things that are detrimental to the health of Seminoles, and not just the Seminoles but most of the Natives throughout the country."[79]

In the 1970s Joe Dan served as the first president of United South Eastern Tribes, a consortium that initially included the Seminoles, Miccosukees, Choctaws, and Cherokees. One of the group's major goals was improvement of Indian health services, and Osceola, who had experience in administering such programs in Florida, became a key figure in the process. "I worked closely with them, even when I was working with the Indian Health Service." In 1955 the U.S. Public Health Service formed the Indian Health Service to provide special care for Native Americans. "I used to be in charge, being the unit service director for directing the health care we have now. It used to be under the state [of Florida] and they did not have hardly any program. No program; the doctor only came once a week to the reservation. If you were going to be sick, you had to be sick that day in order to get any kind of medical attention. If you were not, then you just had to wait one whole week.

"Luckily, we had a man who was involved in it, an Indian from Oklahoma. His name was Key Wolf. He was program director for Indian Health Services. That is the way they [U.S. government] had given us the power to contract the money out of Washington. [That is] what the state was doing, but the state had problems handling their own programs anyway for the state of Florida. So that is why we took the program away from them. . . . We should know the problems better than anyone else. . . .

"From there we were able to maintain our records and have better health care. . . . We have a clinic built on each of the reservations now. . . . A nurse practitioner, and also Dr. Steele comes. If we are unable to handle either clinic, then we have contract doctors in nearby towns and the hospital. . . . A lot of reservations are so isolated. The nearest town could be fifty miles, maybe one hundred miles, but here in Hollywood we have been fortunate enough so we are able to have contract doctors. There are a lot of tribal members out on Big Cypress and Brighton who generally come here for the medical attention, for the hospital. So, we gear towards that instead of building a hospital, the building itself, on the reservation and trying to [operate] it with equipment and staff."[80]

As a nurse, Helene Johns Buster has a clear grasp of the medical issues confronting her people. She agreed with others

in stating, "diabetes is the number one disease that we face out
here [Big Cypress]. Everything else is second to the diabetes.
. . . I have seen it on both reservations and Brighton is probably, health-wise, sicker than this community is, as far as diabetes. I would like to say now it is changing over there because
we have a doctor that works there. This community for years
has had Dr. James Van Gelder, who is a nephrologist and works
with diabetes. He has been coming here for years. He has had
the clients on this reservation on a regimen of medication and
it has been a lot more closely monitored than the Brighton Reservation. Whereas at Brighton we had only a nurse practitioner and nobody that was really into the diabetes like Dr. Van
Gelder is. [That made] a big difference in the diabetic care on
the two reservations."

Buster said there were no Seminole or Miccosukee medical
doctors, but proudly noted, "we have several nurses. There was
a couple out here [Big Cypress]. In Brighton there were only two
of us nurses; one of my cousins was an RN, and myself." Buster
concluded by saying it is a good program to combat diabetes; individuals, however, still have to take responsibility: "It is as good
as you want to make it. You can come in here and eat the free
food and get your blood sugar and go and never care about your
medicine, if you take them or not. . . . Making people responsible for their own health has been a very hard thing here. I mean,
not just here but in our tribe, because you do not have to pay
for health care, the tribe pays for it, but as an individual you do
not see it as money coming out of your pocket. You think that
you are not paying for it, but, in actuality, you are paying for it
because it is tribal money that is being spent on it."[81]

Tribal members discussed problems with alcoholism, but
in far less detail than diabetes. Andy Buster provided the most
graphic description of how drinking and drugs had nearly ru-
ined his life. After years of drug and alcohol abuse, he decided
to reform his life. He joined an Alcoholics Anonymous program

and then joined a church and recovered from his addiction. Like many others, he appreciated the impact that Christianity had on his life. He admitted that in the 1980s, "I used drugs and alcohol, and I lost everything. Then I started looking into recovering from all this substance abuse, recovering in that way. I got into an AA program and started abstaining from all alcohol and drugs. My next step was that I wanted to become Christian. So I did."[82] His wife, Helene Johns Buster, also had trouble with alcohol and drugs. She went to AA and decided to go back and get training as a nurse to help others. She serves as an example to the community, as they know of her past history. "So, if I can have a life and hold a position in the community and be sober, what better way to say something than being an example?" Now, as a recovering alcoholic, she spends the majority of her nursing duties dealing with drug and alcohol abuse.[83]

Lee Tiger put a new spin on the old belief that Indians were more susceptible to alcohol than whites. When discussing the impact of diabetes and alcohol on the Seminoles, he said, "I think, again, that is still part of our cultural shock and not only cultural, but physical shock of adaptation. We are still in that phase. Because our food was a lot different before we met the non-Indian and started eating his food and sugar and different things that we didn't have before. So adapting to those things is a slow process and so we have overweight people with diabetes problems and whatever, also, overweight brings to you. With alcohol, the same thing. I guess we are, also like, maybe Asian people that it has not been in our blood for a long time so it is more pure so the alcohol will probably hurt us quicker than it would a non-Indian or somebody, maybe from Europe, who has had alcohol in their blood maybe for centuries."[84]

Susan Stans, who wrote a dissertation on community attitudes toward alcohol use, concluded that many Seminoles "have come to buy into that belief that they have something about them that compels them to drink that is physical. . . . I believe it is more of a cultural thing, an expectation." Some of the younger tribal members think "that this is what Seminoles do, this is what Indians do, we cannot help it; it is what we are supposed to do. It is in our blood."[85]

When Victor Billie was asked how Seminoles could overcome alcoholism, he placed responsibility squarely on the individual. But he also pointed out that the Seminole community at large was letting the youth down: "An Indian person is a strong person, to me. A female or a male is a strong person. If he wants to, he can put his mind [to it] and can move a mountain and can reach the unreachable star. A teenage Seminole Indian can do that. But he puts an obstacle before himself, like drugs and alcohol, that makes it bigger [so] that he cannot go around and cannot go under and cannot go over. He is making it bigger each day in relying on those drugs to ease the pain or release himself to live better—but it is not. Like I said, they can do anything, they even can quit doing drugs in they believe in themselves, and if somebody, like another Seminole or an elder, believes in them. But today, we do not have a connection among each other; . . . we do not have communication and love for our own brothers and sisters. . . . They are kind of jealous of each other. We are like that. That is how we are killing each other. We do not want to connect anymore. When I was a child, when I was growing up in the village, if somebody got hurt twenty or fifty miles away, and if they heard it, some of our elders used to collect some clothes and some food and walk way down there, or be in a canoe going down there, to help them because they had that connection, that love and respect for each other. Today, we are into too much non-Indian ways and beliefs. We are losing that connection and love and respect for each other."[86]

Some Seminole medical issues cannot be resolved simply by throwing money at them. For example, in the 1970s the Tribal Council became aware of the need for emergency medical services on the outlying reservations that were far removed from cities. The tribe responded initially by buying an ambulance for each reservation and providing EMT training for qualified Seminoles. However, the tribe soon learned that there were not enough emergency cases to justify keeping an ambulance on standby just in case it was needed. They removed the vehicles, and the Indian EMTs resorted to using private vehicles to get the occasional emergency case to a hospital.[87]

Carl Baxley believed that while the tribe had come far it still had a ways to go in offering health services and educating people to use them. "As far as being in today's world and the economic development that we have here on the reservation, I would think that the most important things would be health and education. I say health because I have lost a lot of relatives in the past due to diabetes, or alcohol or whatever. I classify those as unneeded deaths because there was prevention there. But whether they did not go seek prevention or prevention did not seek them, for whatever reason, a lot of it was due to the education part of it, of not knowing. . . . The health and the medical facilities on the reservation may not be the standard that I think they should be at this particular time in our lives, but they are a heck of a lot better than they were when I was a young kid. There are lots more opportunities out there. Not to say that those are things that we highlighted back then. I mean, money changes people. It makes them good; it makes them bad. I guess in the past ten years this tribe has come into some money through our gambling. But the issues are still there. We have better medical facilities on the reservations that were built with those dollars."[88]

Thus the irony of Seminole economic progress is that it has not guaranteed overall better health for the people. Certainly, modern clinical facilities and trained professionals are available on the reservations, but much education must take place before the people will accept the concept of preventive medicine.

The conflict between Christianity and the Green Corn Dance as a religious / medical experience continues into the twenty-first century. There are, of course, significant doctrinal differences between the religious points of view—for example, Baptists have a particularist view of hell and damnation, while traditionalists do not worry about eternal damnation; they have no belief in Jesus, talk about the afterlife rather than heaven, and see God (or their interpretation of him) everywhere. They do share moral values and a belief in one God, but some Seminoles clearly resent the idea of white churches coming into their society and trying to convert them to Western civilization while purging their "pagan" religious practices. They see it as an attempt to deracinate them—to strip them of their cultural identity—to make them Christian and white at the same time. Nonetheless, the Seminoles have proved themselves remarkably adaptive and as indicated, committed to the retention of their culture. They have managed to resolve their theological differences and live in relative harmony. As Harry Kersey expressed it: "Even Seminoles who no longer accept its [the Green Corn Dance's] spiritual significance consider the ritual a crucial link to the past. Thus the ongoing tribal revitalization, encompassing both cultural continuity and dynamic social change, provides contemporary Florida Seminoles with an opportunity to realize the best of both worlds."[89]

In the health realm, the Seminoles reflect the same individualism they do when pondering the cultural dilemmas in religion. Some still use Indian medicine, while others use white doctors and pharmacies. Many take advantage of both areas of healing and find no conflict in shifting from one cure to the other. They are pragmatic in their health choices: if white medicine does not work, they will turn to Indian medicine. The tribe has worked steadily to alleviate the twin scourges of diabetes and alcoholism through community health programs. While some who badly need treatment ignore the opportunity, as always, the choice is up to the individual to take advantage of the tribal-sponsored programs.

4. Housing and Family Transitions in Social Context

Seminole housing has changed dramatically over the past hundred years—from the thatched-roof chikees, to concrete block or wood frame structures, and more recently with increased wealth to elaborate mansions. This chapter addresses the changes in Seminole family and community life that occurred as a result of moving residents from traditional camps to modern housing provided by the tribal government. The changes in housing, especially during the thirty years covered by this study, have modified and influenced tribal values, beliefs, and practices. Most significantly, this shift undermined the extended family and its effectiveness in molding social structures and relationships. The social and economic dislocation, coupled with other political and economic issues on the reservation, led to a period of increasing stress and anxiety among the Seminoles.

Following the Third Seminole War (1855–58), the Seminoles remaining in Florida survived in the pine woods and palmetto scrub north of Lake Okeechobee or made their homes on tree islands known as hammocks in the Big Cypress Swamp and Everglades region. Except for occasional trading at coastal towns such as Miami or Fort Myers, the Indians rarely ventured from these isolated enclaves, and little was known of their numbers or lifestyle. Nevertheless, the Seminoles developed a symbiotic relationship with white settlers in the coastal contact communities, and the commodities they supplied—primarily alligator hides, bird plumes, and otter pelts—were an important aspect of the frontier economy.

During the last quarter of the nineteenth century both federal and state officials took greater interest in the indigenous population. During his 1880–81 survey of the Seminole Indians, conducted for the Smithsonian Institution's Bureau of Ethnology, Clay MacCauley visited five multi-family Seminole communities in southern Florida. He identified these as: (1) Big Cypress Swamp settlement, Monroe County; (2) Miami River settlement, Dade County; (3) Fish Eating Creek settlement, Manatee County; (4) Cow Creek Settlement, Brevard; and (5) Cat Fish Lake settlement, Polk County. MacCauley's census listed 208 men, women, and children, including several "blacks" and "mixed bloods."[1] Captain Richard H. Pratt had visited some of these Seminole communities in 1879 to determine the feasibility of removing them to Indian Territory in present-day Oklahoma (he advised against it), but his report to the commissioner of Indian Affairs was more anecdotal than ethnological.[2]

Nonetheless, MacCauley's report provided the most comprehensive overview of post-removal Seminole culture and subsistence. MacCauley, accompanied by a Mikasuki-speaking Indian interpreter, left a detailed description of the sleeping chikee, the cooking chikee, and other physical aspects of the Seminole camps. He observed that dwellings throughout the Seminole district were practically uniform in construction and that this style of architecture prevailed in the Florida Everglades. The typical shelter was approximately sixteen by nine feet, made primarily from materials taken from the palmetto tree. The house, continued MacCauley, consisted of a "platform elevated about three feet from the ground and covered with a palmetto thatched roof" which was "12 feet above the ground at the ridge pole. Eight upright palmetto logs, unsplit and undressed, support the roof." Many rafters supported the palmetto thatching.

The platform was "composed of split palmetto logs lying transversely, flat sides up, upon beams that extend the length of the building and are lashed to the uprights by palmetto ropes, thongs, or trader's ropes." The platform filled the interior of the building like a floor and "served to furnish the family with a dry sitting or lying down place when," as often happened, "the whole region is underwater." MacCauley saw the thatching of the roof as a work of art: "inside, the regularity and compactness of the laying of the leaves display much skill and taste on the part of the builder"; outside, less care was taken. The palmetto thatching that composed the roof was held in place by heavy logs. "The covering is, I was informed, water tight and durable and will resist even a violent wind."

"The Seminole's house is open on all sides and without rooms. It is, in fact, only a covered platform. The single equivalent for a room is in the space above the joists." Here the inhabitants placed surplus food and household effects out of use. Household utensils were usually suspended from the uprights of the building. MacCauley described three houses that had been placed at three corners of an oblong clearing, perhaps forty by thirty feet. At the fourth corner was the entrance into the elliptical garden. The three houses were very similar, the sole exception being that "in one of them the elevated platform is only half the size of those of the others. This difference seems to have been made on account of the camp fire. The fire usually burns in the space around which the buildings stand."[3]

As for the Seminole family structure, MacCauley provided only a brief account: "The family consists of the husband, one or more wives, and their children. I do not know what limit tribal law places to the number of wives the Florida Indian may have, but certainly he may possess two. There are several Seminole families in which such duogamy exists." MacCauley also provided a brief description of the clan system.[4]

The fluid Seminole communities and camps shifted frequently as the people moved about hunting, fishing, and gathering the zamia root. In the 1890s, outdoorsman and author Charles Cory described his trip up New River to visit the Pine Island settlement at the eastern edge of the Everglades. The New River vicinity had long been a major *coontie* (Indian starch) gathering ground for the Indians, and Cory found a large number of in-

habitants and dwellings, as well as a dance ground for conducting religious ceremonies.[5] By 1900 the Pine Island settlement
had broken up and its inhabitants dispersed into extended family camps throughout the region between the New River and
the Miami River.[6] Cory's observations remained the last report
of a significant number of Seminole camps gathered at a single
location until the reservation era.

In 1930 a government operative, Roy Nash, conducted a
detailed assessment of the Florida Seminoles, including policy
recommendations, for the U.S. Senate. He found that in many
respects little had changed in Seminole life since MacCauley's
visit half a century earlier—with the obvious exception of improvements in technology available to the Indians, such as sewing machines, electric torches, and even automobiles. Matrilineal extended-family camps headed by a clan matron, the *posi* (or
grandmother), were still the norm. Parents raised children in
a close-knit family environment that transmitted the language
and customs. When a man married a woman, he had to live
with her family.[7]

Seminoles and whites intermarried infrequently until the
1920s and not in any great number after World War II. That custom did change by the 1970s with an increase in intermarriage between Seminoles and whites. Even so, when Lottie Baxley married a white male, she could not live on the reservation, whereas
a Seminole male could bring his white wife to live with him on
the reservation.[8] The reason why Seminole women married to
non-Indians were not allowed to live on the reservation was economic rather than cultural. In the early years of tribal government it was assumed, rightly or wrongly, that white husbands
would be better providers. Thus, the few jobs on the reservation
were reserved for Indian men to support their families.

In the 1930s most Seminoles still resided in chikees, cooked
their meals over an open fire with logs radiating from the core,
and sewed the colorful patchwork garments for which they were

known. Gone were the days when hunting and fishing could supplement produce from a family's garden to provide sustenance; Seminoles had to adapt to a cash economy. Many of the women and some of the men engaged in agricultural wage labor on nearby farms and ranches, and some had learned to work with cattle from the tribal herd that the Indian Agency established. In the 1940s, several individuals purchased cattle for their own brand, and the communal herd went out of existence.

Nash's report appeared at a time of Seminole transition from a seminomadic lifestyle to permanent residence on federal reservation lands that had been set aside for their use in the 1890s. Indians had been displaced from many of their traditional campsites and hunting grounds due to the explosive growth of south Florida's population following the arrival of the railroad in 1896, the land boom of the 1920s, and the drainage of the Everglades that began in 1905. In addition, the closing of European markets during World War I effectively killed the Seminole commercial trade in pelts, plumes, and hides destined for the international fashion industry.

Nash described in great detail the Seminole camp, which provided not only a place of residence but also remained the fundamental unit of social structure. The term "camp" referred to the physical site as well as the people living there. In the early stages of the reservation period these chikee camps were replicated on government land at the Brighton and Big Cypress reservations.[9]

Several informants recalled an austere life growing up in a traditional camp. Lorene Gopher, who was a child in the late 1940s, remembered: "Our neighbors were a couple of hammocks away [from] where we lived. We did not actually mingle with other people, if I can remember . . . I mean the way we were brought up, you really did not . . . play. Your time had to be spent meaningfully, like washing clothes or cooking. There were different things, like working in the garden. I mean, you did not waste your time. You just did not lay around. The sun comes up and you had to be up. . . . You just did not lay around unless you were sick or something. That is how we were brought up." As for visitors, "I remember they would come visit or something, but I hardly remember us ever going to visit anybody. I remember there were a lot of people who [were] always coming to see my grandparents, and we always had visitors." In the camp there were "four sisters and one brother and me. That is six. So, we kind of played at times, but I remember that you just had to be doing something all the time. But if we did something, I remember it was building a little chikee or doing stuff like that. . . . Working in the garden was a chore because my grandfather had a big old garden. He would plant corn every year when you were supposed to, and he would always [have] sweet potatoes growing. . . . So, that is a year-round job, it seemed. We were busy doing all that."[10]

Marie Phillips believed that many aspects of Seminole life—particularly the role of elders—changed dramatically with the demise of camps. When pressed on what was different in the treatment of elders, she offered the following: "Well, they are really not taken care of the way they were back when I was growing up. They are, more or less, babysitters. They are raising their grandkids; great-grandkids. But they would not trade it for the world. It is not a burden to them . . . they could not turn away their grandkids. Even if it meant something really bad was happening with the parents and you know they could not really take care of the kids and they ended up with them. But they would not say no; they would not turn them away. [Today] it is different because [previously] if you went anywhere, your grandparents went with you. Now, everybody has their own vehicle; their own homes. Sometimes, they do not even go by and say 'Do you want to go with me?' or 'Do you want me to pick anything up for you?' They are more or less neglected nowadays."

Asked when this change in attitude occurred, Phillips said,

"It is when they started living away from the extended family and then people having to work to provide for themselves. Back when we were growing up, my grandfather and my uncle would go out and they would kill a deer. Everybody would get a little bit of deer here and there. Then, we always had whatever they bought, even if they went off the reservation to buy it. Everybody bought everything together. It was not put aside saying, I bought this; this is for my family and me. My grandparents cannot have any. It was not that way. Everything was just pooled together so that everybody could have whatever was there. They [went to Clewiston for groceries]. And if they did that, back when we were growing up, they were not shopping just for themselves. They were shopping for the whole family."[11]

Many Seminole camps had names based on their location, the persons who lived there, or association with one of the clans. Jacob Osceola recounted:, "I lived in Immokalee. I went through school in Immokalee. Seasonally, after school was out, I returned to Big Cypress to live. But in actuality, for nine months out of the year I lived on the outskirts of Immokalee in a chikee hut, and I went through high school living in one of those huts. But when I would come back to the reservation, at the time we would periodically live at what we called the Pine camp, or Pine Island strand camp, or probably better known as the Panther camp. Then later on, we were able to get a brick house here, one of the new developments they had back in the 1960s. It was kind of ironic. I lived in white society in Immokalee but lived in a chikee, but when I came back here three months out of the year, I would be on an Indian reservation but I would live in a brick home. That was something else. So, I had to play both parts here in both areas, so I think I got to be proficient in each."[12]

Many Seminole families kept their camps on land well away from the federal reservations. Sonny Billie, a medicine man who became a member of the Miccosukee Tribe, said, "My parents never lived on the reservation. Not in a group like today. They were scattered, living throughout the East Naples area, scattered through all the way up to Miami, and even up here [Big Cypress] as well."[13] Mary Frances Johns's family had a village adjacent to U.S. 41, the Tamiami Trail, and they kept animals in pens to attract tourists. When asked if life in a tourist village was different from life in the other camps, she responded, "Well, I did not ever notice any difference between that village and my grandfather's village. . . . We were just traditional people. I mean, we dressed in our clothes the way we are, every day, and my grandmother cooked on an open fire and we had black pots and pans hanging up in the rafters, and whatever. My grandmother used to hate a mess because she said, when tourists come they do not need to see [it]. So, after we ate, she would put a piece of canvas over the food and weigh it down so that the food being left on the table would not be inspected.

"I did not care, . . . I was just being a kid. I would play around. I would do my thing. They [tourists] did not care. They would take pictures of the place and look at the chikees. We had alligators and wildcats and coons and whatever. They were all in cages. . . . I used to hate to have to feed them. It was one of my jobs, to give them some fruit, a piece of chicken. Sometimes my grandmother would kill garfish just to feed the alligators and the wildcats. That was something that I used to find yucky to do."[14]

Jeannette Cypress spent her early years with her grandmother Susie Billie, a venerated medicine woman from the Panther clan who lived to be over one hundred years of age. From this elder she learned not only a unique form of the Mikasuki language but also many traditional beliefs. Jeannette reflected on her early years: "I stayed mostly with my grandmother; that was who I got raised with. I helped them a lot and in return they always wanted me to get an education. They wanted me to learn traditional things but they wanted me to get an education. . . . I got to live in a chikee until I was twelve. We did not have the luxuries, we had to go in the woods to the bathroom, and pump water for baths, and sometimes you heated it up. I grew up more like that. I think it made me appreciate things more."[15]

Before the state launched water-management programs following World War II, the Big Cypress and Brighton reservations frequently flooded. This danger added to the difficulties of those living in traditional camps. When asked how drainage had affected the reservation environment, Mary Jene Coppedge responded: "I remember walking to church with my grandparents, and church was probably a good two or three miles from the house, from the camp, and I remember my grandmother was four foot, eleven [inches tall], and I remember her walking through the water right at her knees, and our platforms were raised, and we had boardwalks underneath our chikees. You could hear eels, or fish, or whatever underneath the platforms that you slept on. And then when they built the canals, it dried everything up. I remember when I was a little girl, well, actually, even twenty years ago, I remember seeing saw grass everywhere; you can't hardly find a blade of saw grass anywhere [now]. There is a lot of different foreign plants that have been transplanted here, or seeded here and has taken over the cypress heads."[16]

Daisi Jumper, a Creek-speaking Seminole from the Brighton Reservation, confirmed the prevalence of standing water when she was a youngster. "The land was very wet and there was a lot of water. You could fish anywhere. You never starved. You could just go out there and get alligator or turtle or deer and you never starved. The water, right. That was our life. But then they made these canals and that is where all the water went."[17]

Before settling on the Big Cypress Reservation, Louise Jumper's family joined a group of Seminoles that moved around frequently seeking farmwork. She recalled how isolated it was for a small child. "We kept moving around because my parents were looking for jobs, like picking vegetables. They would just follow where there was work. We would move here and there until we settled here, in Big Cypress. I was about six or seven, somewhere around there, when we settled here, and we lived here all our lives after that. . . . The roads were not developed that well, it was just dirt roads, and when the rainy season came it was underwater. . . .

"I hardly went anywhere. I probably went to town like once a year, once in a great while. So I do not remember that much about roads. I just remember about the reservation road and remember it being underwater. I kind of joke about that once in a while because I say, our roads used to be underwater and you had to walk everywhere and sometimes in water. We probably were fit people with clean feet. [Laughter] My family had to walk everywhere to places, like to church. I remember walking to school and walking home."[18]

By the 1960s, little more than a quarter century after the first influx of Seminoles to rural reservations, the traditional camp with its social structure began to give way to modern housing on the Big Cypress and Brighton reservations. The funds to provide improved living conditions for Indians came from a government agency, the Department of Housing and Urban Development (HUD). Utilizing these monies, the Seminole Tribe of Florida established its own housing authority to build and manage the home program.

A third Seminole community at the Dania Reservation (renamed Hollywood Reservation in 1966 to more accurately reflect its geographic location) originally opened in 1926 as a home for sick and indigent Indians living in south Florida—although it was immediately occupied exclusively by Seminole families from the New River area. The federal government constructed a number of small wooden homes for Indians, along with a day school and washing facility. Thus the Dania Seminoles were introduced early to living in the white man's style. However, because of the Great Depression and World War II, the Dania Reservation suffered from dire neglect and the original facilities eventually became quite dilapidated.

Fortunately, the residents of this urban reservation also received assistance from the tribal housing program in the 1960s. Joe Dan Osceola, who served as president of the tribe's Board of Directors between 1967 and 1971, recounted how sparse the housing was when he first moved to the Hollywood Reservation: "Well, when I first got here there was no housing authority. And as a matter of fact, the federal government did not have a housing program for a lot of the reservations and this was one of them. They had lived in the huts and they did not know they were eligible for a lot of programs because the tribe had only been organized for ten years. We were so far behind in things; we did not know what was available. And the Bureau of Indian Affairs was no help. . . . And now the tribe took over their own programs, a lot of different programs, and they stress that they do this and this has to be done or lose the job. We like this better because we could not fire civil servants . . . and there was no money available for housing or anything. But being the president, you have to live on the reservation. This is mandatory, it is written in the regulations, the constitution and bylaws, for the tribal officials. This way I was borrowing money out of Washington to build this house and I made it bigger and bigger as I went along."[19]

Merwyn S. Garbarino, an anthropologist who did her fieldwork primarily on the Big Cypress Reservation between 1964 and 1968, offered a final glimpse of a rapidly transforming Seminole camp. She noted many changes that had already taken place and predicted that extended-family camps would eventually disappear. "The physical elements of the camp have changed very little since MacCauley visited the Seminole in 1880, but the small birth *chickee* and the seclusion *chickee* for menstruating women are no longer present. Babies today are born in the hospital and menstruating women are no longer segregated. When the camp is occupied by a matrilineal extended family, each nuclear family has its own sleeping *chickee*. When an extended family moves into a cement block structure, each nuclear family gets a bedroom, one which may actually have been intended as a living room.

"Camps today are permanent. The temporary camps used by hunting parties in the past are rarely built because the hunters make part of their trip by truck and return home to sleep. During the vegetable growing season, some people leave their Big Cypress camps and go to Immokalee to work. There is a camp area in Immokalee where Indians have built *chickees* in which they live when working on the ranches or at shipping depots. . . .

"The number of nuclear families constituting the entire camp has increased to almost half the total number of camps." Garbarino concluded that this trend was probably a consistent one, which meant "that the extended family grouping will eventually disappear." Garbarino found it awkward for an extended family to live in a Western-style house: "When an additional *chickee* could be raised with little effort, new units to the camp caused no stress, but the crowding of an extended family into a non-expendable cement block building puts a strain on all the inhabitants."[20]

Families that owned cattle were the first to secure the ten new concrete block structure (CBS) homes built at the Big Cypress Reservation in 1960. Their cattle were used as collateral for the mortgages, and the homes would revert to the tribe if they defaulted. This was true at the Brighton Reservation as well, and it signaled a growing economic disparity among the reservation Seminoles. The neediest families, without assets to secure a loan, had to wait until self-help housing was made available under a subsequent program. These inequities did not go unobserved but were taken in stride. When questioned about how the tribe selected the people who were to get the first houses, Marie Phillips observed: "I think, well, mainly the ones that did get a home were people that had cattle. And that when they would sell the cows, they would just automatically take monies out of their sales to pay for the homes. . . . Come to think about it, everybody that did get into these ten homes did have cattle. . . . They probably asked who wanted a home or whatever. And they probably asked the people who had cattle so that they could pay for it. Yeah, everybody that did get a home did have cows."[21] Brian Billie confirmed Phillips's account: "I do not know if it is true, but when I was reading a book one time it said that the brick houses, the first ones they had out here, only the cattle owners were the ones that got the houses because the cattle were there against the lien on the deed of the houses. So I am sure that cattle had a big impact within the tribe."[22]

The original CBS homes were designed with a simple rectangular floor plan of about nine hundred square feet and featured one or two bedrooms, a bathroom, a kitchen, and a living-dining area. The homes, sited on a paved semicircle drive, had electricity and were on a central water/sewer system. Reluctant to break up the extended family, in some instances several generations moved from a camp into one of the small houses. As another way to stay connected with their cultural traditions, many families built a "cooking chikee" behind these structures. The people had become accustomed to cooking over an open fire; moreover, they found it too warm in the non air-conditioned kitchens during the heat of a Florida summer.[23]

Marie Phillips's grandparents were cattle owners, and Marie remembered the excitement of moving into the new house: "I believe it was about November or December when we moved in. And then, they were still living back out in the woods at the old camp. . . . So the extended family was still there with the grandparents and the uncles and the aunts and the mothers [in] three bedrooms. And we were all used to sleeping on pallets, anyway, so we had pallets everywhere. Just sleeping everywhere. . . . So, our grandmother got a king-sized bed so there was three of us older girls, we slept with her. . . . So, lots of people moved into this house, at the same time. When you first started moving in, you had a bunch of people go from chikees into the house—

not just your mom and your dad but your brothers and sisters. The house was built for our grandparents, but that is when they started trying to build homes [for] everybody else, too. And my grandmother did not want us living anywhere else but with her. We all moved in with her. . . .

"Oh, yeah, it was [exciting]. Cooking on an electric stove. It seems like everything was cooking faster than what you were used to. My grandmother always had a fire going. She never did let her fire go out in the 'cook[ing] chikee.' And I believe she had a small electric stove that she only used for certain things. . . . But it was exciting. I can still see the day that we moved in. . . . I do not even know where they got the furniture. But they had brand-new furniture in the house. . . . All I know is I was in a house."[24]

Seminole families moved into the upgraded reservation housing for many different reasons. In the case of Nancy Shore's family, they needed to provide for her brother, who was blind. Her father, Frank Shore, a highly respected medicine man and a successful cattleman, preferred to live in the traditional way. "We lived in chikees. When they started building these [houses], my parents did not really come over here to stay or anything, except my brother got blind—Jim Shore—he got blind, and he was coming home and my mother came into this house and stayed with him. That is how they ended up moving up here. But my dad he stayed out at the old camp for all those years. He would come up here every once in a while and then, when he got just a little bit older, he just moved in here. I do not know if we would have ever moved in if it were not for my brother. My mom moved in with him. Then we all moved here with them."[25]

The tribal housing project eventually encountered problems, primarily with HUD. Jacob Osceola had firsthand knowledge of the difficulties. "I was the commissioner for a housing project here. . . . I stayed in there for the early 1980s and early 1990s. The HUD project was terminated or was dismantled."[26]

The shortage of funds severely limited the amount and quality of housing that could be provided for the reservations. Yet, Osceola believed the standard of living "has changed very remarkably, as far as housing is concerned. Houses are a lot better. Maybe there are not enough now. However, I think some of the revenues that are coming from the tribe have built houses. They have gone into their own construction and stuff like that.

"I think housing is going to be a lot better for individuals in the coming years. I think HUD probably only gave us about a nine-hundred-square-foot living space, and it was dependent on how many people needed homes. So, if you had fifty people that were in dire need, and there were people still living in chikees, and we send an application to HUD saying that we had fifty people who need housing, and they only gave us $200,000 for those fifty people. They said, well, you said you [need] fifty houses; you have got to do it with $200,000. And that only gave you a cardboard box, or something. HUD was, in a sense, good some years and some years the square footage was remarkably cut down. I have a house that is out there on the reservation right now about nine hundred square feet. That is probably this room and the next room and that is it. Enough for a bunk bed, that is it."[27]

In 1967 the Seminoles began building wooden frame homes under the tribe's self-help housing program, with the owners contributing much of the labor. These structures made several concessions to Seminole cultural values. A row of screened windows was set high on all sides to allow for a free flow of air, just as in a chikee. These windows could be closed during cold weather. The sleeping area was separated from the cooking and dining area by an open breezeway, emulating the separation of a sleeping chikee from the cooking chikee. Original plans called for each home to have three separate units—one for sleeping, one for cooking and eating, and a bathroom/toilet facility—all joined by a breezeway to simulate a camp. The units were built on a concrete slab with electricity and plumbing connected to a septic system. Due to lack of funds, many of the homes built were of the two-unit variety with an outside toilet facility. Sometimes the high groundwater level made septic tanks difficult to install.[28]

The wooden homes took a bit of getting used to, particularly for the elders. "I remember when my grandparents first got their home," said Mary Jene Coppedge. "I was about thirteen when we moved in—and my grandmother hated it. It was hot. The windows were real tall. You could not see through the walls. . . . After a while she got used to it, but she still did a lot of things outside, whether we cooked outside or whatever. But the whole camp moved over; there were like thirteen people in that three-bedroom house. Both of my grandparents were there, and my mom, my two uncles, and us eight kids were in that house. We made it work. I think that is why my Mikasuki language, my language, is fluent, because my grandparents made sure we made it work."[29]

Jeannette Cypress's family was among the first to get one of the wooden homes. She remembered that it was quite a step up from their former living conditions: "I lived in a chikee because I stayed with my grandmother and . . . my grandfather, and we lived in a chikee until I was about twelve. . . . I remember her when she used to wash her clothes in the canal, there was like a pond behind us. They started making homes for senior citizens and then they started making the wooden homes. My parents got one of the wooden homes, and I ended up living with them."[30]

In addition to the problems of coping with the physical structure of the white man's house, many Seminoles also had a difficult time adjusting to the psychological impact of separation from their extended family. The Seminole camps, either on or off the reservation, had been a model of communal child rearing. Many of these camps were occupied mainly by women of the same clan, who could easily share the discipline and instruction of youngsters. In the Seminoles' matrilineal/matrilocal system, males who were not of the same clan were superfluous except to provide food for the table and perhaps contribute occasional wages. In truth, they were often more welcome at the camp of the women of their own clan, where they served as valued uncles. As might be expected, the move to a new type of living environment on the reservations disrupted this close-knit social system.

Helene Johns Buster became firmly convinced that the transition from chikee camps to HUD housing had a negative impact on Seminole family life. In the late 1960s she left home to attend Chilocco Indian school for a year, "and that was when we were moving from our chikees and our camps to the homes, when we first got brick homes, the CBS homes. In 1969 or 1968, somewhere around there. . . . To me, when that breakup happened, with the camps and the stuff, and we moved into CBS homes, that was probably the biggest, the most sorrowful time in my life. . . . We had already moved into the homes when I left. . . . I was not happy, because we were a family there [in the camp]. And then, all of a sudden, my mother decided she was going to get a home and pull us out—there were three of us at that time. . . . She took us out of there, out of the camp, and put us in this house and became a mom. . . . I think there were families from there [the camp] that got the homes and then a couple of more got [them] in the next round. But, I was really—I felt like everything was kind of destroyed at that time, when we got into those homes, because then we did not have that bonding like we had. We were all very close to each other there, and when we got pulled out and taken with our moms, which at that time you knew who your mom was but everybody disciplined. It was just not one person, just your mom, that you listened to; it was all of your aunts and your uncles that were there that you had better listen to.

"We had one aunt, the oldest aunt, that basically took care of all of us. She did not work; she did not have her own children, and my mother and her sisters and all, they went out to work in the tomato fields and things like that. They were gone from daybreak to nightfall. My aunt was the one that took care of us, so we called her 'Mama.' . . . We all looked at her as if she was our mom. So, when they decided to break up into these homes, move into CBS homes, they just kind of broke up that structure that were used to. . . . She [her aunt] stayed in the camp."[31]

Jacob Osceola, a politically astute individual who served on the Tribal Council from 1979 to 1985, questioned the federal government's motivation for promoting the Seminole housing program at a time when the tribal government was still relatively new and inexperienced. Tribal leaders, eager to improve living conditions for their people, depended on government funding, and HUD would support only certain types of projects. In later decades, the Tribal Council pushed to provide reservation housing in settings more congenial to Seminole cultural values. But in the 1960s the federal Indian policy was still strongly committed to termination of tribes and the assimilation of Indians. Therefore, Osceola could declare: "I think there was some period in time when the government needed to get the Indian out into the flow stream, so the only way to actually break that tie and disseminate them into the mainstream was to get them to get away from their culture. And housing was one of the avenues that they used. The reason why I say that is because we had a camp setting, like I was talking about the Panther camp, then the male had to move into that camp. . . . However, the main, basic culture was given to each offspring by the grandmothers and the mothers. And so when HUD came along, or housing came along, and built houses side by side in a little subdivision, then you had a Panther clan [person] that may be living here in a brick building, and you might have a Bird clan [person] sitting side by side, so that family structure was disassembled. So, that was the purposes of trying to get the Indian to wear the white man's suit. That was one way of actually breaking up the system."[32]

Mary Jene Coppedge also lamented the social cost of moving into the new government-funded houses. She also suspected that the federal government had an ulterior motive in pushing the housing program. The Seminoles had been forced to learn English, "and housing is the same way . . . I mean, yes, sure, I enjoy my house. But if they would have asked me how I wanted my house to be built, I think I would have told them that, okay, I have lived in a camp setting all my life, where we had my aunts and uncles in the same place, my grandparents, there was not a child that went undisciplined or [not] watched. We did not have any such thing as latchkey kids. Children were constantly being taught. I think if they would have come out and asked, 'How would you like your house?' I would have told them, put me in a camp setting. Fine, if you want to build us nice, single-family dwellings. I would much rather have had my grandmother's house here, mine here, my mother's here, my uncle's or aunt's here, in this same location in a cluster so that I still had my extended family. And the government knew exactly what they were doing when they brought single-dwelling homes into this reservation, because they knew that would eventually break up the extended family and the language would die from there. Trying to kill the culture, they knew that all along. I have always felt that way."[33]

Coppedge complained that living in homes had stifled the people's ability to interact the way they used to. She believed it definitely had undermined the Seminole communal value of sharing: "I do not think hardly anybody has a garden anymore. I know my uncle George, . . . he likes to garden. Of course, he is in his sixties, probably close to seventy, but he always tries to have something in his backyard. And he had some great pumpkins sometimes, and my grandmother, her specialty was pumpkins. . . . [T]hey would plant a lot, and it did not matter if one family planted it, it was for everybody. So, if anybody wanted pumpkin they could come get it. But my grandmother was always like that, too. She always shared.

"As far as sharing, it is probably a little bit different, but I know still a lot of our people, like if you go visit someone, it is 'Come on, sit down,' and whatever food was on the table or they would provide even just a glass of water, glass of tea, or whatever. It is still there. It is just that it is not in the open anymore because we have four walls and a house. You do not get to see it as often as if you were in a chikee. You could see people visiting there under the chikee and you could see them exchanging whatever and having a drink, or you could see someone carrying a bucket of water. But you cannot see that anymore because we have four walls. It is not that it is not here, it is just that it is not as noticeable."

When asked if the children were still learning traditional cultural values such as sharing, Coppedge responded positively: "Well, I am sure there are some changes, but not to the degree that it is not there. It is there but it is just not as visible. Because you can tell it [in] your kids. Some of the kids, whatever we are doing, you can tell that the culture is still there just by the way they act, and the way they share, and the way they talk, and the way they act. It is still there. They are still being taught."[34]

Nevertheless, some question what Seminole youth are learning about their history and culture, information that the elders used to impart and which cannot be learned in books. Few Seminoles today know much about the history of the tribe—for example, the Florida Indian wars of the nineteenth century or who Andrew Jackson was. Nor do they understand the significance that era had for the naming of children. The naming of children was the prerogative of the clan matron, and Nancy Shore told how the Seminole wars influenced the naming process in her family: "I think that is where my grandmother picked it up. When my grandmother gives her names out to her grandkids—

she did not do that until my great-grandmother passed away. . . .
After she passed away (she was 109 years old), then it was her
[my grandmother's] turn to start picking the names. . . .

"Her mother, Polly Parker, is in some history [books]. You
hear about her every once in a while, but not much. Anyway,
she was one of those who got on the ship to go to Oklahoma,
and she and the other people on the ship were going to get
some medicine for the people that were on the ship because
they were getting sick. So, they got permission to get off and
gather some herbs and stuff like that, but instead of going back
they left [escaped]. There are lots of stories, like that they had
to sleep during the daytime and travel at nighttime. How they
survived was picking some berries and some fruit, to survive
on, to get back over here. I think it was her aunt and one of her
cousins who escaped from the ship and came back. The story
goes on like that.

"My mother kind of visions how they were back in those
days. Like she referred [to] that story, that is how she gives names
out to her grandchildren, she refers to my [great] great-grandmother's escape. . . . Like in that case, she said they were scared,
and I guess you would have to be scared, so she named one of the
kids [a name] that means scared: *Ingalee*, scared. And they said
that they had to keep turning around, looking back to see if any
body was coming, and she named some of her kids *Ahichakitag*,
looking back. And that is how she named most of the people.
. . . She tells them what she is referring to, so it is usually back
to Polly Parker being in the state. That is what she tells. All the
kids know. The mothers know that the names came from that
story."[35]

The move to modern housing also modified some Seminoles' views on ownership of land. Merwyn Garbarino reported
that families who occupied new houses tended to be possessive
of the land on which the house were built. Even though owners could leave a house to heirs, they had no deed and could not

sell the underlying property, which belonged to the tribe. Moreover, in case of a default on the mortgage, the house reverted to tribal ownership. By contrast, those Seminoles who remained in their camps did not think of owning the land; however, they would speak of owning the pumps and wells that they had paid to have installed. Garbarino concluded that "the camps are usually traditional sites in the sense that people now represent second or third generations on the site, but it is the camp and buildings, not the land, which they conceive as theirs."[36]

Marie Phillips confirmed this process of de facto transfer. After her family left their camp and moved into one of the new homes, the campsite went through several transitions. The family did not destroy the abandoned chikees but rather "stayed over there for a little while. And then, they finally got everything out of there and my grandfather left that homesite to my youngest uncle, and he could do with [it] whatever he wanted to do. And when he got married, he moved over there for a little while. And, then, he got divorced and came back. We had to move out of his room. And then, he gave up the homesite to his sister-in law. So, that is who lives there today."[37]

The transition from traditional chikee camps to modern housing was not the only issue affecting Seminole families. There was an increasing number of single-parent families headed by women, the most economically insecure group on the reservations. Moving these families into modern housing removed them from the security and support network that the family camps had offered. Furthermore, some of the mothers had never been married to their children's father, and that presented another set of issues for both mother and children to deal with.

One single mother, Helene Johns Buster, recounted that she met her future husband when she was in eleventh grade: "I met him in April and we got married in September. . . . Actually things did not work out well . . . he passed away. We were married in September; he died in July the following year. I was two months pregnant with my oldest daughter at the time. I guess it worked out, but it didn't work out—not what I thought. But I think if he did not die, we would probably have still been married today. That is how sure I was of it at that time. I was seventeen and two months' pregnant. That was one of the main things, probably in my whole life; I was not going to have children without knowing who their fathers were, because we were all raised that way. That was my goal in life. That was not going to happen to me. And that was very acceptable at that time, to have children whether the father was there or not. . . . The major thing was to have children, and that is how we were produced. But, I do not think they [their mothers] ever realized how traumatic it was for us, for everybody else to have fathers and us not. . . . Or not being a part of our lives. . . . But then, I think that kind of makes us who we are today, too, because we struggled a little bit harder, a little bit more, because we did not have that other parent."[38]

Jeannette Cypress offered some insight into the complexities of how unwed mothers occasionally passed their children around to be raised by different families—not an uncommon practice in tribal societies where the important issue is to ensure that the child is taken care of in a stable, loving home environment. Cypress explained: "My mom, before she got with my stepfather, met another Indian man and she ended up pregnant: she thought they were going to get married and he did not. . . . When my stepfather married my mom, she was pregnant with my sister Wanda, who would be the second child. Financially, they were just trying to get on their feet. He had come back from the service. So they made the choice to give my sister to his mom and dad, because they were better off at the time. They had a nice house and everything else, and they wanted a child too. They felt like she would still be in the family but she would be taken care of, so my sister got adopted out to my stepfather's mom and dad. That was who she grew up with."[39]

Marie Phillips remembered how hard her mother worked to keep the family together. As a small child she also learned to work in the fields to help support the family. [40] Later, as a single mother herself, Marie encouraged her children to be self-sufficient by teaching them to sew. "And then I was, all of a sudden, a single mother with two kids that were only two and four. And when they were old enough to thread a needle, I taught them how to do it. I told them it is always something good to have, even if you have an education." [41]

The Seminoles have historically been a matrilineal people; that is, they reckon an individual's lineage and clan membership through the female line. They were also matrilocal, which meant when a man married, he and his family went to live in the camp of his wife's clan. This provided a secure, multigenerational setting for rearing children surrounded by their mother's kin. Thus children learned the language, customs, and traditions of their clan from aunts, uncles, and grandparents. Many families moved frequently seeking employment, and children were often left with elderly grandparents or other relatives.

By the mid-twentieth century these traditional patterns remained in place but were severely strained. The construction of new CBS houses on the reservations beginning in 1960, followed by the HUD program's wooden homes, accelerated the breakup of extended-family chikee camps. Anthropologist Jessica Cattelino has identified the control of reservation housing as a domain of contested sovereignty. For some forty years the BIA was able to force an assimilationist policy on the tribe through control of where and how the people lived. However, because of an explosion of gaming revenues during the 1990s, the Seminole Tribe developed the means to wrest control over delivery of social services—including housing—to its people. Modern tribal housing programs attempt to take into account traditional social structure and patterns of settlement. [42]

Once the extraordinary largesse from gaming became available, the Seminoles purchased large, luxurious homes. Tribal leaders built million-dollar homes, and some owned vacation homes around the country. Still others bought homes in gated communities away from the reservation, and their ownership of new trucks and s u v s gave them the freedom to travel and live away from the influence of the community. This shift to the procurement of lavish new homes was a far cry from the days of simple c b s or wood-frame homes. The new homeowners were further estranged from the tribe both in terms of distance from the reservation and in lifestyle. The dramatic increase in housing options is another major impact on the Seminole culture due to soaring incomes. The provision of modern housing definitely improved the general quality of life on the reservations. Yet, without access to the wisdom and knowledge of their clan elders, the depth and consistency of what Seminole youngsters have learned about being Indian has varied greatly. Thus the transition from traditional camps to modern housing has tendered mixed results.

5. Dilemmas of Language and Culture

Like many other American Indian tribes, the Seminoles continue to struggle to define what it means to be Indian in a world dominated by non-Indians. Although there is disagreement over how effectively the Seminoles have defined their worldview, at its core, culture retention requires an effort to preserve one's language, material culture, and essential values as handed down by elders who are rapidly passing from the scene. Their traditions, ceremonies, and languages, guarded so carefully during the years of self-imposed isolation, are disappearing as the Seminoles emerge increasingly into an overwhelmingly white world. Many of the individuals interviewed reported that the skills and values they learned as children were slipping away. William Boehmer noted in 1971 that the young people "are sort of torn between two cultures. There is the old culture that's fading away and it's not important anymore. They're trying to adjust to this new one. . . . They could pick up the worst that the new culture [white culture] has to offer sometimes." The Seminole children, continued Boehmer, were simply not as careful and honest about preserving the past as were their grandparents.[1]

Several tribal members have struggled with the dichotomy of cultures. As one young man put it, "There are good white things and good Indian things. We want the best of both." A young woman had a similar view: "We don't want to be white people; we want to be Seminoles. We want the modern things and we want to live nicely, but we want to do it among friends."[2]

Therefore, there is general consensus that tribal leaders did the right thing in trying to sustain Native culture by opening the multimillion-dollar Ah-Tah-Thi-Ki Museum on a sixty-acre site at the Big Cypress Reservation, by building a museum at the Okalee Indian Village in Hollywood, and by supporting cultural classes in the tribal school. These decisions were part of a move to revitalize the Seminole heritage and constituted a commitment to increase tourism. Tribal Chairman James Billie proclaimed in 1997 that the tribe wanted everyone "to come see what we are about." He explained that "if we don't preserve our culture then as a people we will die."

The first comprehensive museum dedicated to the culture and heritage of Florida's Seminole Indians opened in August 1997. Ah-Tah-Thi-Ki, which means "a place to learn, a place to remember," not only preserves Seminole history but also offers visitors a chance to learn about Indian society. Tourists can enjoy Seminole culture through a variety of experiences. The new facility features a one-mile boardwalk through a natural bald cypress dome and a replica of an authentic Seminole village. The five-thousand-square-foot exhibit gallery includes rare artifacts and dioramas on Indian life. The museum's five-screen theater offers orientation films, while a resource library and computers enable interested parties to research in-depth information about the Seminoles. The gift shop sells Seminoles arts and crafts. Outside the museum, tribal members show how Seminoles lived more than a hundred years ago, and local artists demonstrate the making of beadwork, small canoes, and Seminole clothing.

The Okalee Indian Village that opened in 1960 was one of the first enterprises established by the Seminole Tribe of Florida. The Seminoles, proud of their heritage and progress, wanted a facility to attract tourists and also to demonstrate to non-Indians that not all Indians lived in teepees and hunted buffalo. It featured a traditional village, an alligator and snake show, a theater, living history demonstrations, and crafts produced by local artisans. However, gaming became paramount and the attraction had been closed for ten years when the tribe decided to restore it in 1988. The new Okalee Indian Village and Museum was designed so that Seminole children could learn the tribe's history. When the Hard Rock Hotel and Casino opened at the Hollywood Reservation in 2004, Okalee Indian Village was incorporated into the complex, and its revamped museum was renamed Ah-Tah-Thi-Ki Museum at Okalee Village.[3]

A well-respected Seminole elder and craftsman, Jimmy O'Toole Osceola, gave a ringing affirmation of the importance of preserving the culture. He acknowledged, "it is very difficult because some young generations like to learn, some do not. Some do not care. Some do, and some older people also do not care to practice. . . . Some are interested in practice. It is different for individual people. I think it is hard to get the people who are interested together and work on it. I think it would be hard because they do not live in the same area. Some live in Big Cypress, or Brighton, or the [Tamiami] Trail. I think it is very important that people should take time for that and learn about the culture and also [the] language. I am interested in [the museum], in favor of it 100 percent. I was hoping the Seminole Tribe would establish a museum like that for a long time before it materialized. I am very happy with what we have today. I think that [it would be good if] the museum would make more room for the other kind of items to be seen in there. It is mostly clothes in [there] now, and some wood [items]; there should be more than that, like also jewelry, Seminole dolls, and things like that."[4]

When asked his opinion of the Ah-Tah-Thi-Ki and Okalee museums, Joe Dan Osceola responded, "I think the tribe needs to put a little bit more money in it. If you ask the tribe, they would probably say that they put too much money in it already. But this one tribe in Connecticut, Fox[woods] . . . has a casino and they spend like $50 million on a museum and the village and all that. And when you go there, you see a certain object, like a village, and you push one button. . . . They are high-tech. You get an earphone and you push a button and they will tell you everything. We have not been able to spend that much money on

modern technology for the Indian village. Right now it is just
more of an Indian village, and gator wrestling, and more of an
Indian village of a souvenir type, and we have this museum that
is up to date about what of the Seminoles has been recorded in
the history. So, that is something good for the public to know. It
is better than not having anything. I would think it is good for
the public and good for the tribe."[5]

Although Brian Billie approved of the tribal museums, he
thought the Green Corn Dance remained the major vehicle for
preserving the Seminole culture. "That is the main place [where]
you can learn everything. Well, not everything, but [the] most
important stuff, at the Corn Dance. All the elders are together
at the Corn Dance, mostly. Everybody is sharing stories; being
with different families that you have not seen in a long time. So,
that is the most traditional, right there, meeting all the people
from the other reservations. If you go see an older one, even
of your own clan, you might meet another older man that you
never met before and hear what he has to say." When asked if
the teaching was all oral, he responded, "Yes. Orally, you just sit
and listen. . . . It is the place to go learn it. The museum is good,
too. You can hear it orally out there, but it is only once a year,
so it is very important. . . . It [going to the Corn Dance] will set
in a lot more . . . than coming here [to the museum], looking
around and reading."[6]

Most Seminoles interviewed did not see the tribal fair and
powwow or the tribal rodeo primarily as a means for preserving traditional Indian culture. These annual events draw professional Indian performers, artists, and craftspersons from across
the nation to sell their wares and compete for prize money. Held
during the winter tourist season, they draw large crowds of non-
Indians to the reservations. When queried about whether these
annual events preserved or changed Seminole culture, Andy
Buster expressed skepticism: "I think much of it has to do with
arts and crafts and [the] food booths that they do. Most of them

now travel to different powwows throughout the country and do their selling that way. That has changed within the last ten or fifteen years."[7]

The origin of the Seminole rodeo is obvious, since the Seminoles are cattle people who have owned large herds since the 1930s. For many years the U.S. Indian Service (forerunner of the Bureau of Indian Affairs) sponsored "field days" on the reservations in which the Indians participated in a variety of athletic competitions and other contests, including rodeo-style events. Only in recent years did the tribe turn rodeos into commercial ventures drawing paying customers. Regarding the origins of the rodeo, Jacob Osceola commented: "I do not know that much about them. I think it is part of the cattle program that stemmed off from it. You can't work cattle all the time, you have got to have [some recreation]."[8] Mary Jene Coppedge saw the skills required for the rodeo as being important in Seminole life. When asked if rodeos are more important today than they were in the 1970s, she answered, "I do not know if they were so much important or more important, but the family values have always been there whether you played a ball game, whether you played with horses, it was a family gathering. It was always [to] get together and share things. Whether you were teaching one person to ride a horse, teaching a person how to ride a bucking horse, or just being around animals, it has always been that way. It is not so much more important today than it was thirty years ago. It is just that the availability is more, we can do more with the same things that we had thirty years ago."[9]

Jeannette Cypress expressed ambivalence about how the annual fair and powwow had affected Seminole culture. "It is hard to say. I think, to me, it is more of a get-together, for everyone to see each other that they have not seen in a while, but culturally I guess maybe it makes the women want to do the patchwork and their artwork and their crafts. That is probably a good thing, because they compete. They try to be better at the basket or the clothes, and in that way that is probably helping preserve [those skills]. It is cool to make a jacket or wear your own traditional clothes. In that way, it probably does. We have other tribal members from other places come and they socialize and they have powwows. I guess if you just want to get together and see people in powwows, I think it is good. I think if you really want to try to teach your child, some people do not like to go, but I think the Green Corn Dance is probably your best bet for culturally wanting to ask questions or learn certain traditions."[10]

The most caustic appraisal of the powwow and rodeo mentality came from Lorene Gopher. "It is somebody's culture. I do not know, [but] it is not ours. But I guess . . . since they are not into anything else, they need something to keep them off drugs and everything else, to keep them busy. I am thinking about the rodeo. And the powwows, that is not even our thing. I know it is not a way to make money, so I do not know why they have them. I do not know. [It is entertainment] for, probably, the non-Indians. I mean, I guess it is entertaining to us too, but it [isn't us]."[11]

Some Seminoles seek to express their Indian identity in wearing the distinctive patchwork clothing that the tribe is noted for producing. Others take pride in replicating the traditional garments worn by their forebears in a past age. Most Seminole women of the generations that grew up in a family camp learned to sew from their mothers and grandmothers. The elders passed on skills such as carving, basketmaking, and beadwork. Beadwork, like many other traditional Seminole crafts, was produced both for personal use and for sale to tourists. These skills, however, are rapidly dying out as Seminoles seek employment that provides a bigger, more stable income. As a result, only a handful of true artisans remain to keep alive these traditions in the tribe.

One of these artists, Mary Frances Johns, made a good living selling her craftwork and telling stories for folklore gatherings and school groups. Other artists still make baskets woven from sweetgrass and palmetto fiber. They are produced primarily for the tourist trade, but are also used in the home. Another area where skilled craftspeople have passed on their knowledge is the art of fashioning dugout canoes. Hunting by canoe in the Everglades has generally disappeared, so there is very little demand for canoes. Over the years, dugout canoes have gone from being the primary conveyance to a symbol of Seminole identity. Bobby Henry, who fashions miniature canoes for tourists, learned the art from his father and grandfather. Canoes are usually made from cypress trees that have died and dried out. Henry cuts the tree to a fifteen- to twenty-foot log and then strips off the bark. He then burns out part of the inside and hollows out the rest with an axe. The finished product is durable and, when powered by a pole, moves easily through the swamps.[12]

After attending school to learn nursing, Mary Frances Johns decided that she did not want to go any further with formal education. She took a position as artist-in-residence at a museum in Tallahassee, where she painted, made baskets, designed clothing, and did beadwork. This convinced her that she could make an independent living from her art. "I went into the business of selling crafts. You know, these museum festivals in places like that go begging for Indians to travel there and make presentation of themselves. Take your sewing, your beadwork, or whatever, and if you demonstrate, some of these people will let you [add] on fees in exchange for demonstrating. Others will pay you extra for the time to demonstrate. Take time to talk to people and things like that and you can sell your crafts on the side. I really got into it. I traveled from the middle of August until the first part of November; I was not [ever] home. And I am still doing it."

But Johns believes appearing at museum festivals is more than economic; it is an opportunity to teach about the culture and present a positive image of her people. "This is a big part

of what you are doing. What you are doing is publicizing your
people. . . . To me it is [important], because they see us in the
newspapers, they see us on television, they see us in other places,
but a lot of times what you see written up in newspapers and
things like that does not present the whole people. So, I feel like
if there were not people doing these other, more positive things,
then the image presented by the public media would be the only
thing there would be. . . . I think that what I am doing is counter-
acting stereotyping. Seminoles do not wear feathers. Seminoles
do not live in teepees. But that is all they see, the Plains Indians,
southwestern stuff, and they think that Indians that live around
here have to be [like] that, too. But along the eastern seaboard,
none of the Indians have the same type of housing as the Plains
Indians, because housing is dependent on the region where you
live. . . . My people up in north Florida, Georgia, and Alabama,
places like that, they used to live in log cabins. Wherever you
are, the climate is different, so you have to be adaptable to the
climate. It does not occur to these people, to these students, so
they assume that everybody wears feathers and lives in teepees
and does powwow dancing." Johns demonstrated her commitment to explaining her people's culture by participating with
a group of storytellers sent to Washington DC to help prepare
the Seminole exhibit for the Museum of the American Indian,
which opened in 2004.[13]

Seminoles have no problem differentiating between making crafts for profit and passing along cultural skills to their offspring. When asked if sewing patchwork garments for sale to
tourists preserved Seminole culture, Sadie Cypress, an accom-
plished seamstress, offered, "No, I think the way that we could
preserve the Seminole culture is to teach our children how to
do it, to learn how to do the patchwork and do the sewing and
the baskets and so on. I have taught all my girls how to sew. She
[my daughter] knows how to sew. She knows how to do beadwork. She can do a lot of that. But she does work, so she just

seems like she does not have the time to do it. . . . I have taught
both the boys and girls, when they were growing up, because
that was all I did. They watched me doing it, sewing and bead-
ing and all that. . . . He [my son] knows how to do beadwork.
He knows how to bead and how to sew. He knows how to do
all that but he just does not."[14]

Historically, the Seminole men first learned to use treadle
sewing machines available at the Stranahan trading post on the
New River and at Brickell's store in Miami. The men later purchased portable models, carried them back to their camps, and
taught the women how to use them. Youngsters of both gen-
ders learned the skills of sewing garments and doing beadwork.
Moreover, in recent years, one man has figured prominently in
the renascence of Seminole historical garb. Jimmy O'Toole Osceola, once a noted maker of traditional Seminole garments, was
an expert in sewing leather chaps, moccasins, and ceremonial
clothing, worn primarily for dances and festivals rather than in
daily life. Jimmy explained how he learned to sew as a matter
of necessity: "When our mother passed away, we had to make
our own clothes, and also mending or fixing. My sisters and I
helped together [to] make clothes and cook, too. That was when I
learned to sew. They were doing [it] by needle, sew[ing] by hand.
For a long time we did not have a sewing machine. For a long,
long time. Then my sisters got [a] sewing machine. They went
on sewing their clothes, and [some] for selling, also.

"Back in 1952, I think it was, I decided to make something
and try to sell it. I sewed with my sisters' machine. I think the
first garment I made at that time was an apron, and I sold it. It
gave me a good idea, so I continued to improve my sewing. And
that is what I am doing today. . . . I am interested in keeping the
Seminole clothing tradition, keeping it going so . . . the younger
generation can learn, or see what they used to wear back in the
old days. I hope that someone is interested in making that kind
. . . I think many of them make that kind of clothing today. Some

of them are difficult to make. It is the medicine men's coat that is difficult to make. . . . The reason they call it the medicine men's coat is that when a Seminole medicine man fixed the medicine, he had to wear the coat to fix it."[15]

Until the late 1930s many Seminole men wore some variation of the big shirt, a knee-length garment that began as a plain dress item that was functional for hunting in the Everglades. This shirt evolved into an elaborate patchwork garment which a few individual Indian men wore at almost ankle length. By the time of World War II, the men had adopted long pants (mostly jeans), which were worn with plain work shirts and a patchwork jacket, and usually topped with a cowboy hat. That was distinctively Seminole garb. Today, tribal members generally wear the same clothing as the general public. However, virtually all Seminole men own one or more of the patchwork jackets that are worn on practically any occasion.[16]

Joe Dan Osceola spoke to the importance of this symbol of his ethnicity and its relation to language and other aspects of the culture. "Yes, I believe in wearing the traditional jackets. That is a modern jacket, however, that I generally wear. There are two different types of, I would say, shirts or jackets. The older type, as I call it, is where the Natives used to wear one long shirt all the way down to the knees. That is really traditional, and the leggings—when they used to be out in the Everglades and [the] tall grass that may cut their legs . . . saw grass has blades that are pretty sharp, so they used to wear leggings [to protect their legs]. Then they got the modern sewing machine that they [used to] make the jackets and the other small designs and everything— and a matter of fact, I was wearing one today, a modern jacket. I do believe in wearing jackets. And it is exposure to the public to tell them who you are.

"A lot of times, nowadays, when they see you, they think that you could be Italian, or you could be Cuban, or a Latino, other than Seminole. When they see you wear jackets, that tells them that you are a Seminole. A lot of times you do not have to tell them. Of course, anyone can wear a jacket and everything, but it was hot so not many people are wearing jackets. But I do. I encourage my children to wear them and keep the culture and the tradition going. . . . All of our children, they take part in the Corn Dance, and we encourage them to speak Indian language. It is like fighting a losing battle. It is hard, especially when it is not written down. But you just have to keep talking to them, and they would say a word. But a lot of times it is where you put the accent in our language. Our language is very simple, but it is hard to speak it if you do not put [the accent] in the right [part, the] front part, the middle part, or the last part."[17]

From her earliest days working with the Seminoles, Ivy Stranahan noted that the tribal elders feared they would lose their language.[18] Other observers complained that the parents were simply not teaching their children the language. Virgil Harrington understood why, as he found the language very difficult and laughingly recalled his botched attempts to master Seminole. Harrington always tried to learn a few words in the local language, but "they always got a good laugh when I tried to express myself in Seminole. So, sometimes, during the serious moments, I would throw in one of my off-brand Seminole words that was always good for a laugh. The nature . . . and the ability of the Seminoles to laugh in trying times and when there's deep trouble was a trait that I really respected them for." This was contrary to the belief that "Indians don't have a sense of humor. This was certainly not true with these people, and I hope they never lose it."[19]

The evolution of Seminole women's clothing as a distinct marker of ethnicity has been thoroughly cataloged by anthropologists and historians from an abundance of photographic evidence dating to the nineteenth century. The clothing went through a number of distinct periods that were identified by specialists such as William Sturtevant, Dorothy Downs, and David Blackard. The initial phase featured skirts made from plain gingham and calico bolt cloth, and adorned with a few bands of rickrack; these were often worn with a short jacket and cape, as seen in photographs from the 1890s. The second phase came with the availability of sewing machines, which led to the development of patchwork patterns for the tourist trade around the time of World War I. This quickly evolved into skirts made from bands of patchwork.

The third phase culminated in a post–World War II explosion of designs that has marked Seminole women's clothing to the present day. When asked if she ever wore traditional Seminole clothing, Jeannette Cypress responded, "I do. I wear it to work sometimes, but not all of the time. I have different types of dresses, some for when we dance at Corn Dance, I have the longer ones and the capes and sometimes I wear a jacket, but I do not wear it all the time. When I was growing up I had to wear quite a bit of it because my grandparents sewed it a lot, so that is what we wore."[20]

The Green Corn Dance is the most revered cultural artifact of the Florida Seminoles and their Miccosukee counterparts. However, as noted in a previous chapter, this ceremony has taken on new meaning for the contemporary Indian community. Today, most individuals who attend the annual affair do so for its sociocultural value rather than because they adhere to its religious content. Only a handful of older Indians still believe in Breathmaker as the primary cosmological force, or invoke other figures of the spiritual world known by their ancestors. Nevertheless, some persons still recall the old songs and understand why "blood scratching" was a fundamental part of the sacred ceremony.

Carl Baxley had some experience with Indian medicine and religious ritual, which he believes is rapidly disappearing. He spoke at length about the relationship between Seminole medicine, family values, and the practice of scratching the arms (and occasionally the back) to draw blood. There were two types of scratching: the first was a form of punishment administered primarily to children for unacceptable behavior; the second was a ritual drawing of blood usually associated with the Green Corn Dance. When asked how Seminole values had changed, Baxley responded: "From what I remember, being a young child the values were instilled in you from your grandparents and your parents. We all had aunts and uncles, and those were the people who passed down punishment to you. I mean, my mother could be out of town and my mother's aunt would scratch me, or spank me, or whatever the case would be. And that was acceptable. . . .

"But back to the Green Corn Dance and the tradition: if one generation misses that cycle, then it is hard to get any other generation back into it. . . . I know some of the songs, as far as the Indian songs go. I know some of the medicine; I know a lot about the medicine plants, only because I wanted to know. I know what plant is called what, what this plant will do and not do, and different things like that, which probably surprises the full-bloods, that I know as much as I know. But when they were going to school, I did not go to school; I was hanging around the village and the camp working with the elder people. So I learned a lot more than anyone could imagine. . . .

"I was never an apprentice [medicine man], but I have learned, and I do know songs, and I have led dances at the Green Corn Dance when I was younger. I would say in my twenties I used to lead dances out there, like the Firefly and the Catfish, songs like that. I know them; I still know them. Most of the songs, whether they relate to Indian medicine or the Green Corn Dance, are all Creek. So you sing in Creek and speak Mikasuki; but to my knowledge the majority of them are Creek."[21]

Baxley described his own experience of being scratched, and speculated that the tradition had disappeared in a more humane era. "That was a form of punishment. Absolutely. . . .

A lot of that [punishment] has kind of died off, I guess, with the elders. But back then they wore a lot of beads and they had safety pins on them all the time because they always needed a safety pin. Somebody would bring you up there, and they would grab that arm, take a safety pin off, and tear you up. And you would run off crying. Not a lot of spanking; more of discipline through the scratching and through verbal and through teaching, I guess."[22] Yet the tradition of scratching has not altogether disappeared. Jeannette Cypress, a mother who observes traditional ways more than most of her contemporaries, confirmed that she occasionally scratched her young son: "My little boy gets scratched so sometimes he will fast for half a day . . . and I do not want to eat in front of him. A lot of times the women will fast with their little boys."[23]

Joe Dan Osceola agreed that scratching was one of the sacred rituals associated with the Green Corn Dance. "A child who is old enough to get the manhood name, that is one of them; the wedding took place; and it is to make the things they go through [meaningful]. To scratch the body, to let the blood drain from the arm, chest, and legs for the new blood to come in. This was May or June, it depends on what part of the month that it comes up, the full moon, then that is the new year, that is how it starts. Then they cannot eat the corn, green corn on the cob . . . from January on up until they go through the rituals. You get scratched and that is the only time you can eat."[24]

The practice of having both English and Indian names is dying out. Historically, at or near the time of birth, a child received an Indian name (males also received an adult name at their coming of age) that the elders always used in addressing that person. The Seminoles adopted English names as a convenience for interaction with a white community, especially at the frontier trading posts where most traders could not, or would not, learn the pronunciation of their Indian clients' names. Moreover, a person's Indian name was once considered very private and its use was not allowed when younger persons addressed their elders. The way Seminoles receive their names has also changed, and indeed many people living today have not received an Indian name or hesitate to recall them.

Others are unclear on the meaning of their names. When asked his Seminole name and its meaning, Paul Bowers Sr. responded, *"Machu Witchee.* From what they tell me, it means that you can throw somebody down or be on top, in strength." He received that name from his grandparents but is not sure why. "I don't know. I looked tough when I fell out, I guess. I wasn't born in a hospital or anything, so they thought I was tough. My parents were picking tomatoes and stuff at that time, and when they had me, it was near a tomato field or somewhere. I survived, though, and I guess that is why they named me that. . . . It is all right to have both an Indian and an English name. Right now, everybody knows how to speak English. But your grandma and your grandpa, in their days, they did not speak English. . . . They had to know your Indian name so they could call you by that, so you could answer to them. I mostly prefer English because it is common, I guess. My mom does not know how to speak English. She just calls me by my Indian name, and I answer to her."[25]

Mary Frances Johns, a member of the Panther clan, has a Mikasuki name but declined to share it because "you do not use those names after you start having children. Yes, because it is like disrespectful to call people by their names after they have children. Children should call you Mother or Father, they should give you a name of honor, like Aunt or Uncle, but they should never call you by your given name. . . . I always get kind of embarrassed to call myself by my given name." Other adults who are her peers or elders can call her by either her Indian name or the given name, Mary. However, most would call her the mother of so and so, or Monica's Mom. "They all know what my [Indian] name is but they do not ever call me that." Each of her children has an Indian name, but she will quit using it when they marry and have children of their own.

As for picking a name, Johns believed it is not really an issue. "You just pick a name and you give it to a child and they carry it for the rest of their life. But, if it is somebody else's name, like if I pass on, somebody will be given that name. They say if it is a recent person that is still in memory, then the name should be blessed before you give it to a new child. I am not sure how they do that, but they have songs to sing to bar it from being remembered as the previous owner's name. I guess it is supposed to keep the other person's destiny or run of luck or whatever [from] intruding on the next life."[26]

Andy Buster explained how Seminole males get two names. "Yes, I have two. My childhood name would be *Shatee*. Coming into manhood, when I was about twelve, they gave [me] another name, *Fos-Shoc-Chee-Mathee*. Now we have bilingual schools, and they have a unique way of spelling the Mikasuki-Seminole language, but I try to spell [it] phonetically. The first one came from my parents. Basically, the way that works is that the grandparents will be asked to name the child, the grandparents or the aunts or even the parents themselves if they are knowledgeable about the medicine, for preparing the medicine. What they do is, when they do the medicine, they do the chant. So those names come from those chants, and that would be the healing of different illnesses. My name is for the cleansing medicine.

"Then the other name is the name from my grandfathers or my uncles or the people who are well respected and knowledgeable with the culture. When they chose the name from that person, then I have to carry that name. I represent that to society. From what I understand, [the name] is like a leader within whatever they happen to be in: a leader of dancing, or within the camp setting or in the household, or even nowadays in different programs and stuff like that. . . . The name clears that person to really do the things that . . . the name represents." As for having two names, one English and the other Mikasuki, he said, "I grew up with it, so actually I don't think anything of it. That is just the way it is when I have that name. I have this name, but the English name is used more than my other name. Back when my parents were alive and my grandparents, they would use my traditional names, but since they left, a new generation came in and basically they use the English names."[27]

One of the more interesting stories about how Seminoles acquired their anglicized names was related by the late Jimmy O'Toole Osceola. When asked about how he acquired such an unusual middle name for an Indian, Osceola replied, "My English name? O'Toole? I bought it. [Laughs] I had a friend from Ireland. He was from Dublin, Ireland. I never met him. He came to the United States but then all of a sudden just stopped writing. I do not know what happened to him, but I took that Irish name to honor him. . . . I liked the name and asked a lawyer to make it legal, and he told me to go up to the courthouse and look up name changing or removing, and all that. It has descriptions on how to do it. He asked me to get a copy for him. I did that and he passed it for me, to make it legal, my attorney. I paid him $107, I think it was."[28]

Joe Dan Osceola provided another variation on how male Seminoles receive their adult names. "At birth they named me; the little boy's name is *Tipehyih*. *Tipehyih* means whipping someone with a whipper—to whip with something. And the warrior's name is *Golahatee*. That is my name. Golahatee is the name of a warrior or leader during the Indian war. They did not identify who this individual was, but that is how they pick the names, by a medicine man, and they give it to you when you are just a little boy, ten, twelve, fourteen years old. You have to go through the ritual of the Green Corn Dance. At the Green Corn Dance, that is where you get the name, little boys get their name." When asked if he still used his Indian name, Osceola replied, "Hardly ever. Now about the only time I do use that as a formal name is during the Corn Dance. At the Corn Dance, that is about the only time they are used. Everyday life is, I would say, the English name."[29]

Helene Johns Buster, a Brighton Reservation resident, never received an Indian name at birth. When asked if she had a Creek name, she answered, "No, I do not. My oldest brother, he was about twelve years older than I, he had an Indian name, but I have another brother and sister and we do not. I do not know why. I asked my mother why we did not have a name, why she did not give us an Indian name, and she said [it was] because the people that could name you—there was not anybody that could name you. So I do not know. . . . They take you to somebody to name you, like an uncle or somebody like that. I guess their uncles—it would have been her uncle—and all those people in that family were already gone. I never knew my grandparents. They were already dead before I was born." However, for Helene, not having an Indian name was not a great disadvantage while growing up. "No. We all used the English names, so it was not [a disadvantage]. It actually did not become a big deal until I got older, and then I am starting to question why, you know. Now [it] is like not too many people remembers everybody else's Indian name. Just the older people use those names."[30]

Alice Johns Sweat, at the time forty-one years of age, believed her Indian name, *Lugayee*, described her lifestyle. "Well, my activities come to me [naturally]. That is what I do. It is kind of like, *Lugayee* is wanderer. That is how I understood it to be, and I am just all over. . . . I guess I was [named], maybe after four months or something, four moons or something. I do not know. . . . A lot of people do not know [me] by that name. No one calls each other by Indian names anymore, not like back then. . . . When you talk to Indian elders these days, when you are talking to them about somebody, if they do not remember you, they will ask you, what was your mother's name or Indian name? When you tell them, they kind of remember whose child you are. A lot of them will say: you know this so-and-so, and they will call them by their Indian name." Even Alice's sisters do not call her by the Indian name, and certainly her children would not use it, even though they know her Creek name. Alice also confirmed that the practice of naming Seminole children has become a problematic affair. When asked if her own children had Indian names, she responded, "Some do, and some do not. The problem with me was, I married away from the tribe, and my husband was really down on the Indians. He was Spanish, and he did not want me talking my language in my home, and he did not speak his language in the home, so my kids wound up not knowing either. They speak English."[31]

The role of Indian elders in perpetuating the culture has also undergone a significant transformation. Gone are the days when a council of elders and the medicine men conducted the affairs of the people at the annual Green Corn Dance, adjudicating transgressions, giving young men their adult names, solemnizing marriages, and setting the political course that the busk group would follow. Since the federal government recognized the Seminole Tribe of Florida in 1957, governmental functions have been handled by an elected Tribal Council and a Board of Directors, while the strictures associated with the Green Corn Dance are followed by relatively few individuals. Nevertheless, most Seminoles interviewed expressed a strong sense of obligation to the elders and wanted them taken care of by the tribal government.

Jeannette Cypress explained that some of her work as administrative assistant to Tribal Chairman James Billie entailed working with elders. "I do different stuff, it could be anything, like if someone dies there is only a few of us that collect the plants, so I will collect the plants and help people get ready for the medicine. Or I might sometimes shop for an elderly person if she cannot do it herself, or drive her to a doctor's appointment, and I attend meetings."[32] Jimmy O'Toole Osceola explained the origin of the senior citizens center and its hot meals program for elders at the Hollywood Reservation. "From the beginning for Hollywood, we had a most difficult time to get the program with the Seminoles, because Florida . . . says that we are in the city of Hollywood. Why don't we get up and go eat with the white people's hot meals in the city? And they all just arose and said they did not want to do it. The next suggestion was meals on wheels; they would deliver food in their homes, but the food would be cold. They did not want that either. So, they turned that one down. We had one tribal representative at that time and he worked hard and decided to try to start it [a hot meals program] and the Florida state would pay the other half, half and half they would cooperate. To that [the elders] agreed and that is how we got it."[33] There are also senior citizens centers at the Big Cypress and Brighton reservations.

Marie Phillips epitomized the view that a great debt was owed to the elders. She recounted how the children often intervened to protect the elders from being cheated: "There were times when [merchants] would try to cheat them out of their money. . . . And when we learned to read and write and do our math, we could tell them, no, that is not right. This is how much she owes—not that much. You know, things like that. Just little things that made them so proud that we had an education. . . . I think they helped us a lot and we helped them a lot. It was like we could probably never repay what they had helped us with, but we felt that we were obligated to help them because they really pushed us to get an education. And it was not a burden; it was an obligation that you were glad to do—to help them out. I guess that is why I more or less get along with the seniors around here, because I grew up with them and I relate to the seniors more than I do anybody else."

As head of the senior center at Big Cypress, Marie was well qualified to speak about the special dietary needs of elders, particularly their fondness for the traditional foods and cooking the old-fashioned way over an open fire. She explained that in the tribe's hot meals program, "it is two meals a day. They get breakfast and lunch. Well, usually we come in about six a.m. . . . and we have breakfast ready by seven-thirty. They can come in between seven-thirty and eight-thirty. And then they have lunch. We also have home deliveries for the homebound clients. We have a couple of them that are actually young people; they are not even seniors yet, but they have medical problems. Their meals are paid for under different programs, but since we deliver breakfast and lunch, we go ahead and deliver to them."

Phillips continued: "We try to accommodate everybody. It is not a therapeutic meal. It is not just for diabetics or just for people with high blood pressure. Just a nutritious, balanced meal. But we do not cook with salt or anything and that is why we have salt on the table. They can put it [on] if they want. Yes, I believe there is a need for it, especially for some of them that are alone. . . . There are some of them who would rather be alone, but sometimes you are scared to let them be alone because they try to cook. We try to tell them, do not be cooking and we will bring your food. But, then sometimes it is like they are not used to this type of food. They want their old Indian food, old ways or whatever. . . . Well, a lot of them eat a lot of stewed chicken or beef, you know, a lot of stewed meats. A lot of grains like rice and grits and stuff like that, and they want their traditional drink, which is what we call *oklee* (*sofkee* in Creek; *oklee* is Mikasuki). It is made out of corn. You can make it out of just about anything. And it is real bland to other people who are not used to it. And they want that or they want fry bread, which they cannot have all of the time, but you cannot tell them that. So they always want to cook their own foods, but then we bring the food to them. Sometimes, they eat it and sometimes, they do not. Depending on what it is."[34]

Alice Johns Sweat often served as an interpreter for the elders who went to the medical clinics on the Seminole reservations. Asked if she saw any reluctance among elders to use the white man's medicine, or if they would use both Seminole remedies and modern drugs, she offered, "Yes, you can do both, and I have done both. . . . I will use both because I respect the traditional healing still. . . . You know, there is something to that. So, if it is there to help me, then I am going to go there first. But, there are some things that we do not—and traditional healers do not—have that the clinic can provide, like . . . something where they give you a shot. We do not have that in the traditional [medicine]. I do not know if they [the elders] do [go to the medicine man]. Like, some Creeks do not understand Mikasuki and some Miccosukees do not understand Creek. So, some of the medicine men speak Creek only in the song and singing and stuff. So, I have been asked to translate for the elders for the Mikasuki language. So, I know they use both."[35]

Sweat also commented that she thought elders suffered a type of depression as a result of moving from traditional villages into modern housing. "When they lived in chikees, it was like a big old camp with family members [and] extended-family members living in and around that camp all the time. Now, being put in a home, it is kind of like they have isolated the seniors into this building. Since there are no chikees or family members nearby, I feel like they get lonely and they get depressed, isolated. Yes, even though we are in a community [and] we know everybody, [because] everybody knows each other, [like] they know whose grandma that is, they just feel there is no one around them now." A related problem Sweat observed was Seminole parents dumping their children on aging grandparents who were not well. "Now, the biggest problem I face working for this program is . . . the children of the elders would bring their kids to the elders. The elder is not being well today and, yet, the parents still bring their kids over and leave them for the elder to watch. That just burns me up, . . . but of course grandma is not going to say no anyway, you know, bring them on. They feel lonely [and] they want company. But they are not capable of taking care of them. In fact, I know of a situation where she had below her knee amputated and, yet, the grandkids would go out the door and go running down the road or something and she would not be able to go after them, not that fast anyway. [What] if something happened to her grandkid? She worries about that. And this is a situation where neither parent worked."[36]

Even so, grandparents served as the primary caregivers for many young children, now adults, who were interviewed for this study. The younger adults described the elders as being an invaluable resource for passing along language and folkways, as well as teaching the significance of clan and kinship. One such tribute came from Lorene Gopher. "I am sure my grandma named all of us. . . . She got names always related to wartime or something. Especially the little boys . . . because her grandmother told her a lot of things about the war that her grandmother's grandmother had told that grandmother. So, she kind of told us, like, firsthand what went on, [how] they ran, and how they had to cross the river and everything. I do not know if anyone knew that much about it, but they lived to be over one hundred. I guess I was kind of fortunate in a way because my mother died when I was young. She did not want our father to raise us, so she took us [to] my grandmother and my grandfather and my aunt, [who] raised us. That was a blessing, I guess, because then we could learn all we could from her. We all went to school except for one of my sisters. They wanted to keep her so they could teach her the traditional ways every day, instead of getting her confused with the white man's ways and everything. So, she did not go to school but, to this day, she can read and write and everything. I guess she learned from us."[37]

One area where the elders had a profound effect on the young was through the telling of legends and folktales. Betty Mae Jumper wrote *Legends of the Seminoles* and explained the importance of passing on stories about the early days of the tribe—"at time when the world was very young—a time when animals talked and walked on two feet. This was in the very beginning, before Jesus was born." It was mostly the older people who disseminated these legends, and they did so primarily to teach the children the ways of the tribe and to help them go to sleep. These stories, argued Jumper, "provided a comfortable consistency in the lives of children forced to contend with the clashing cultures of dual worlds." These tales "became a vital means of passing on tradition, teaching moral lessons, facilitating child development, molding character and . . . they were just plain entertainment in the absolutely mundane world of the swamp Indian. More than anything, the myths sought to create bonds with the surrounding environment."[38] Lottie Baxley fondly remembered being told "old stories [passed] from generation to generation" to either get them to sleep or teach them some discipline. She described one of the stories that her aunt told her. After the rain, you could see the smoke (steam) coming up, and her aunt would say: "The witch is cooking her supper. If you don't be quiet, she'll come and cook you too."[39] A ploy used by millions of parents from every culture in the world—if children did not behave, some bogeyman or alien would come and snatch them away.

Louise Jumper recalled that "sometimes I would spend most of the time with my grandparents, both sides. My grandmother from my father's side would teach me stuff. She would sing medicine songs to me, but I could never catch on to them. . . . Sometimes it is hard for people, and sometimes it is the people that are meant to have the music [that] catch [it]. It is just something about you, I guess, that you can grasp it but some others cannot, and I am one that cannot. She would teach me to know people's Indian names, the older people. When I [would] go to my other grandmother and then I would use that knowledge, she said, no, you are not supposed to do those things, you are a child. And then I would get all confused. And that is [why] I think I did not learn that much."[40]

Her grandmother also taught Louise practical skills needed around the camp. "She taught me things by doing it, by doing stuff. It was hard work she put me through. You know that *sofkee*, that corn *sofkee* that we drink a lot? We had to go out and find the whitest sand and fill it up in a five-gallon bucket, carry it back in her jeep, and we had to build a big fire and roast the corn in the sand, and then grind it down. It took all day; I guess it took a whole week to do that. I remember that. I remember the steps but I do not remember how brown the corn had to be. That is the only step I do not remember. . . . I remember grinding it and grinding it and grinding it. With a hand-cranking grinder. . . . But at the same time she was teaching me the language. . . . She did not speak English. She talked in Indian. But the names of people and stuff like that, and the ways that you have to go, I do not remember her telling me those things. But she taught me how to work. [Laughter.]"[41]

As detailed earlier, Jeannette Cypress learned an great deal about preparing Indian medicine from Susie Billie, the grandmother who raised her. She realized that the old woman would not live too much longer, and that with her passing an important piece of Seminole folk knowledge would disappear. So it was with great admiration that she discussed her grandmother's remarkable life. "My grandma is over one hundred. . . . She still does really well. And I think a lot of it is because of the exercise and the work. They didn't have all of that junk food that we eat today. She had to work hard. They traveled a lot. They walked a lot. She had lots of exercise. So I think that has a lot to do with it."[42]

The preservation of Native languages is crucial to the survival of Indian cultures. Language is the cultural lifeblood that transmits the essential beliefs, values, and history of a people from one generation to another. Loss of the highly nuanced

Muskogee/Creek or Mikasuki languages spoken by Seminoles would create a discontinuity of contact with past generations. Many contemporary Seminoles and Miccosukees believe that their languages are already disappearing, and with them the ability to transmit traditional knowledge to youngsters.

Part of the problem of transmitting language is that some parents are themselves less than fluent in Indian languages, or have married a non-Indian spouse and thus focus on speaking English in the home. However, there are also families that have worked hard to preserve languages for the next generation. Helene Johns Buster recounted how her family, although the children were of mixed-blood ancestry and attended a white English-speaking school in Okeechobee, retained the Creek language spoken on her reservation. "The majority of us were half-breeds and so that was a problem. . . . We were probably more prejudiced against, on the Brighton Reservation, for being half-breeds than we were in the white community for being half-Indian. That is the way I always felt about it. It is funny to me today and I laugh about [it] that the full-bloods were always down on us because we were half-breeds. But today, when you go to the community meetings and stuff like that, the full-bloods are up there asking us half-breeds to interpret for them to the community because the full-bloods do not know how to speak it but the people in my family know how to speak it, because we hung onto it, the language. But the full-bloods out there did not. I do not know why they did not. I always have a hard time with that because both parents—and most of them had both parents— they both spoke the language and everything, but the kids all spoke English. And they did not pick it up well enough to where they feel comfortable enough to speak to the community in the language. So, they always get [people] like my cousins to interpret for them."[43]

The preservation of Indian language remains a crucial issue for many tribal members. When asked major developments were taking place in Seminole culture and society and where he would like to see things going in the next generation, Brian Billie had a clear focus: "Language. The language and traditions of the medicine, how to do medicine. Hopefully, a lot of people are interested in it to carry it on as the older people dwindle down. And also our culture, as to the blood line of the Indians, is getting thinner and thinner, there are less full-bloods; I think that is where we are losing them, too. We need more full-blooded Indians." As for his own children, he would like to raise them on the reservation and teach them Indian ways until they are old enough to choose how they want to live. "I would like to keep them, teach them, let them learn, maybe from my mother, who speaks more fluently than me. I try to get them to go over there and speak with her, like every day or every other day." Billie is one of those parents who is frustrated by a limited knowledge of the language. "I speak to them in my native language, Mikasuki language. I speak to them and make sure they know some words, anyway. My son, he is the oldest, he is five, he always asks me, 'What does it mean?' If I say something, he is very curious. So, I am pretty sure he will learn how to talk. . . . He can say the words, but he does not put them in a sentence yet. He should already know. If I spoke it more fluently, like every day, he would probably know."[44]

Mary Frances Johns's family was one in which both parents were fluent in the Indian languages, but this was not totally passed down to the next generation. Johns noted, "I think we speak predominantly English . . . [my husband] is trilingual. His first language is Mikasuki, I think, because he was one of the ones that traveled a lot, like me. They lived a lot of times more in Hollywood and the Big Cypress area. So, I think he grew up probably speaking both languages, but I think his mother probably started him out in Mikasuki. But whatever language is spoken, it is understood. Now my youngest son, I am not sure of how much grasp he has of the Indian dialects because he is in English most of the time."[45]

Marie Phillips was proud of her five-year-old granddaughter's bilingualism: "I would say [Mikasuki] is her primary language. I would want it to be. She speaks English very well. She is five, going on twenty-five. But she is really smart. She does really well in school. . . . There are a lot of kids that speak only English and she has got to be there with the culture teacher telling the kids how to say this or that. . . . She speaks Mikasuki to her dolls and her teddy bears and she says, you have to learn the language. My two girls, they speak it. And they speak to her. Sometimes they will catch themselves speaking English and Mikasuki at the same time. I will catch them and I will say, either you speak one language or the other to her."

Although Marie's immediate family has done a good job of perpetuating the language, she realizes that others have not. "My own sister, Maryjean, was married to a non-Indian. They had two children and they are only a quarter Seminole and they do not speak the language because her husband did not want them learning [it]. He felt left out when she would speak to them in Seminole. And today, he kicks himself. He admits that he was wrong. That he deprived them of that. They understand it. You can speak to them in Seminole and they understand it but they do not speak it. So, now, Maryjean has a grandson. He is not even two, yet. And she speaks [Seminole] to him and he understands. And he tries to talk and he hears English from his grandfather and Seminole from her. He more or less understands if you tell him to do something or go get something or just talk to him; he understands. . . .

"I guess [the language] is just, personally, important to me. Maybe I see it as a tribute to my grandparents. Because they taught me and I have taught my kids and I want my granddaughter to know. Because I grew up listening to my grandfather say that there will be a day when nobody will even know the Semi-

nole language; the arts and crafts; the way of the Seminole. He
said there would be a day. That day will come when everybody
will probably be speaking one language and it will probably be
English. I hear him, every day, telling me these things. And I just
want to keep it going for as long as we can."[46]

Another reason for language loss is that Seminole youngsters are attending schools, both public and tribal, that focus on
learning English, often to the detriment of their native tongue.
Helene Johns Buster is from that generation of Brighton Reservation youngsters who attended the public school in Okeechobee during the 1950s and 1960s. She recalled the efforts that were
made to encourage her to speak English came mostly from her
family: "It was kind of like, to me—and I always said that—our
being an Indian was kind of put aside so that we could go out
and learn to be white, so that we could help them [adults] to be
able to live in this life that was changing, because they had to go
to Okeechobee to do their business and they could not because
they did not speak the language. They always had to take one
of us kids to town with them. And here we were, making con-
tracts for cars and translating all this stuff for vehicles and just
bills and things like that. And we were little kids, just translating all that stuff. It was very important to them for us to learn
how to live out here in this world.

". . . I never heard anything from anybody in our family,
anything negative about going to school. It was always pushed
to get there, that you needed to go to school and learn whatever you could. This was really pushed on us. I never felt like
it was a negative to be going there, being mixed with non-
Indians and stuff. I know a lot of people talk about that and . . . I
never felt like that. . . . And we were pushed more to speak English than to speak the [Creek] language so we would be able to
handle things."[47]

The Indian-language program instituted at the Ahfachkee
School was a somewhat belated attempt to rectify this situa-

tion; furthermore, it reaches only a limited segment of Seminole children, since most attend public schools. Louise Jumper, who spent a number of years working for the tribal education department, reflected on the gradual loss of the Mikasuki language: "Ahfachkee has been trying to get that language going for a few years now . . . through the whole school. And we even took some tests on the kids; if we were lucky, we would have gotten one child or two children out of the whole class that could speak the language. They understood it but they could not speak it. That is what we found out. They only took those tests a couple of years ago."[48] When asked when this began, she replied, "That is what I was wondering. When? Why didn't I catch it? I would say in the last ten years. Really gradually, that I did not realize it. Now I think they—what do they call it, immersion, that was the Mikasuki-speaking children, they wanted them to be speaking English more—now they wanted it switched around. . . . And now I am wishing . . . maybe I should have taught them to keep their language alive and well but yet try to grasp onto the English language and use it, instead of taking up one and losing the other. I hope it is not too late."

At the time of this interview (1999), Jumper, with strong backing from the chairman and Tribal Council, developed a preschool program aimed at language development. "The whole idea behind this preschool," she said, "where they have the native language project going, is to start with preschool, the babies; they have got to hear the language, talk to them. Even though they can not speak it, you have to just keep talking to them until they learn it along the way."[49]

Victor Billie reflected the concern of some Indian adults that the schools might be a detriment to Seminole youngsters in learning their culture. "When I got my knowledge of traditional ways and our laws and how to behave among people was when I talked to my elders. I was taught to listen, and when he is breathing at me, that is the lesson, in there, put in my mouth and my nostrils. The way that schools are teaching, they cannot get that effect. What they are learning from school about traditional ways and the language is from a book. It has no feelings. It has no soul.

"When I learned my ways, I learned them from a person that was alive, experiencing, teaching me and giving me the feelings and the pain and everything about him and about tradition. I cannot get that from a book or from a VCR or cassette. And I want them to learn that way [the traditional way]. I do not want them to learn from a book. . . . Today's kids, there is a non-Indian influence around them every day, even in the cars, even when they walk around, even if they are driving. It is making them lose touch with our beliefs and our people. Some of the young kids today, they do not even know how to speak their language. Even if they have a full-blood mom and a full-blood dad, all they know is English, and sometimes they try to speak it and they speak broken-Seminole language."

Billie believes that Seminole children should not be forced to attend school at an early age. "Do not do that. Let them learn about themselves, about their culture and their language [until] they are about ten or eleven years old. Let us teach them first, then let them go to school, if they want. They do not do that. They let them go to school when they are about one or two years old, and they forget. My elders once said, when an Indian boy or an Indian girl goes to school, they have two brains. Two brains cannot work together, like Indian and white. They fight among each other, and the Indian way will die and the white man will take over and [the Indian] will lose his language and lose his way and lose his direction. That is what happens today on the reservations. They do not know what they are going to do, which direction they have to go. That is why they are using drugs and alcohol. They do not know who they are. . . . And the Indian dies inside of them and they want to kill the pain. That is why they use drugs and alcohol. . . . I used to do drugs and al-

cohol, too. I am not a perfect man. But, when I found my direction, it was an Indian way and it made me stronger, so I do not
drink alcohol or do drugs now."[50]

The existence of two tribal languages that are not mutu-
ally intelligible has also created a problem in transmitting the
cultural past. For example, much of the Green Corn Dance is
based in the Creek language, but most Seminoles speak Mikasuki. But as Jeannette Cypress points out, to a great extent a person's ability to speak one or more of the languages depends on
where they grew up and who their elders were. "Our language
is kind of dying out to a certain point. You will have some families that still speak the language, and then you will have some
where they go down the generations. Like myself, I am fluent
because I grew up with grandparents and they did not speak
English. All of my brothers and sisters are fluent. . . . My oldest
son is fluent; the next one, she understands everything you say
but responds in English. She does not feel comfortable talking
the language, I think because she thinks she is not going to pro-
nounce them right or something. My other daughter, she understands here and there, and she will speak a little, but it is not
enough really. . . . And my youngest ones understand some, but
they are the same way. A lot of it is because—I think if I could
have stayed home and spoken to them all the time, it probably
would have worked.

"But when you send them to Head Start and preschool, most
of the employees are not Indian and they do not speak the language. So, they lose a lot of that because they spend the whole
day hearing English. I always tell them, even if you only learn a
little bit, it is better than none at all, so I try to teach them things
at home. But as far as traditional things, like how to behave, or
how you are supposed to respect your elders, they know that."
As pointed out earlier, Jeannette Cypress confirmed that many
of the medicine chants her grandmother used contain a mix-

ture of Creek and Mikasuki terms that even she found difficult to understand.[51]

Joe Dan Osceola expressed pleasure that his people have preserved as much of the language and culture as they have. "The Bureau of Indian Affairs wanted us to forget who we were so we will not know our history, culture, and language, and the whole nine yards. But the tribes, the Seminoles and the Miccosukees, are the only two tribes that have been able to maintain their culture, meaning the Green Corn Dance, and that has been one of the highlights of their lives. . . . I can tell you the purpose of that [Corn Dance], why I think it is still important. It was important in the earlier days of recorded history of the Seminole Tribe and the Miccosukee. The Green Corn Dance represents the culture and language."[52]

Few of the Seminoles interviewed spoke both Creek and Mikasuki. However, this issue is compounded when an Indian person marries a non-Indian, or even an Indian who speaks the other language. In such homes it is unlikely that the children will learn to speak an Indian language; instead, they will learn English as a compromise. Carl Baxley is one of the exceptions. "I grew up in Brighton, which speaks Creek, but I lived in Big Cypress for about eight to ten years, something like that, and I am married to a girl out there, so I can probably speak more Mikasuki than I can Creek. I certainly understand more Mikasuki than I do Creek—to this day. I also sit on the Board of Directors as an elected official, and we were in a briefing the other day and one of the tribal members was talking to the president and started speaking Mikasuki, thinking that I did not know what she was saying. So, as she finished, I just kind of broke in [using] English and threw her for a loop. I know a lot of the language. I speak it if I have to. Most of the time I don't have to."[53]

Despite seeing the importance of retaining the native tongue, Helene Johns Buster, a Creek-speaker from the Brighton Reservation, admits that her own children do not speak the language. "No. They do not, because I married a Mikasuki-speaking person. Well, my first husband was an English-speaking person, and he was white. The second husband was a Mikasuki-speaking person, so I did not understand him, and he did not understand me, so, of course, we spoke English. And that is what my child speaks. I have really been thinking about it back then, they should have learned both languages. They should have been trilingual, but they are not. They speak English. My daughters try hard now to learn the language, but they do not speak it. My grandsons speak more than they do."

Helene told of her own problems in trying to learn Mikasuki after years living at Big Cypress. "I am catching it a little. [Laughter] It is hard for me. With some [people] I can sit in a conversation and I can hear talk and I catch things here and there and by the time the conversation is through I kind of think I know what they were talking about. Then I will lean over to somebody and say, 'Did they say this?' And they will say, yes. Sometimes I think I know a little bit more than I am comfortable saying I know, I think because I do not want to say yes and then be totally wiped out. It is hard. . . . I think I have only run into two—two of the elderly women—that speak the Creek language, too. But, then they are determined that I am going to learn how to speak Mikasuki, so they quit talking to me in Creek. But most of the time it is all in Mikasuki and I might have to get an interpreter. If I cannot pick up the gist of what they are saying, then I have to get an interpreter."[54] Nancy Shore, a Creek-speaker, claims limited speaking ability in the Mikasuki language. "I can understand it but I really cannot speak it fluently. Just a little bit, not much. But if you sit and listen to them talk, you can really pick up what they are talking about. That is what I go by, listening, because it is almost like our language. That is how I pick up what they are talking about."[55]

As the Seminole Tribe moves into the twenty-first century it still struggles to maintain a balance between preserving traditional language and culture while preparing youngsters to adapt and survive in an increasingly synergistic technological world. Like other tribes, the Seminoles mourn the rapid passing of traditional elders who are the bearers of a rich cultural heritage. Their most fundamental ceremony, the Green Corn Dance, is no longer attended frequently by most of the tribe, and those who do attend attach little religious significance to it. The role of the medicine men as political figures has been greatly attenuated, and they share the position of healer with white doctors. Seminoles still learn and appreciate the ways of their elders, but most live very modern lives and share the hopes and aspirations of non-Indians. It is difficult to remain Indian in today's world.

Conclusion

Over the thirty-year span between 1970 and 2000, members of the Seminole Tribe of Florida underwent an extraordinary sociocultural, economic, and political transformation. By the opening decade of the twenty-first century, the tribe had created a workable governmental system and had established itself as an economic powerhouse. Gone forever were the days of having to wrestle alligators or selling patchwork and basketry to tourists to eke out a living. All of the tribal members interviewed understood and fully appreciated this dramatic improvement.

By 2000 the tribe had enjoyed more than twenty years of steadily increasing prosperity. Nevertheless, on their journey to security and prosperity, the Seminole people realized that many of their old ways and values were being challenged or, in some cases, had already disappeared. They faced the difficult task of maintaining the languages and folkways that uniquely defined them as Indian and passing these along to succeeding generations while at the same time coming to grips with life in a new century. Most of the interviewees recognized that it was exceedingly difficult to remain a traditional Indian in the modern world, and they pointed out many ways in which their culture had changed in a mere three decades. Although individual opinions occasionally varied widely, a broad consensus emerged on some issues, and these are presented here in no particular hierarchy.

Virtually all of the Seminoles interviewed agreed that it was important to preserve their languages and culture as markers of both personal and group identity, but there was no consensus on how this could be achieved. They generally supported the elaborate Ah-Tah-Thi-Ki Museum as a place where Indians and non-Indians alike could learn more about Seminole culture, although a few individuals held it was no substitute for traditional ways of learning from the elders and medicine men. They acknowledged that many societal forces were working against language retention among the young. For the most part, except for the Ahfachkee School at Big Cypress, Seminole youngsters attend public or private schools where their teachers and classmates primarily use English, and that is what they hear on television and in public places.

In the 1970s and 1980s, observers acknowledged that the Miccosukee Tribe was more successful with its bilingual education programs in creating language fluency and self-esteem than were the Seminoles. This was largely due to the fact that all Miccosukee children attended the tribal school, where Mikasuki was a central language of instruction. Furthermore, it was a living language spoken by all members of the community at home and in daily discourse.

Seminole children did not enjoy the same extent or degree of language reinforcement. Moreover, English had become the primary language in most Seminole homes. Even in reservation homes where one parent is fluent in one of the two Indian languages, it is not always transmitted to the children. This is certainly true where the other parent or partner is non-Indian or speaks a different Indian language from his or her spouse. In such cases English is usually employed as a compromise. Even a consummate Mikasuki-speaker like Jeannette Cypress, who was raised by her grandmother (the venerated medicine woman Susie Jim Billie) and knew both the archaic and modern forms of Mikasuki, admitted that her own children were not learning the language of their people as well as they should. Thus language maintenance depends on the individual family's ability and willingness to reinforce Indian language by speaking it at home and, in the case of Big Cypress, supplementing what is taught by native-language instructors at the Ahfachkee School.

Preservation of such cultural artifacts as patchwork, bead-work, basketry, carving, and storytelling lies in the hands of an ever-shrinking number of individuals. Interviewees acknowl-edged that fewer and fewer young people, even though they might have learned the requisite skills, choose to practice these traditional folk arts. The Seminole oral tradition is at particular risk. When the older generation, some in their eighties and nine-ties, has passed away, their collective wisdom will reside primar-ily in written materials, such as Betty Mae Jumper's *Legends of the Seminoles* (1994), which contains stories handed down by her grandmother. Another of Jumper's works, *And with the Wagon Came God's Word* (1985), is a personal account of her youthful in-teraction with Indian Baptist missionaries and her acceptance of Christianity. She also coauthored an autobiography, *A Seminole Legend: The Life of Betty Mae Tiger Jumper* (2001), which recounts many aspects of her remarkable life. Aside from these works, and perhaps the Miccosukee leader Buffalo Tiger's own coau-thored autobiography, *Buffalo Tiger: A Life in the Everglades* (2002), the knowledge of the elders is in danger of slipping away.

Among the next generation, however, there are gifted art-ists, poets, and musicians. One of these, Mary Frances Johns, made a good living selling her craft creations and serving as sto-ryteller-in-residence at many museums throughout the nation. Her goal was to keep the folk culture of her people alive and make it understandable to non-Indians as well. It is important to understand that some of the Indian legends and stories, al-though often dismissed as mere mythology by whites, have as much validity as recorded history. For example, some years ago Mary Frances related to one of the authors a story concerning her family and the Seminole clan system. Early in the twenti-eth century the Panther clan had been greatly reduced in num-ber and just a few of the survivors were women, one of whom was Mary Frances's maternal grandmother. Since the Seminole clans are matrilineal and descent is determined through the woman's line, the Panther clan was in danger of disappearing, as had happened to other clans over time; some had literally "died out" from a dearth of procreation. Since each clan plays a special role in the Green Corn Dance, the loss of a clan would have been disastrous. However, her grandmother married as a very young woman, bore ten daughters, and almost single-handedly regenerated the Panther clan, which remains the largest among both the Seminole and Miccosukee tribes. Thus this little-known and as yet unconfirmed family vignette reveals how the clan structure of the tribe has remained stable over time. Such stories are an integral part of the folklore that should not be lost, but many are still not written down anywhere.

Perhaps the strongest difference of opinion manifested itself over the role of the Green Corn Dance in contemporary Seminole life. Many informants believe that the growth of Christianity among tribal members after the 1940s, mostly in Baptist churches, marked the beginning of the end for traditional beliefs. And certainly the devout Baptists are adamantly opposed to what they consider a pagan ritual, and their opposition increased when the amount of alcohol consumed at the annual ceremony reached damaging proportions. Some interviewees admitted that it had become a drunken orgy. The celebration of the Green Corn Dance was banished from the Seminole reservations until the early 1990s, when a reformed "non-alcoholic" version was reinstated by Tribal Chairman James Billie and the Tribal Council. In part this revival was a response to a resurgence of interest in traditional Indian religion during the 1970s and 1980s, when some leaders of the Red Power movement, such as Vine Deloria Jr., in his work *Custer Died for Your Sins: An Indian Manifesto* (1969), called for Indians to abandon the colonialism of the white man's church. Currently an increasing number of Indians attend the ritual each year. Interestingly, most informants believed that the ritual was important as a connection with their past as a people, and a surprising number thought that an individual could attend the ceremony and still remain a Christian. In truth, however, the spiritual role of the Green Corn Dance had already declined by the late twentieth century due to the demise of so many leading medicine men. Others had converted to Christianity and limited themselves to essentially curative medicine. The social roles of medicine men also changed drastically as they lost their political authority after the Seminole Tribe organized an elected government in 1957.

The conflict between Christianity and the Green Corn Dance as a religious/medical experience continues to the present day. The differences seldom damage interpersonal or tribal relationships, but many devout Baptists stay away from the Green Corn Dance, and the traditionalists rarely set foot in a church. Others, however, embrace both Christianity and the Green Corn Dance. Nonetheless, the Seminoles retain individual opinions and respect one another's point of view.

The Seminoles interviewed proudly acknowledged that their health care had improved dramatically over the last three decades thanks to gaming profits, which help support modern health clinics. There was also a surprisingly strong consensus regarding the compatibility of traditional Indian cures and the white man's medicine. The interviewees generally used the Indian Health Service (IHS) facilities and the doctors available to them in reservation clinics. However, except for a few very devout Baptists, they have no compunctions about also going to the medicine man or woman to seek traditional cures as well. To a great degree their willingness to do so corresponded to the individual's religious preferences. The medicine men employed their spiritual powers, including prayers and incantations to make the medicine work; therefore the patient had to believe as well if it was to be effective. Eventually, some medicine men and women converted to Christianity, and individuals such as Susie Billie limited herself to the medicinal world, but even that required knowledge of curing songs and the like.

The interviewees almost universally recognized that diabetes remained the tribe's greatest health threat. The disease had reached near epidemic proportions in the Seminole community, and only dietary changes and the medicines administered by white doctors held any promise to stem its spread. Tribal members also saw alcoholism as a lingering Indian health problem. Tribal-run meals programs for the elderly and follow-up social services became part of an all-out attack on ailments such as diabetes, high blood pressure, and heart disease, but generally poor health among seniors remained a problem. It is somewhat ironic that medicine man Buffalo Jim and IHS physician David Hilton shared similar concerns that their patients would not follow directions. Thus in the health realm, the Seminoles reflected the same individualism they did when confronting the cultural dilemmas in religion. Some still use Indian medicine, while others patronize white doctors and pharmacies. Many are pragmatic in their health choices and take advantage of both types of healing. As always, it is up to individuals to take advantage of the tribal-sponsored clinics. Some who badly need treatment either ignore the opportunity or refuse to change their lifestyles. This attitude changed little over the period studied.

One of the more startling revelations to emerge from the interviews was the negative impact of tribal housing programs on Indian families, especially in the rural settings of Big Cypress and Brighton. When the urban Hollywood Reservation opened in 1926, the federal housing was immediately occupied by a diverse group of displaced families representing a cross-section of clans. On the rural reservations, however, people lived in extended-family camps with all members of one clan. The traditional Seminole camp was both matrilineal and matrilocal; that is, women of the same clan and their families settled together for mutual support and to raise their children under the tutelage of the senior clan matron (known as the *posi*, or grandmother) and any male members of their clan who might reside there.

Seminole husbands, being from another clan, were extraneous to child rearing, and their main role was to provide sustenance. The clan camps were effective in protecting, instructing, and disciplining the children, as all adult women were "mothers" to all children of the camp. This was important, because some Indian families moved frequently to seek employment, and children were often left in the care of the grandmother and other adult females.

The construction of modern housing initiated by the Seminole Tribe with government funding in the 1960s and 1970s became a culturally disruptive element in the lives of these Mikasuki-speaking people at Big Cypress, and to a somewhat lesser degree among the Creeks at Brighton. The construction of concrete block structure (CBS) houses on the reservations in the 1960s, followed by the Housing and Urban Development (HUD) program's wooden homes, accelerated the breakup of extended-family chikee camps. BIA officials based the long-range goals for these programs on the best of intentions—to improve living conditions for people residing in substandard settings—and many chikee camps were deemed substandard. However, the move into CBS homes bewildered some of the older people, who had spent their lives without electricity, running water, or indoor plumbing. They found the CBS houses strange, dark, and hot; they missed the openness of the chikee camp with the free-flowing breezes and the outside cookfire. Some of the cattle-owning families welcomed the upgraded housing as well as an obligation to pay for it, but this was not the case for the less-acculturated and nearly destitute Indian families. Even when federal officials ostensibly designed the wooden homes to emulate a chikee camp with multiple screened-in structures and open air flow, many still found them unsuitable.

Aside from the structures themselves, however, many interviewees complained no thought had been given to the fact that the old clan system was being violated. Families were moved into housing without regard to who their neighbors might be. In addition, the homes were designed to hold one family at most, and were not expandable like the old camps to accommodate several generations. Thus elderly parents might be placed in an upgraded home at some distance from other women of their clan. Without the closeness of the camp setting, it was difficult to collectively supervise, instruct, or discipline the children, and many single mothers found that they had no support system. This contributed to growing delinquency as well as drug and alcohol abuse on the reservations. On the whole, interviewees believed that tribal officials could have handled this transition period much better. Over time, and as the older people passed away, the Seminoles adapted to living in modern housing but frequently retained a chikee out back as a connection to their cultural past. By 2000, complaints about the negative influence of new housing had dissipated, as more Seminoles built and enjoyed fancy homes or moved away from the reservation.

All of the Seminoles interviewed had participated in some type of formal schooling. Those from the older generation, such as Betty Mae Jumper and Jimmy O'Toole Osceola, attended reservation schools in the 1930s and were later sent to Indian boarding schools in other parts of the country. Most of the middle-aged Seminoles had experienced a combination of reservation day schools and public schools in nearby towns, while children at the Hollywood Reservation had attended the Broward County schools for at least two generations. Thus they brought a diversity of experiences and opinions to the discussion of Indian education, and readily critiqued what their own children and grandchildren encountered. Without doubt the most cynical group was those from Brighton who, as youngsters being bused to public school, had been pawns in the struggles of the early 1950s over where Indians would attend. They realized that much of the white community's belated acceptance was related to Indian athletic prowess, and they were suspicious of white teachers and school officials. Several reported that as parents they fought to get their children into schools where they knew and trusted the teachers regardless of whether the children belonged there or not. The first Seminole graduated from the Okeechobee public high school in 1957, the same year the tribe was formally recognized by the federal government. That graduate, Joe Dan Osceola, provided a positive account of his experiences in public school and later in college.

The residents of Big Cypress Reservation have heavily invested psychologically in the successful operation of the Ahfachkee School. Many of them attended the day school when it was run by the Bureau of Indian Affairs and recall what a minimalist operation that was. For years they fought to have the tribe operate the school through direct contracting with Washington, just as the Miccosukee Tribe did, but representatives from the other reservations resisted, fearing that Ahfachkee would be a drain on funds. The income from gaming rendered that point moot. Now there is great community pride in the strides the school has made since it came under tribal control in the early 1980s. A community school board works with the professional staff to provide a meaningful learning environment and curriculum for the children. The school has a strong culture- and language-retention program that resonates with community values, and the Tribal Council is committed to providing the funding necessary to develop structured educational programs through the secondary level. But the success of Seminole education depends on many factors other than funding.

The Seminole Tribe cannot afford to become complacent. Although tribal revenues from gaming are currently secure, legal and political conditions change. In many jurisdictions Indian tribal sovereignty is being challenged on a variety of issues and could be eroded through unfavorable judicial decisions of congressional enactments. Several individuals interviewed voiced these same concerns. The U.S. Supreme Court's ruling in *Sem-*

inole Tribe of Florida v. State of Florida (1996), which blocked the tribe from suing the state to force a casino gaming settlement, was a wake-up call after decades of victory in the courts. Seminoles understand that in the future the tribe will continue to need attorneys and other professionals to defend their rights, as well as an educated and involved polity to make good decisions and elect enlightened leaders. Thus it would be shortsighted for tribal leaders to accept anything less than high educational standards in preparing youngsters for citizenship. This challenge calls for a new mind-set among the people and will require continuous, unified effort on the part of Indian families, the public schools, and tribal educational programs.

There are always questions about who speaks with authority for an Indian community. This is true even with the voices being heard are virtually all Native, as there are always competing agendas within tribal communities. Certainly, excerpts from the Seminole interviews incorporated into this volume provide a broad, if not totally definitive, picture of how tribal members viewed the changes they confronted between 1970 and 2000. Moreover, the compilation provides a predominantly "bottom-up" view from a diverse demographic within the tribe, crossing all reservations and most occupational strata, including Christians and traditionalists, cattlemen and craftspeople, men and women, old and young. Nor is it overbalanced with the rhetoric of tribal political leaders, who tend to voice the mantra of Indian economic progress without sufficiently considering its impact on family life and cultural values. Not all of the Indians interviewed were completely happy with the direction the tribe had taken, and those dissenters did not hesitate to articulate their concerns. We have encouraged the Seminole people to speak for themselves on topics they found important, and attempted to place their statements in a broad historical context. Having spoken of the past, the Seminoles must resolve the issues that confront them in the present.

Notes

1. Economic Change

1. *Seminole Tribune*, November 10, 2000, 1.
2. *Palm Beach Post*, February 4, 2007.
3. Seminole Tribe of Florida, "History: Seminoles Today," http://www .seminoletribe.com.
4. Joe Dan Osceola, interview by Tom King, 31.
5. Covington, *The Seminoles of Florida*, 252–56; Kersey, "The Florida Seminoles," 94–96.
6. Carl Baxley, interview, 22–23.
7. Louise Jumper, interview, 32–33.
8. James Billie, interview by Tom King, 9.
9. Marie Phillips, interview, 15–16.
10. Carl Baxley, interview, 20.
11. Covington, *The Seminoles of Florida*, 12–13; *Seminole Tribune*, April 30, 2001, 7.
12. Capron, "Florida's Emerging Seminoles," 729.
13. Cattelino, "High Stakes," 45.
14. Covington, "Brighton Reservation," 60–61.
15. Mary Jene Coppedge, interview, 21.
16. Stanlo Johns, interview, 4–6, 15, 27–30.
17. Richard Bowers, interview, 7.
18. Joe Frank, interview, 21.
19. Carl Baxley, interview, 18.
20. Don Robertson, interview, 3.
21. Mary Jene Coppedge, interview, 22.
22. *Seminole Tribune*, April 30, 2001, 7.
23. Richard Bowers, interview, 7–10.
24. Don Robertson, interview, 15–17.
25. Polly Osceola Hayes, interview, 18.
26. Andy Buster, interview, 34.
27. Cattelino, "High Stakes," 46–48.
28. Betty Mae Jumper, interview by Rosalyn Howard, 9–10.
29. Mary Jene Coppedge, interview, 21.

30. Lorene Gopher, interview, 49–52.
31. Nancy Shore, interview by James Ellison, 32–33.
32. Marie Phillips, interview, 25.
33. Polly Osceola Hayes, interview, 11–12.
34. Daisi Jumper, interview, 15.
35. Paul Bowers Sr., interview, 12.
36. Paul Douglas Buster, interview, 221, 9.
37. Richard Bowers, interview, 8.
38. Don Robertson, interview, 13.
39. Richard Bowers, interview, 10.
40. Paul Bowers Sr., interview, 16.
41. Don Robertson, interview, 14.
42. Paul Douglas Buster, interview, 2, 10–11.
43. Covington, "Brighton Reservation," 61.
44. Joe Frank, interview, 5.
45. Marie Phillips, interview, 4–5.
46. Alice Johns Sweat, interview, 5.
47. Jeannette Cypress, interview, 4.
48. Victor Billie, interview, 6.
49. Jacob Osceola, interview, 15.
50. Paul Bowers Sr., interview, 4.
51. Joe Frank, interview, 20.
52. Jacob Osceola, interview, 9.
53. Mary Jene Coppedge, interview, 19.
54. Louise Gopher, interview, 8.
55. Joe Frank, interview, 17.
56. Lorene Gopher, interview, 18–19.
57. Carl Baxley, interview, 9.
58. Mary Frances Johns, interview by James Ellison, 9.
59. Victor Billie, interview, 6.
60. Don Robertson, interview, 2, 3, 4.
61. Stanlo Johns, interview, 31–33, 47.
62. *Seminole Tribune*, November 26, 2004, 5.
63. Covington, *The Seminoles of Florida*, 253–54; Kersey, "The Florida Seminoles," 94.
64. Carl Baxley, interview, 31–32.
65. Joe Dan Osceola, interview by Rosalyn Howard, 31–32.
66. Jacob Osceola, interview, 30.
67. Covington, *The Seminoles of Florida*, 254–55; Kersey, "The Florida Seminoles," 94–95; *Seminole Tribune*, July 9, 1997, 1.

68. *St. Petersburg Times*, December 19, 1997.

69. *St. Petersburg Times*, July 13, 2000.

70. *Seminole Tribune*, March 23, 2001, July 4, 2003, and May 21, 2004; *St. Petersburg Times*, February 5, 2003.

71. *Miami Herald*, December 5, 2003.

72. *Seminole Tribune*, March 23, 2001.

73. James Billie, interview by James Ellison, 16–17; *St. Petersburg Times*, December 18, 1997.

74. *St. Petersburg Times*, December 19, 20, 1997.

75. *St. Petersburg Times*, December 19, 1997; *Seminole Tribune*, September 5, 1997.

76. *St. Petersburg Times*, February 18, 1999.

77. *Seminole Tribune*, January 19, 2001, and April 30, 2001.

78. *Seminole Tribune*, September 27, 2002.

79. *Seminole Tribune*, April 11, 2003.

80. *Seminole Tribune*, May 23 and June 13, 2003.

81. *St. Petersburg Times*, February 25, 2004.

82. *South Florida Sun-Sentinel*, November 25, 26, 2007.

83. Cattelino, *High Stakes*, 108–11.

84. Cattelino, *High Stakes*, 169–73.

85. *St. Petersburg Times*, March 1, 2002, and February 5, 2003.

86. *New York Times*, December 8, 2006.

87. *New York Times*, December 8, 2006; *USA Today*, December 8, 9, 2006; *Gainesville Sun*, December 8, 2006.

88. *South Florida Sun-Sentinel*, November 25, 2007.

89. *Gainesville Sun*, November 15, 2007; *St. Petersburg Times*, November 14, 15, 2007.

90. *St. Petersburg Times*, November 18, 2007.

91. *St. Petersburg Times*, December 4, 2007; *Palm Beach Post*, July 3, 2008; *Miami Herald*, September 20, 2008.

92. *Seminole Tribune*, May 30, 2008.

93. *Palm Beach Post*, February 4, 2007; Cattelino, "High Stakes," 132–36.

94. Cattelino, "High Stakes," 129; *Miami Herald*, July 30, 2007, A1.

95. Mary Jene Coppedge, interview, 23–24.

96. *Miami Herald*, July 30, 2007, A1.

97. Joe Dan Osceola, interview by Rosalyn Howard, 25–27.

98. Jim Shore, interview, 14.

99. Richard Bowers, interview, 14.

100. Joe Frank, interview, 19–20.

101. Paul Bowers Sr., interview, 176.

102. Paul Douglas Buster, interview, 8.

103. Joe Dan Osceola, interview by Rosalyn Howard, 33.

104. Samuel Tommie, interview by Rosalyn Howard, 8–9.

105. Louise Gopher, interview, 8.

106. Betty Mae Jumper, interview by Rosalyn Howard, 243, 20.

107. *Palm Beach Post*, February 4, 2007.

108. Sadie Cypress, interview, 20.

109. Marie Phillips, interview, 36–37.

110. West, *The Enduring Seminoles*, xiv–xv, 9–31.

111. West, *The Enduring Seminoles*, xi, 30–33.

112. *Seminole Tribune*, September 11, 1998, 1, 4, 7; brochure for Billie Swamp Safari; brochure for Okalee Indian Village and Museum.

113. *New York Times*, September 20, 2000, A 23, 1.

114. Jeannette Cypress, interview, 33.

115. Jacob Osceola, interview, 31–32.

116. Joe Frank, interview, 17.

117. Carl Baxley, interview, 29.

118. Daisi Jumper, interview, 16.

119. Victor Billie, interview, 16.

120. Lee Tiger, interview, 15–16.

121. Andy Buster, interview, 13.

122. Lee Tiger, interview, 16–17.

123. Mary Jene Coppedge, interview, 25.

124. Marie Phillips, interview, 17.

125. Daisi Jumper, interview, 17–18.

126. Samuel Tommie, interview by Rosalyn Howard, 8, 10–12, 14–15.

127. Victor Billie, interview, 4–5.

128. Helene Johns Buster, interview, 22.

129. Mary Jene Coppedge, interview, 31.

2. Seminole Education

1. Bob Mitchell, interview by Harry A. Kersey Jr., April 25, 1969, 9.

2. Bob Mitchell, interview by Harry A. Kersey Jr., April 25, 1969, 4; Kersey, "Educating the Seminole Indians," 20–23.

3. Billy Cypress, interview, 14.

4. Mary Frances Johns, interview by Tom King, 4–5.

5. Billy Cypress, interview, 15.

6. Lottie Baxley, interview by Harry A. Kersey Jr., 10.

7. Ivy Stranahan, interview, 21, 29, 31, 60; Kersey, *The Stranahans of Fort Lauderdale*, 131–32.

8. Kersey, "The Dania Indian School," 42–53.

9. Covington, *The Seminoles of Florida*, 194–200; William Boehmer, interview by Sam Proctor, 9–10.

10. Betty Mae Jumper, interview by Harry A. Kersey Jr., 10.

11. Betty Mae Jumper, interview by Rosalyn Howard, 5, 10.

12. Billy Cypress, interview, 3.

13. Interviews by Mabel B. Francis and W. R. Thomas, November 15, 1938, in Francis and Thomas, *American Life Histories*.

14. Betty Mae Jumper, interview by Rosalyn Howard, 8.

15. Vivian Crooks, interview, 10.

16. Vivian Crooks, interview, 39.

17. Richard Bowers, interview, 5–6.

18. Jimmy O'Toole Osceola, interview by Rosalyn Howard, 5.

19. Paul Douglas Buster, interview, 4.

20. Mary Jene Coppedge, interview, 10–11.

21. Mitchell Cypress, interview, 6.

22. Marie Phillips, interview, 7.

23. Marie Phillips, interview, 26.

24. Daisi Jumper, interview, 7–8.

25. Kersey, "The Ahfachkee Day School," 93–94; Kersey and Greene, "Educational Achievement," 25–28; Garbarino, *Big Cypress*, 55–62.

26. Kersey, "The Federal Day School," 1–10; Kersey, "Educating the Seminole Indians," 16–18.

27. William Boehmer, interview by Sam Proctor, 3–35.

28. Lottie Baxley, interview by Harry A. Kersey Jr., 12.

29. Joe Dan Osceola, interview by Rosalyn Howard, 6, 21.

30. Joe Dan Osceola, interview by Tom King, 15–16.

31. Lorene Gopher, interview, 3–4.

32. Joe Dan Osceola, interview by Rosalyn Howard, 6–7.

33. Stanlo Johns, interview, 13.

34. Joe Dan Osceola, interview by Rosalyn Howard, 6–7.

35. Helene Johns Buster, interview, 9–12.

36. Nancy Shore, interview by James Ellison, 14–17.

37. Joe Dan Osceola, interview by Rosalyn Howard, 130.

38. Peter B. Gallagher, "Ahfachkee: Happy School," *Seminole Tribune*, August 4, 1995, 1–2.

39. *Seminole Tribune*, May 23, 1997, 1–5.

40. *Seminole Tribune*, May 23, 1997, 1–5; *Port Huron (MI) Times Herald*, June 19, 2000, 9A.
41. Sharon Byrd-Gaffney, interview, 1, 2, 4.
42. Sharon Byrd-Gaffney, interview, 5–6, 8, 19, 22.
43. Vivian Crooks, interview, 15–16.
44. Sharon Byrd-Gaffney, interview, 17.
45. Jeannette Cypress, interview, 12.
46. Joe Frank, interview, 5–6.
47. Louise Gopher, interview, 3.
48. Louise Gopher, interview, 4–5.
49. Lorene Gopher, interview, 9.
50. Nancy Shore, interview by James Ellison, 45.
51. Billy Cypress, interview, 1, 2, 3, 12, 13.
52. Jim Shore, interview, 5–17, 19.
53. Carl Baxley, interview, 19, 26.
54. Helene Johns Buster, interview, 22.
55. Virgil N. Harrington, interview by William D. Boehmer, 10.

3. Transformations in Religion and Medicine

1. Weisman, *Unconquered People*, 90–93.
2. Sturtevant, "Medicine Bundles," 30–71; Capron, "Medicine Bundles of the Florida Seminole, 155–210."
3. Buswell, "Florida Seminole Religious Ritual."
4. Joe Frank, interview, 7.
5. Ivy Stranahan, interview, 39, 59; Kersey, *The Stranahans of Fort Lauderdale*, 131.
6. Betty Mae Jumper, interview by Rosalyn Howard, 4.
7. Bob Mitchell, interview by Harry A. Kersey Jr., 1971, 9, 37–39.
8. Bob Mitchell, interview by Harry A. Kersey Jr., 1971, 37–39; Bob Mitchell and Josie Billie, interview, 37–39.
9. Covington, *The Seminoles of Florida*, 229–32.
10. Billy Osceola, interview, 4.
11. Billy Osceola, interview, 7.
12. Kersey, *An Assumption of Sovereignty*, 81–83.
13. Paul Douglas Buster, interview, 8–10.
14. Victor Billie, interview, 13.
15. Lorene Gopher, interview, 28.
16. Joe Dan Osceola, interview by Rosalyn Howard, 17, 21.
17. Paul Douglas Buster, interview, 7–10.

18. Helene Johns Buster, interview, 34–35.

19. Alice Johns Sweat, interview, 21–27.

20. Jeannette Cypress, interview, 20–21.

21. Carl Baxley, interview, 11–12.

22. Louise Jumper, interview, 25–30.

23. Jacob Osceola, interview, 16–20.

24. Virgil N. Harrington, interview by William D. Boehmer, 8.

25. Ivy Stranahan, interview, 66.

26. William D. Boehmer, interview by Sam Proctor, 22.

27. Wall, *Wisdom's Daughters*, 68–92.

28. Martin, *Sacred Revolt*, 38–40.

29. Mary Jene Coppedge, interview, 13–14.

30. Betty Mae Jumper, interview by Rosalyn Howard, 21–22.

31. Andy Buster, interview, 23–24.

32. Joe Frank, interview, 10.

33. Paul Douglas Buster, interview, 7.

34. Jeannette Cypress, interview, 20–21.

35. Carl Baxley, interview, 13.

36. Jeannette Cypress, interview, 31–32.

37. Betty Mae Jumper, interview by Rosalyn Howard, 14.

38. Mary Frances Johns, interview by James Ellison, 38–39.

39. Stanlo Johns, interview, 23.

40. Lorene Gopher, interview, 8.

41. Helene Johns Buster, interview, 46–51.

42. Nancy Shore, interview by James Ellison, 21–27.

43. Lorene Gopher, interview, 26–33.

44. Daisi Jumper, interview, 11–12.

45. Andy Buster, interview, 4–12; Mitchell Cypress, interview, 1.

46. Jeannette Cypress, interview, 30.

47. Sturtevant, "Medicine Bundles," 43–45.

48. Capron, "Florida's 'Wild' Indians," 839.

49. Jacob Osceola, interview, 25 (quote); Covington, *The Seminoles of Florida*, 150–51; Weisman, *Unconquered People*, 101.

50. Capron, "Florida's 'Wild' Indians," 839–40.

51. Carl Baxley, interview, 15.

52. Andy Buster, interview, 9.

53. Capron, "Florida's 'Wild' Indians," 840.

54. Joe Frank, interview, 15.

55. Joe Frank, interview, 14.

56. Joe Dan Osceola, interview by Rosalyn Howard, 34.

57. Betty Mae Jumper, interview by Rosalyn Howard, 24.

58. Jimmy O'Toole Osceola, interview by Rosalyn Howard, 10.

59. Paul Douglas Buster, interview, 8.

60. Louise Jumper, interview, 26.

61. Brian Billie, interview, 13–14.

62. Joe Frank, interview, 11.

63. Helene Johns Buster, interview, 40–42.

64. Lorene Gopher, interview, 38.

65. *Four Corners of the Earth*, videotape produced by Florida Folklife Programs and WFSU-TV (Tallahassee, 1984).

66. Sadie Cypress, interview, 6.

67. Capron, "Florida's Emerging Seminoles," 732–33.

68. Sonny Billie, interview, 7.

69. Marie Phillips, interview, 44.

70. *Four Corners of the Earth*.

71. William Boehmer, interview by Sam Proctor, 6.

72. Joe Dan Osceola, interview by Tom King, 20.

73. Helene Johns Buster, interview, 52.

74. Andy Buster, interview, 15.

75. Jacob Osceola, interview, 26–27.

76. Jeannette Cypress, interview, 16–17.

77. William Boehmer, interview by Sam Proctor, 7.

78. Nancy Shore, interview by Tom King, 12.

79. Joe Dan Osceola, interview by Rosalyn Howard, 28.

80. Joe Dan Osceola, interview by Tom King, 18–19; Joe Dan Osceola, interview by Rosalyn Howard, 30–31.

81. Helene Johns Buster, interview, 35–39.

82. Andy Buster, interview, 20–21.

83. Helene Johns Buster, interview, 53–54.

84. Lee Tiger, interview, 11.

85. Susan Stans, interview, 3–4.

86. Victor Billie, interview, 15.

87. Helene Johns Buster, interview, 7.

88. Carl Baxley, interview, 23–24.

89. Kersey, "Seminoles and Miccosukees," 96.

4. Housing and Family Transitions in Social Context

1. MacCauley, *Seminole Indians of Florida*, 477–78.

2. Sturtevant, "R. H. Pratt's Report," 1–24.

3. MacCauley, *Seminole Indians of Florida*, 500–501.

4. MacCauley, *Seminole Indians of Florida*, 495.

5. Cory, *Hunting and Fishing in Florida*, 96–97.

6. West, "Seminole Indian Settlements," 43–56.

7. Nash, *Survey*, 1–12.

8. Lottie Baxley, interview by Harry A. Kersey Jr., 14; William Boehmer, interview by Sam Proctor, 43.

9. William Boehmer, interview by Sam Proctor, 40; Nancy Shore, interview by Tom King, 14; Nash, *Survey*, 1–12.

10. Lorene Gopher, interview, 26–28.

11. Marie Phillips, interview, 15–17.

12. Jacob Osceola, interview, 2.

13. Sonny Billie, interview, 3.

14. Mary Frances Johns, interview by James Ellison, 9–10.

15. Jeannette Cypress, interview, 14–17.

16. Mary Jene Coppedge, interview, 26.

17. Daisi Jumper, interview, 18.

18. Louise Jumper, interview, 3–4.

19. Joe Dan Osceola, interview by Rosalyn Howard, 35–36.

20. Garbarino, *Big Cypress*, 19, 69.

21. Marie Phillips, interview, 20.

22. Brian Billie, interview, 29.

23. Garbarino, *Big Cypress*, 17–19.

24. Marie Phillips, interview, 19–21.

25. Nancy Shore, interview by James Ellison, 13–14.

26. Jacob Osceola, interview, 4.

27. Jacob Osceola, interview, 28–29.

28. Garbarino, *Big Cypress*, 17–19.

29. Mary Jene Coppedge, interview, 31–32.

30. Jeannette Cypress, interview, 34–35.

31. Helene Johns Buster, interview, 26–29.

32. Jacob Osceola, interview, 29–30.

33. Mary Jene Coppedge, interview, 35.

34. Mary Jene Coppedge, interview, 20–21.

35. Nancy Shore, interview by James Ellison, 5–7.

36. Garbarino, *Big Cypress*, 19.

37. Marie Phillips, interview, 23.

38. Helene Johns Buster, interview, 32–33.

39. Jeannette Cypress, interview, 13.

40. Marie Phillips, interview, 4.

41. Marie Phillips, interview, 37–38.

42. Cattelino, *High Stakes*, 140.

5. Dilemmas of Language and Culture

1. William Boehmer, interview by Sam Proctor, 24, 42.

2. Capron, "Florida's Emerging Seminoles," 719, 730.

3. *Seminole Tribune*, September 5, 1997, 6.

4. Jimmy O'Toole Osceola, interview by Rosalyn Howard, 18.

5. Joe Dan Osceola, interview by Rosalyn Howard, 33.

6. Brian Billie, interview, 16.

7. Andy Buster, interview, 25.

8. Jacob Osceola, interview, 13.

9. Mary Jene Coppedge, interview, 38.

10. Jeannette Cypress, interview, 31.

11. Lorene Gopher, interview, 13.

12. Stuempfle, *Florida Folklife*, 26; Capron, "Florida's 'Wild' Indians," 833.

13. Mary Frances Johns, interview by James Ellison, 27–31.

14. Sadie Cypress, interview, 13.

15. Jimmy O'Toole Osceola, interview by Rosalyn Howard, 11–13.

16. William Boehmer, interview by Sam Proctor, 17.

17. Joe Dan Osceola, interview by Rosalyn Howard, 33–34.

18. Ivy Stranahan, interview, 61.

19. Virgil N. Harrington, interview by John Mahon, 15.

20. Jeannette Cypress, interview, 34.

21. Carl Baxley, interview, 14–15.

22. Carl Baxley, interview, 16.

23. Jeannette Cypress, interview, 31.

24. Joe Dan Osceola, interview by Rosalyn Howard, 16.

25. Paul Bowers Sr., interview, 1–2.

26. Mary Frances Johns, interview by James Ellison, 2–5.

27. Andy Buster, interview, 1–2.

28. Jimmy O'Toole Osceola, interview by Rosalyn Howard, 2.

29. Joe Dan Osceola, interview by Rosalyn Howard, 1–2.

30. Helene Johns Buster, interview, 2–3.

31. Alice Johns Sweat, interview, 2–3.

32. Jeannette Cypress, interview, 16.

33. Jimmy O'Toole Osceola, interview by Rosalyn Howard, 18–20.

34. Marie Phillips, interview, 9, 12–13.

35. Alice Johns Sweat, interview, 31–32.

36. Alice Johns Sweat, interview, 34–36.

37. Lorene Gopher, interview, 3.

38. Jumper, *Legends of the Seminoles*, 12–14.

39. Lottie Baxley, interview by Harry A. Kersey Jr., 1971, 4–5.

40. Louise Jumper, interview, 7.

41. Louise Jumper, interview, 9.

42. Jeannette Cypress, interview, 19–20.

43. Helene Johns Buster, interview, 15.

44. Brian Billie, interview, 20, 33–34.

45. Mary Frances Johns, interview by James Ellison, 35–36.

46. Marie Phillips, interview, 28–29, 37–38.

47. Helene Johns Buster, interview, 13–14.

48. Louise Jumper, interview, 32.

49. Louise Jumper, interview, 17–18.

50. Victor Billie, interview, 10–12.

51. Jeannette Cypress, interview, 3, 9–10, 18.

52. Joe Dan Osceola, interview by Rosalyn Howard, 15–17, 34.

53. Carl Baxley, interview, 12.

54. Helene Johns Buster, interview, 15–17.

55. Nancy Shore, interview by James Ellison, 3.

Bibliography

Interviews

Material is housed in the Samuel Proctor Oral History Program, University of Florida, Gainesville.

Baxley, Carl. Interview by Rosalyn Howard, 1999.

Baxley, Lottie. Interview by Harry A. Kersey Jr., 1971, and interview by Tom King, 1972.

Beaver, Fred. Interview by Jack Gregory, 1971.

Billie, Brian. Interview by James Ellison, 1999.

Billie, James. Interview by Tom King, 1973, and interview by James Ellison, 2000.

Billie, Sonny. Interview by Rosalyn Howard, 1999.

Billie, Victor. Interview by James Ellison, 1999.

Bird, E. F. Interview by Jean Chaudhuri, n.d.

Boehmer, William. Interview by Harry A. Kersey Jr., 1969, and interview by Sam Proctor, 1971.

Bowers, Paul, Sr. Interview by Rosalyn Howard, 1999.

Bowers, Richard. Interview by Rosalyn Howard, April 19, 1999.

Buster, Andy. Interview by Rosalyn Howard, April 21, 1999.

Buster, Helene Johns. Interview by James Ellison, 1991.

Buster, Paul Douglas. Interview by Rosalyn Howard, 1999.

Byrd-Gaffney, Sharon. Interview by Rosalyn Howard, 1999.

Coppedge, Mary Jene. Interview by Rosalyn Howard, 1999.

Crooks, Vivian. Interview by Rosalyn Howard, 1999.

Cypress, Billy. Interview by Tom King, 1972.

Cypress, Jeannette. Interview by Rosalyn Howard, 1999.

Cypress, Mitchell. Interview by Rosalyn Howard, 1999.

Cypress, Sadie. Interview by Rosalyn Howard, 1999.

Frank, Joe. Interview by Rosalyn Howard, 1999.

Gopher, Lorene. Interview by James Ellison, 1999.

Gopher, Louise. Interview by Rosalyn Howard, 1999.

Harrington, Virgil N. Interview by William D. Boehmer, 1971, and interview by John Mahon, 1976.

Hayes, Polly Osceola. Interview by Rosalyn Howard, May 10, 1999.

Johns, Mary Frances. Interview by Tom King, August 16, 1972, and interview by James Ellison, 1999.

Johns, Stanlo. Interview by Rosalyn Howard, 1999.

Jumper, Betty Mae. Interview by Harry A. Kersey Jr., 1969, interview by Jeannette Cypress, 1985, and interview by Rosalyn Howard, 1999.

Jumper, Daisi. Interview by Rosalyn Howard, 1999.

Jumper, Louise. Interview by James Ellison, 1999.

Mitchell, Bob. Interviews by Harry A. Kersey Jr., April 25, 1969, and 1971.

Mitchell, Bob, and Josie Billie. Interview by Harry A. Kersey Jr., 1962.

Osceola, Billy. Interview by Tom King, 1973.

Osceola, Jacob. Interview by Rosalyn Howard, 1999.

Osceola, Jimmy O'Toole. Interview by Billy Cypress, 1992, and interview by Rosalyn Howard, 1999.

Osceola, Joe Dan. Interview by Tom King, 1972, interview by Harry A. Kersey Jr., August 31, 1972, and interview by Rosalyn Howard, 1999.

Phillips, Marie. Interview by James Ellison, 1999.

Robertson, Don. Interview by Rosalyn Howard, April 24, 1999.

Shore, Jim. Interview by Rosalyn Howard, 1999.

Shore, Nancy. Interview by Tom King, 1973, and interview by James Ellison, 1999.

Smathers, George A. Interview by Harry A. Kersey Jr., 1992.

Stans, Susan. Interview by Rosalyn Howard, 1999.

Stranahan, Ivy. Interview by Sam Proctor, 1970.

Sweat, Alice Johns. Interview by James Ellison, 1999.

Tiger, Lee. Interview by Rosalyn Howard, 1999.

Tommie, Samuel. Interview by Harry A. Kersey Jr. and Eleanor Mooney, 1969, and interview by Rosalyn Howard, 1999.

Published Sources

Adair's History of the American Indians. Ed. Samuel C. Williams. Johnson City TN: Auspices of the National Society of the Colonial Dames of America, 1930.

Bemrose, John. *Reminiscences of the Second Seminole War*. Ed. John K. Mahon. Gainesville: University of Florida Press, 1966.

Blassingame, Wyatt. *The Seminoles of Florida*. Gainesville: University Press of Florida, 1993.

Buswell, James O., III. "Florida Seminole Religious Ritual: Resistance and Change." PhD diss., Washington University, St. Louis, 1972.

Capron, Louis. "Florida's Emerging Seminoles." *National Geographic*, November 1969, 730–39.

———. "Florida's 'Wild' Indians." *National Geographic*, December 1956, 819–40.

———. "The Medicine Bundles of the Florida Seminoles and the Green Corn Dance." Bureau of American Ethnology, Bulletin no. 151, pp. 155–210. Washington DC: Government Printing Office, 1953.

Cattelino, Jessica. *High Stakes: Florida Seminole Gaming and Sovereignty*. Durham NC: Duke University Press, 2008.

———. "High Stakes: Seminole Sovereignty in the Casino Era." PhD diss., New York University, 2004.

Coe, Charles. *Red Patriots: The Story of the Seminoles*. Gainesville: University Presses of Florida, 1974.

Cory, Charles Barney. *Hunting and Fishing in Florida*. Boston: Estes and Lauriat, 1896.

Covington, James W. "Brighton Reservation, Florida, 1935–1938." *Tequesta* 36 (1976): 55–65.

———. *The British Meet the Seminoles*. Gainesville: University Press of Florida, 1961.

———. "Federal and State Relations with the Florida Seminoles, 1875–1901." *Tequesta* 32 (1972): 17–27.

———. *The Seminoles of Florida*. Gainesville: University Press of Florida, 1993.

Deloria, Vine, Jr. *Custer Died for Your Sins: An Indian Manifesto*. Norman: University of Oklahoma Press, 1988.

Drake, Ella Wells. "A Choctaw Academy Education: The Apalachicola Experience, 1830–1833." *Florida Historical Quarterly* 78, no. 3 (2000): 289–308.

Emerson, William Canfield. *The Seminoles: Dwellers of the Everglades: The Land, History, and Culture of the Florida Indians*. New York: Exposition Press, 1954.

Fairbanks, Charles. "The Ethnoarcheology of the Florida Seminole." In *Tacachale: Essays on the Indians of Florida and Southeastern Georgia during the Historic Period*, ed. J. T. Milanich and Sam Proctor, 163–93. Gainesville: University Press of Florida, 1994.

———. *The Florida Seminole People*. Phoenix: Indian Tribal Series, 1973.

Fixico, Donald L. *Termination and Relocation: Federal Indian Policy, 1945–1960*. Albuquerque: University of New Mexico Press, 1986.

Foreman, Grant. *The Five Civilized Tribes*. Norman: University of Oklahoma Press, 1934.

Francis, Mabel B., and W. R. Thomas. *American Life Histories: Manuscripts from the Federal Writer's Project, 1936–1940*. November 1938.

Garbarino, Merwyn S. *Big Cypress: A Changing Seminole Community*. New York: Holt, Rinehart and Winston, 1972.

———. *The Seminole*. New York: Chelsea, 1989.

Gibson, Arrell M. *The American Indian: Prehistory to the Present*. Lexington MA: D. C. Heath, 1980.

Gifford, John C. *Billy Bowlegs and the Seminole War*. Florida: Triangle Company, 1925.

Glenn, James L. *My Work among the Florida Seminoles*. Ed. Harry A. Kersey Jr. Gainesville: University Presses of Florida, 1982.

Green, Michael D. *The Politics of Indian Removal: Creek Government and Society in Crisis*. Lincoln: University of Nebraska Press, 1982.

Hartley, William, and Ellen Hartley. *Osceola: The Unconquered Indian*. New York: Hawthorn Books, 1973.

Hudson, Charles M., ed. *Four Centuries of Southern Indians*. Athens: University of Georgia Press, 1975.

James, Marquis. *Andrew Jackson: The Border Captain*. New York: Grosset and Dunlap, 1933.

Jumper, Betty Mae. *Legends of the Seminoles*. Sarasota: Pineapple Press, 1994.

———. *And with the Wagon Came God's Word*. Hollywood FL: Seminole Communications Department, 1985.

Jumper, Betty Mae, and Patsy West. *A Seminole Legend: The Life of Betty Mae Tiger Jumper*. Gainesville: University Press of Florida, 2001.

Kersey, Harry A., Jr. "The Ahfachee Day School, 1927–1936." *Teacher's College Record*, September 1970, 93–94.

———. *An Assumption of Sovereignty*. Lincoln: University of Nebraska Press, 1996.

———. "The Dania Indian School, 1927–1936." *Tequesta* 39 (1979): 42–53.

———. "Educating the Seminole Indians of Florida, 1879–1970." *Florida Historical Quarterly* 44, no. 1 (1970): 16–35.

———. "The Federal Day School as an Acculturational Agent for Seminole Indian Children." Paper delivered at the AERA conference, Minneapolis, March 1970.

———. "The Florida Seminoles, 1888–1990." In *Florida's Heritage of Diversity: Essays in Honor of Samuel Proctor*, ed. Mark Greenberg et al., 83–96. Tallahassee: Sentry Press, 1997.

———. *The Florida Seminoles and the New Deal, 1933–1942*. Gainesville: University Presses of Florida, 1989.

———. "Give Us Twenty-five Years: Florida Seminoles from Near Termination to Self-Determination, 1953–1967." *Florida Historical Quarterly* 67 (1989): 290–309.

———. "The 'New Red Atlantis': John Collier's Encounter with the Florida Seminoles in 1935." *Florida Historical Quarterly* 66 (October 1987): 131–51.

———. *Pelts, Plumes, and Hides: White Traders among the Seminole Indians, 1870–1930.* Gainesville: University Presses of Florida, 1975.

———. "Seminoles and Miccosukees: A Century in Perspective." In *Indians of the Southeastern United States in the Late Twentieth Century,* ed. J. Anthony Paredes, 102–19. Tuscaloosa: University of Alabama Press, 1992.

———. *The Stranahans of Fort Lauderdale: A Pioneer Family of New River.* Gainesville: University Press of Florida, 2003.

Kersey, Harry A., Jr., and H. Ross Greene. "Educational Achievement among Three Florida Seminole Reservations." *Schools and Society* 100 (1972): 25–28.

Kersey, Harry A., Jr., and Voncile Mallory. *The Seminole World of Tommy Tiger.* Tallahassee: Florida Department of State, 1982.

Kersey, Harry A., Jr., and Donald E. Pullease. "Bishop William Crane Gray's Mission to the Seminole Indians in Florida, 1893–1914." *Historical Magazine of the Protestant Episcopal Church* 42 (1973): 257–73.

King, Robert T. "Clan Affiliation and Leadership among the Twentieth Century Florida Indians." *Florida Historical Quarterly* 55 (1976): 138–52.

———. "The Florida Seminole Polity: 1858–1977." PhD diss., University of Florida, 1978.

Knight, Vernon J. *Tukabachee: Archeological Investigations of an Historic Creek Town, Elmore County, Alabama, 1984. Report of Investigations 45.* Tuscaloosa: Office of Archeological Research, University of Alabama.

Lancaster, Jane Fairchild. *The First Decades: The Western Seminoles From Removal to Reconstruction, 1836–1866.* Starkville: Mississippi State University, 1986.

———. *Removal Aftershock: The Seminoles' Struggle to Survive in the West, 1836–1866.* Knoxville: University of Tennessee Press, 1994.

Laumer, Frank. *Massacre.* Gainesville: University Press of Florida, 1968.

Lefley, Harriet P. "Acculturation, Child-Rearing, and Self-Esteem in Two North American Indian Tribes." *Ethos* 4 (1976): 385–401.

Levine, Stuart, and Nancy O. Lurie, eds. *The American Indian Today.* Baltimore: Penguin Books, 1968.

MacCauley, Clay. *The Seminole Indians of Florida.* Gainesville: University Press of Florida, 2000. Reprint of 1887 Bureau of Ethnology Report with an introduction by William C. Sturtevant.

Mahon, John K. *History of the Second Seminole War*. Gainesville: University Press of Florida, 1967.

Martin, Joel. *Sacred Revolt: The Muskogee's Struggle for a New World*. Boston: Beacon Press, 1991.

Nash, Roy. *Survey of the Seminole Indians of Florida*. Senate Document 314, 71st Cong., 1st sess. Washington DC: Government Printing Office, 1931.

Philp, Kenneth R. "Turmoil at Big Cypress." *Florida Historical Quarterly* 56, no. 1 (1977): 28–44.

Porter, Kenneth W., ed. *The Black Seminoles: A History of a Freedom-Seeking People*. Gainesville: University Press of Florida, 1996.

Remini, Robert. *Andrew Jackson*. New York: Harper and Row, 1966.

Schlesinger, Arthur M., Jr. *The Age of Jackson*. Boston: Little, Brown, 1945.

Stirling, Gene. "Report of the Seminole Indians of Florida." Applied Anthropology Unit, Office of Indian Affairs, document 126657. Washington DC: Government Printing Office, 1936.

Stuempfle, Stephen, ed. *Florida Folklife: Traditional Arts in Contemporary Communities*. Miami: Historical Museum of South Florida, 1998.

Stull, James. "Seminole Rejection of American Education." PhD diss., Bowling Green State University, 1950.

Sturtevant, William C. "Creek into Seminole." In *North American Indians in Historical Perspective*, ed. Eleanor H. Leacock and Nancy O. Lurie, 92–128. New York: Random House, 1971.

———. "The Medicine Bundles and Busks of the Florida Seminoles." *Florida Anthropologist* 7 (May 1954): 30–71.

———. "The Mikasuki Seminole: Medical Beliefs and Practices." PhD diss., Yale University, 1955.

———. "R. H. Pratt's Report on the Seminoles in 1879." *Florida Anthropologist* 9 (1956): 1–24.

Swanton, John R. *Early History of the Creek Indians and Their Neighbors*. Smithsonian Institution, Bureau of American Ethnology Bulletin No. 73. Washington DC: Government Printing Office, 1922.

Tiger, Buffalo, and Harry A. Kersey Jr. *Buffalo Tiger: A Life in the Everglades*. Lincoln: University of Nebraska Press, 2002.

Tozier, Morrill M. *Report on the Florida Seminoles*. Commissioner of Indian Affairs, 1954.

Tyler, Lyman S. *A History of Indian Policy*. Washington DC: Government Printing Office, 1972.

U.S. Department of the Interior, Bureau of Indian Affairs. *Constitution and By-laws of the Seminole Tribe of Florida, Ratified August 21, 1957*. Washington DC: Government Printing Office, 1958.

————. *Corporate Charter of the Seminole Tribe of Florida, Ratified August 21, 1957*. Washington DC: Government Printing Office, 1958.

Wall, Steve. *Wisdom's Daughters: Conversations with Women Elders of Native America*. New York: Harper Collins, 1993.

Weeks, Philip. *Farewell My Nation: The American Indian and the United States, 1820–1890*. Arlington Heights IL: Harlan Davidson, 1990.

Weisman, Brent R. *Like Beads on a String: A Cultural History of the Seminole Indians in North Peninsular Florida*. Tuscaloosa: University of Alabama Press, 1989.

————. *Unconquered People: Florida's Seminole and Miccosukee Indians*. Gainesville: University Press of Florida, 1999.

West, Patsy. *The Enduring Seminoles: From Alligator Wrestling to Ecotourism*. Gainesville: University Press of Florida, 1998.

————. "The Miami Indian Tourist Attractions: A History and Analysis of a Transitional Mikasuki Seminole Environment." *Florida Anthropologist* 34 (1981): 200–224.

————. "Seminole Indian Settlements at Pine Island, Broward County, Florida: An Overview." *Florida Anthropologist* 32, no. 1 (1979): 43–56.

————. "A Very Private Battle: Why the Florida Seminoles Refused to Join in America's War." Florida Humanities Council *Forum* 22, no. 3 (1999): 38–39.

Wickman, Patricia R. *Osceola's Legacy*. Tuscaloosa: University of Alabama Press, 1991.

————. *The Tree That Bends: Discourse, Power, and the Survival of the Kaskoki People*. Tuscaloosa: University of Alabama Press, 1999.

WPA Writer's Program. *The Seminole Indians In Florida*. Tallahassee: Florida State Department of Agriculture, 1941.

Wright, J. Leitch, Jr. *Creeks and Seminoles: The Destruction and Regeneration of the Muscogulge People*. Lincoln: University of Nebraska Press, 1986.

INDEX

In the Indians of the Southeast series

The Payne-Butrick Papers, Volumes 1, 2, 3
Edited and annotated by William L. Anderson, Jane L. Brown,
and Anne F. Rogers

The Payne-Butrick Papers, Volumes 4, 5, 6
Edited and annotated by William L. Anderson, Jane L. Brown,
and Anne F. Rogers

Deerskins and Duffels
The Creek Indian Trade with Anglo-America, 1685–1815
By Kathryn E. Holland Braund

Searching for the Bright Path
The Mississippi Choctaws from Prehistory to Removal
By James Taylor Carson

Demanding the Cherokee Nation
Indian Autonomy and American Culture, 1830–1900
By Andrew Denson

Cherokee Americans
The Eastern Band of Cherokees in the Twentieth Century
By John R. Finger

Creeks and Southerners
Biculturalism on the Early American Frontier
By Andrew K. Frank

Choctaw Genesis, 1500–1700
By Patricia Galloway

The Southeastern Ceremonial Complex
Artifacts and Analysis
The Cottonlandia Conference
Edited by Patricia Galloway
Exhibition Catalog by David H. Dye and Camille Wharey

The Invention of the Creek Nation, 1670–1763
By Steven C. Hahn

Bad Fruits of the Civilized Tree
Alcohol and the Sovereignty of the Cherokee Nation
By Izumi Ishii

Epidemics and Enslavement
Biological Catastrophe in the Native Southeast, 1492–1715
By Paul Kelton

An Assumption of Sovereignty
Social and Political Transformation among
the Florida Seminoles, 1953–1979
By Harry A. Kersey Jr.

The Caddo Chiefdoms
Caddo Economics and Politics, 700–1835
By David La Vere

The Moravian Springplace Mission to the Cherokees, Volume 1: 1805–1813
The Moravian Springplace Mission to the Cherokees, Volume 2: 1814–1821
Edited and with an introduction by Rowena McClinton

Keeping the Circle
American Indian Identity in Eastern North Carolina, 1885–2004
By Christopher Arris Oakley

Choctaws in a Revolutionary Age, 1750–1830
By Greg O'Brien

Cherokee Women
Gender and Culture Change, 1700–1835
By Theda Perdue

The Brainerd Journal
A Mission to the Cherokees, 1817–1823
Edited and introduced by Joyce B. Phillips and Paul Gary Phillips

Seminole Voices
Reflections on Their Changing Society, 1970–2000
By Julian M. Pleasants and Harry A. Kersey Jr.

The Yamasee War
A Study of Culture, Economy, and Conflict in the Colonial South
By William L. Ramsey

The Cherokees
A Population History
By Russell Thornton

Buffalo Tiger
A Life in the Everglades
By Buffalo Tiger and Harry A. Kersey Jr.

American Indians in the Lower Mississippi Valley
Social and Economic Histories
By Daniel H. Usner Jr.

William Bartram on the Southeastern Indians
Edited and annotated by Gregory A. Waselkov and
Kathryn E. Holland Braund

Powhatan's Mantle
Indians in the Colonial Southeast
Edited by Peter H. Wood, Gregory A. Waselkov,
and M. Thomas Hatley

Creeks and Seminoles
The Destruction and Regeneration of the Muscogulge People
By J. Leitch Wright Jr.

To order or obtain more information on these or other
University of Nebraska Press titles, visit www.nebraskapress.unl.edu.